FROM
Literature TO Literacy

Bridging Learning in the Library and the Primary Grade Classroom

JOY F. MOSS

The Harley School and the
  University of Rochester Warner
  Graduate School of Education
  and Human Development
Rochester, New York, USA

MARILYN F. FENSTER

The Harley School
Rochester, New York, USA

INTERNATIONAL
Reading Association
800 Barksdale Road, PO Box 8139
Newark, Delaware 19714-8139, USA
www.reading.org

The International Reading Association attempts, through its publications, to provide a forum for a wide spectrum of opinions on reading. This policy permits divergent viewpoints without implying the endorsement of the Association.

Director of Publications Joan M. Irwin
Editorial Director, Books and Special Projects Matthew W. Baker
Senior Editor, Books and Special Projects Tori Mello Bachman
Permissions Editor Janet S. Parrack
Production Editor Shannon Benner
Assistant Editor Corinne M. Mooney
Editorial Assistant Tyanna L. Collins
Production Department Manager Iona Sauscermen
Supervisor, Electronic Publishing Anette Schütz
Senior Electronic Publishing Specialist Cheryl J. Strum
Electronic Publishing Specialist R. Lynn Harrison
Proofreader Charlene M. Nichols

Project Editor Corinne M. Mooney

Cover Design: Linda Steere
Photo Credit: Image 100 Ltd.

Library of Congress Cataloging-in-Publication Data
Moss, Joy F., 1937–
    From literature to literacy : bridging learning in the library and the primary grade classroom / Joy F. Moss, Marilyn F. Fenster.
        p.   cm.
Includes bibliographical references (p.   ) and index.
    ISBN 0-87207-345-9 (pbk.)
1. Literature—Study and teaching (Primary)—United States.   2. Children—Books and reading.   I. Fenster, Marilyn F.   II. Title.
    LB1527 .M68 2002
    372.64'044—dc21

                                                          2002007434

To our students
whose voices enlivened this story
of our literary journey

CONTENTS

● ● ●

ACKNOWLEDGMENTS

• • •

This book is about literature in the lives of children, and we are indebted to all the children who have explored the world of literature with us over the years. From them, we have learned a great deal about literary response and literacy learning and the nature of dialogue that evolves out of a community of learners.

We also would like to express our appreciation to Margie Siegel at Columbia University Teachers College, who encouraged us to record our year-long collaborative study in order to share it with other teachers. We also want to thank Matt Baker and Corinne Mooney for their support and thoughtful involvement in this project, as well as the reviewers, whose comments and suggestions helped us to revise the early drafts of this manuscript.

Finally, we want to express our gratitude to our families:

- To Art and Remy, for their love and understanding as we pursued our goals as teachers over the years, and more recently, as we prepared this manuscript for publication

- To the young parents in the Moss family—Kathy and Jeff, Debbie and Keith, and Abby and David—who have passed on their own passion for reading to their children

- To the new generation of readers in our families—the Moss grand-children, Daniel, Rachel, Aaron, Yonah, Adam, Julia, Joshua, Tamar, and Emily; and the Fenster children, Jason and Aaron

JFM and MFF

INTRODUCTION

• • •

This book is the product of a collaborative partnership in which we, Moss and Fenster, developed a yearlong literary/literacy program for 11 first-grade children and recorded what happened when we translated our plans into practice. Moss is the librarian and literature teacher for a private elementary school in Rochester, New York, USA. Fenster teaches in a combined K–1 classroom in the same school. The purpose of this book is to describe our program and to suggest the possibilities inherent in a curriculum that integrates literary and literacy learning.

We have been working together as colleagues for many years, and we have become increasingly interested in bridging learning in the library and the classroom. Fenster has been using library books to teach literacy skills and strategies and to motivate her students to become active and thoughtful readers and writers. Moss has been helping Fenster find appropriate and interesting books that would meet the learning needs of each child as he or she progressed from one stage of literacy development to the next. Thus, our collaboration began with the challenge of finding appropriate library books for children to use in the process of learning how to read and write meaningful language, as well as in the application of their growing literacy skills to become independent readers and writers. The literature program that Moss developed in the library was designed to promote literary learning through the study of carefully selected texts in the context of thematic units. The cumulative experiences with literature in these thematic units provided opportunities for children to learn about literature, build their literary histories, develop strategies to generate meaning in their transactions with literary texts, and discover new possibilities for independent reading and writing. Accordingly, the literary learning in the library became linked with the literacy learning in the classroom.

Over the years, we have studied the growing body of professional writing about literary and literacy learning, and we have attempted to translate this theory and research into practice as we developed learning experiences for our students. We particularly have been impressed with the research that highlights the critical role of literary experiences in the development of literacy skills (for example, Clark, 1976; Cohen, 1968; Durkin, 1961; Wells, 1986). This research has corroborated our own observations as teachers and our growing conviction that the quality and extent of a child's literary background is a major determinant in his or her response to the challenge of learning to read and write. Our convictions about the importance of literature as a context for literacy learning led to our decision to develop an integrated program in which the literary experiences in the library would enrich the literacy instruction in the classroom. The literary/literacy program we developed is based on the theory and research that has informed our practice as teachers. In chapter 1, we discuss in depth the theoretical background for this program that grew out of our collaborative partnership.

We began our work as teacher-researchers by formulating a list of objectives that would guide the development of our literary/literacy program. We derived these objectives from the theory and research described in chapter 1, and we used them to plan our program and evaluate the children's involvement in the literary/literacy experiences that evolved out of this program. The objectives are as follows:

- To provide opportunities for children to experience personal enjoyment and growth through literature

- To provide opportunities for children to develop the motivation, skills, strategies, and knowledge necessary for them to become active and thoughtful readers and writers who explore books on their own and engage in inquiry and discovery

- To provide experiences in which children are challenged to engage in critical thinking and stretch their minds and imaginations

- To provide opportunities for children to learn to work together and to form a "community of readers" (Hepler & Hickman, 1982, p. 279) in which they explore and build meanings together and learn from one another in the process

- To expose children to diverse literary genres

- To expose children to their literary heritage by introducing traditional tales from around the world

- To provide opportunities for children to engage in independent reading and writing and to discover new possibilities for developing personal reading interests

- To provide children with a context for studying literary themes about the human experience and exploring literature-life connections

- To provide children with a context for learning about literature, the language of literary analysis, and the craft of authors and artists

- To provide opportunities for children to engage in comparative analysis of multiple texts, to use intertextual links to generate meaning, and to learn to respond to each new story in light of previous stories

- To provide opportunities for children to study literature with a "writer's eye" (Portalupi, 1999, p. 6) in preparation for creating original narratives

In order to realize these objectives, we developed cumulative literary experiences in the context of a series of thematic literary units, which served as the core of the literary/literacy program. We organized each thematic literary unit around a particular focus, such as a topic or issue; a literary motif, theme, or genre; a narrative element; or a specific author. We feature two of these units in this book, the Dog Tale Unit and the Transformation Tale Unit, to illustrate the nature of the cumulative literary experiences that were introduced in the library by Moss and recorded by Fenster. These two units are featured in this book for several reasons. First, Moss developed these two units in the library. A significant dimension of our collaborative partnership was our study of the effect of literary learning experiences in the library on subsequent literary/literacy learning experiences in the classroom. We view this book as an invitation to librarians and classroom teachers in other elementary schools to enter into collaborative partnerships and to discover possibilities for building their own literary/literacy programs. Another reason we chose to feature these two units was to illustrate some of the ways we realized our objectives for this program and translated theory into practice. For example, the Dog Tale Unit had personal appeal for the children because most of them had dogs as pets and all of them had very positive experiences with dogs. Therefore, the children could bring these prior experiences and positive attitudes into their transactions with the diverse literary texts introduced in this unit, which in turn, allowed us to fulfill our objective to provide opportunities for children to experience personal enjoyment and growth through literature. This unit, as the introductory unit, also was intended to initiate an approach to literary study that involved the integration of diverse literary genres, including traditional and modern tales, fantasy, realistic fiction, poetry, and nonfiction, thus allowing us to realize another objective. Because this approach was used throughout the school year, this unit set the stage for the use of multiple genres to explore the particular focus selected for each of the units. Also, in the course of the Dog Tale Unit, we had observed that the books introduced in this unit became popular choices for the children's independent in-class reading. In addition, their reading experiences outside of school expanded as they discovered new possibilities for developing personal reading interests. Over time, it became apparent to us that the read-aloud selections in each unit piqued the children's interest in particular authors, artists, topics, or genres, which motivated them to engage in wider reading (another objective we had established for this program).

We selected the Transformation Tale Unit as the second thematic unit to feature in this book because it introduced literary concepts that would contribute significantly to the children's literary awareness and growth as readers and writers. This unit, which Moss implemented in the library during the second semester of the school year, provided opportunities for the children to acquire the prior knowledge needed for transactions with the increasingly complex literary selections they would encounter beyond first grade.

Each of the units introduced in the library provided opportunities for children to engage in a comparative study of conceptually related literary texts in a sequence of cumulative group sessions, to use intertextual links to generate meaning, and to learn to respond to each new text in light of previous ones. The focus of each unit guided the selection of conceptually related texts to be read aloud or independently. In a carefully planned sequence of group sessions, the children listened to and discussed these selections or shared texts. In the context of these cumulative group sessions, Moss invited the children to respond to each story as it unfolded. At the completion of each story, the children shared their thoughts, feelings, understandings, and interpretations and searched for intertextual links between each new text and those encountered previously in the unit. Ultimately, the thematic units featured in this book exemplify a translation of theory into practice.

Organization of the Book

Chapter 1 presents our theoretical rationale for the thematic literary units featured in this book and discusses our translation of this theory into practice. This chapter also gives an overview of the thematic literary units.

Chapters 2–4 provide an in-depth study of the Dog Tale Unit, whereas chapters 5–6 provide an in-depth study of the Transformation Tale Unit. We present the sessions in these units chronologically to demonstrate how the children's learning progressed in the context of these *cumulative* literary units.

Chapter 7 focuses on the collaborative writing project in which the children worked together to create an original transformation tale. Their original story reveals the depth of their learning and their knowledge of literary craft. The story the children created, "The Magic Library," is included at the end of the chapter.

Chapter 8 provides our personal reflections, as well as a follow-up of some of these children as they moved beyond their first-grade year.

The dimension of this literary/literacy program that sets it apart from most traditional language arts programs in elementary schools is the collaborative partnership between a classroom teacher and a librarian. Cumulative literary experiences that evolved in regularly scheduled read-aloud sessions in the library provided a structure for this program. Our collaborative partnership enabled Fenster to integrate the literary learning in the library with the literacy learning in the classroom. We worked together to plan a cohesive program in which the literary experiences in the library served as a springboard for literacy experiences in readers' and writers' workshops. A great deal has been written about readers' and writers' workshops in the elementary school. For example, Lucy Calkins's *The Art of Teaching Writing* (1994) and *The Art of Teaching Reading* (2001) are excellent resources for teachers who want to develop readers' and writers' workshops in their own classrooms. Additional resources for teachers on these workshops are *Creating Classrooms for Authors: The Reading-Writing Connection* by Jerome Harste, Kathy Short, and Carolyn Burke (1988) and *Lasting Impressions: Weaving Literature Into the Writing Workshop* by Shelley Harwayne (1992). Many teachers who are responsible for larger groups of students have established these workshops as the core of their language arts curricula. Even though we were responsible for a smaller number of students, we believe that teachers can develop a similar program for 30 students. For instance, a classroom teacher could send half the students to the library at a time so that all the students would have opportunities to engage in small-group literature sessions in the library. The librarian, working with smaller groups, can introduce the literary experiences that set the stage for the literary/literacy program described in this book.

We believe that *any* classroom teacher who is interested in forming a partnership with a librarian has the potential for building rich literary experiences into his or her curriculum. Readers of this book are invited to embark on literary journeys with their own students and to explore with them the rich world of language and ideas.

CHAPTER 1

From Theory to Practice: Integrating Literary and Literacy Learning

This chapter focuses on the theoretical foundations for the central features of the literary/literacy program that we developed during our collaborative partnership. Over the years, numerous studies of young readers have served to underscore the impact of rich and meaningful literary experiences on literacy learning (for example, Clark, 1976; Cohen, 1968; Durkin, 1961; Wells, 1986). Therefore, in our program, we invited the children to listen to and discuss a wide variety of literary selections. Dialogue was a significant feature of this program. Through dialogue, the children engaged in collaborative construction of meaning as they explored literature in a social context. Studies of literary discussion in the elementary school have revealed that book talk offers students opportunities to discover new ways to think about literary texts, to enrich their responses as readers, and to extend their language competence (for example, Cazden, 1988; Hansen, 1987; Leal, 1993; McGee, 1995; Peterson & Eeds, 1990). In the context of the thematic literary units we developed in the library and the classroom, respectively, we invited the children to compare multiple texts and to consider each new text in light of those introduced in previous read-aloud sessions. Research of reading comprehension has illuminated readers' use of intertextual links to generate meaning and to enrich their understanding of literary texts (for example, Beach, 1990; Hartman, 1995; Wolf, 1988).

Another feature of our program was the use of questions as teaching and learning tools. Research also has shown that questioning is effective in teaching and guiding the meaning-making process and in fostering critical thinking (for example, Ausubel, 1960; Carroll & Freedle, 1972; Chambers, 1985; Frase,

1967; Probst, 1990; Zarillo, 1991). In addition to our focus on reading as a cognitive process, we focused on reading as an aesthetic experience. Drawing from Louise Rosenblatt's (1982) transactional theory of reading, we encouraged the children to engage in aesthetic reading and invited them to reflect on and share their unique personal responses to the literary texts introduced in the read-aloud sessions that were central to our program.

The Social Context and the Role of Talk

In the context of the literary/literacy curriculum, our students explored with us a wide range of literary selections in a series of weekly read-aloud sessions in the school library. Literature served as a springboard for talk in these cumulative, interactive sessions; that is, as the children responded to the literary selections, they shared their thoughts, feelings, associations, memories, understandings, interpretations, questions, and concerns. Talk about literature opened paths of intellectual inquiry that led to explorations of issues about human values, motivation, and behavior and about personal responsibility and the consequences of one's deeds. Talk led the children into deeper understandings about a particular text, about the structure of the texts selected for each unit, about literature in general, about themselves, and about one another. Disagreements during this group talk led to the children's discoveries about multiple perspectives of individuals, multiple layers of meanings, and multiple interpretations that a single text can generate. As the children articulated their responses to the shared texts in these group sessions, special bonds developed, and the children gradually became a community of readers. Susan Hepler and Janet Hickman (1982) use the term *community of readers* to describe children working together to become readers of literature and to explore and build meanings together. The ongoing dialogue that formed the core of the literary experiences in the library emerged in a supportive environment that enabled children to take the risks necessary to become active participants in the exploration of this unfamiliar territory in the world of literature.

Through dialogue, the children engaged in a collaborative study of literature in a social context. In her discussion of young children's conversations about books, Lea McGee (1995) notes that "children who talk together about books create what Fish (1980) calls an interpretative community—a group of readers who share their idiosyncratic interpretations and negotiate a group-constructed view of a story or a poem" (p. 108). In her book *When Writers Read*, Jane Hansen (1987) records what she learned from an extended study of reading and writing in classroom settings and highlights the central role of community as a context for learning. Dorothy Leal's study of peer-group discussions of literature provides evidence that "the acquisition of knowledge is not only found in the personal construction of meaning from a text but also in a context of social interactions with peers" (1993, p. 115). Leal's conclusions are consistent with those of other researchers such as Courtney Cazden (1988) and Ralph Peterson and Maryann Eeds (1990). For example, Peterson and Eeds note, "When one child expresses his or her personal prior knowledge, the prior knowledge of other participants is activated. These shared thoughts stimulate further ideas from others in the group and result in the collaborative construction of meaning for all" (p. 116). In the foreword to *Book Talk and Beyond: Children and Teachers Respond to Literature* (Roser & Martinez, 1995), Bernice Cullinan shares the words of the linguist and educator James Britton, who wrote that "reading and writing float on a sea of talk." The "beyond" in the title of this book refers to "what happens when rich, fulfilling literature surges into the classroom" (p. ix). We introduced our students to a wide variety of quality literature in the library and the classroom. This book tells the story of what happened when these children became immersed in "rich, fulfilling literature."

Experiences With Literature

Rich and fulfilling experiences with literature served as the core of our literary/literacy program. Various studies have yielded evidence that positive and meaningful experiences with books and written language play a critical role in the development of literacy skills. For example, Dolores Durkin (1961) studied children from diverse backgrounds who learned to read before entering first grade. Durkin found that all these readers had been read to regularly at home and that their families had a high regard for books and reading. Since Durkin's report, other studies of young readers have served to underscore the importance of rich and meaningful experiences with literature for the developing child (for example, Chomsky, 1972; Clark, 1976; Cohen, 1968; Teale,

1978; Wells, 1986). Such research corroborates our observations as teachers. Our own work with young children over the years convinced us that the quality and extent of a child's literary background are major determinants in his or her response to the challenge of learning to read and write and in his or her development as a thoughtful and independent reader and writer. Moreover, we observed that children's experiences with quality literature helped smooth the transition from beginning reading to fluent reading and contributed to their sense of story and literary awareness. That is, as the children became actively involved in exploring diverse literary selections together, they became increasingly aware of literary genres, narrative elements, and the craft of authors and artists who created these texts. Exposure to rich and meaningful literary selections provided the children with the linguistic input and motivation necessary to undertake the challenge of learning to read and write.

Read-aloud experiences expose children to decontextualized language, which challenges them to make sense of ideas outside their immediate personal experiences. Because the meaning in books is conveyed textually or by language itself, readers need to learn to read the vocabulary, text structures, and complex sentence patterns that are characteristic of decontextualized language. Studies of literacy learning have provided evidence that talking about books contributes to language development and helps build the decontextualized language skills associated with literacy (for example, Dickinson & Tabors, 1991; Freppon, 1991; Morrow, 1992; Snow, Tabors, Nicholson, & Kurland, 1995). When Moss introduced picture storybooks in the read-aloud sessions in the library, she usually read the text on each page before showing the illustrations to the children. As a result, the children learned to attend to the linguistic content and to construct meaning from the story language prior to their encounters with the illustrations. In most books read during these sessions, the illustrations complemented as well as enhanced the text by offering information that was not revealed through the text. In some books, however, the pictures contradicted the text or revealed an embedded story, or a story within a story, that was not in the text. The children discovered the interrelationship between text and illustrations in these picture books and consequently learned that they could not comprehend the whole story without attending to both.

The research above suggests that children who listen to carefully selected literary texts have opportunities to build the linguistic background necessary to become literate. As children listen to and talk about books, they become increasingly aware of and familiar with the language of literature. Literary texts are a rich source of new vocabulary and concepts, which are important components of the linguistic background that readers bring to their transactions with texts. Researchers have found that vocabulary plays a significant role in reading proficiency and in academic success (see Anderson & Freebody, 1981; Sternberg, 1987).

Reading research carried out since the 1960s has highlighted the active role of readers in generating meaning and the impact of prior knowledge and personal experience on comprehension (for example, Adams & Collins, 1977; Golden & Guthrie, 1986; Goodman, 1967, 1985; McKeown, Beck, Sinatra, & Loxterman, 1992; Rosenblatt, 1982; Rumelhart, 1976; Smith, 1978, 1988). That is, readers make sense of a text by bringing to the text what they know about language, literature, and the world. The more a person reads, the more knowledge about language, literature, and the natural world and human experience that person has to bring to the text. In large part, the quality of a person's comprehension of text is determined by the quality of the background knowledge that he or she is able to retrieve and integrate with the text content. In the context of the read-aloud sessions in the literary/literacy program, we encouraged the children to invoke relevant background knowledge and to integrate it with the text to help them construct meaning before, during, and after the read-aloud experience.

Because a reader's literary history is an integral part of the prior knowledge he or she brings to the text, we designed our program to provide the wide reading necessary to help build the children's literary histories. Through the cumulative literary experiences we provided in our program, we invited the children to search for connections among diverse texts and to read new texts in light of other texts they had heard in previous read-aloud sessions. The students discovered their own literary histories played a central role in each new literary experience.

We also introduced the children to diverse literary genres, which included traditional folk tales, legends, and fables; modern fantasy; realistic fiction; poetry; and informational books. In the sixth edition of *A Critical Handbook of Children's Literature* (1999), Rebecca Lukens defines *genre* as "a kind or type of literature that has a common set of characteristics" (p. 13).

Once readers identify the genre of a text, they generally know what to expect from that text. Both authors and readers generate meaning with an awareness of genre and the set of expectations associated with a particular genre. Exposure to a range of genres helps students discover the distinguishing features of each genre, what to expect of each, and the relationship between traditional and modern literature. Students' knowledge of genre is a critical factor in their ability to generate meaning as readers and writers.

Intertextual Links

We invited the children to search for and explore connections among diverse literary texts introduced in the group sessions. They were encouraged to consider each new literary text in light of all previous texts introduced along the way and to use intertextual links to generate meaning. Eventually, the children began to initiate the search for intertextual links on their own as they listened to or read thematically related stories, and the number of intertextual comments in the group dialogue increased as well. In his discussion of intertextual links, Richard Beach (1990) notes,

> With each new text, readers apply an evolving literary "databank" of prior literary experiences.... By learning to conceive of texts as representative of certain types or genres...or of text aspects in terms of prototypical concepts ("villain," "happy ending," "foreboding event," and so forth), readers learn to evoke prior knowledge of related literary experiences. (p. 70)

In his study of readers' understanding of texts, Beach found that "the more stories they [the students in this study] read, the richer their intertextual linking, which, in turn, related to the quality of their interpretations of the story" (p. 70). According to Beach, the results of his study are consistent with other studies of intertextual linking that, taken together, suggest the value of "continually relating current texts to past texts so that students build a sense of their own histories as readers" (p. 70). In the concluding segment of a report of his study of intertextual links of readers who read multiple passages, Douglas Hartman (1995) discusses some of the following implications:

> Thus, the results of this study indicate that prior knowledge is not something that readers merely bring to the passage and unload before they read; rather, it

is something that is utilized, constructed, and reconstructed by readers throughout reading. Understandings of one passage can influence or color understanding of subsequent or previous passages—implicitly or explicitly—throughout the reading encounter.... As many of the students in the study demonstrated, their understandings of one passage spill into their understandings of other passages—both past and future—such that a reading is always open to further interpretations. (p. 558)

We endeavored to provide the children with an "intertextually rich environment" (Hartman, 1995, p. 528). In the context of this environment, the children developed the habit of reading intertextually and engaging in comparative analysis as a natural dimension of literary study.

Readers' Response to Literature

Rosenblatt's (1982) transactional theory of reading provides a framework for exploring readers' responses to literature. According to Rosenblatt, reading is a "transaction, a two-way process, involving a reader and a text at a particular time under particular circumstances" (p. 268). The nature of this transaction is determined by the reader's stance or mental set. Rosenblatt uses the term *efferent* to refer to the stance of the reader who "focuses on accumulating what is to be carried away at the end of the reading" (p. 269). She uses the term *aesthetic* to refer to the stance of the reader whose "attention shifts inward" (p. 269), centering on what is being created *during* the reading experience. The aesthetic reader enters into a story and "lives through" it as a personal and emotional experience. Readers bring to the text their personal memories, literary histories, feelings, beliefs, and expectations. Rosenblatt calls for literature instruction that emphasizes aesthetic reading: "Precisely because every aesthetic reading of a text is a unique creation, woven out of the inner life and thought of the reader, the literary work of art can be a rich source of insight and truth" (pp. 276–277).

In the group sessions of our literary/literacy program, the children were invited to live through each story as a personal and emotional experience and to share their subjective responses to this aesthetic experience as the story unfolded and at its conclusion. Following their immersion in the story world and their spontaneous personal responses, we asked the children to step back from the aesthetic experience to explore the story objectively as a literary text and to engage in reflection, analysis, and interpretation. The term *critical/analytic* has been used to refer to a third stance, which is defined as "a focus on a major dilemma or problem facing a character, a consideration of reasons for different courses of action, and appeals to the text for evidence and for interpretive context" (Chinn, Anderson, & Waggoner, 2001, pp. 381–382). By stepping back from the text, the children could shift smoothly from the aesthetic stance to the critical/analytic stance. As they analyzed each text, they searched for intertextual links with texts previously shared in the read-aloud sessions, which they then used to generate meaning as thoughtful readers.

The comparative study of thematically related literary texts in these cumulative sessions enabled the children to (a) build their literary histories; (b) deepen their understanding of literary genres, themes, language, and narrative elements, as well as the craft of authors and artists; (c) discover connections among diverse texts and between literature and life; and (d) gain insights about the human experience. Literature is about life and what it means to be human; that is, "the province of literature is the human condition. Literature illuminates life by shaping our insights" (Huck, Hepler, Hickman, & Kiefer, 1997, p. 6).

Selecting Books for Read-Aloud Sessions and Independent Reading

Literature has the power to touch the minds and hearts of aesthetic readers and to transform readers who make emotional connections as they enter into the lives of literary characters. Therefore, we selected the literature used in each thematic unit to inspire the children to stretch their minds and imaginations, to respond to characters with empathy and compassion, and to imagine beyond the boundaries of their own experience. We selected literary texts that would provide opportunities for the children to gain new insights and perspectives about the universality of human experience and the uniqueness of individual human beings. As Judith Langer (1995) writes, "All literature...provides us with a way to imagine human potential. In its best sense, literature is intellectually provocative as well as humanizing, allowing us to use various angles of vision to examine thoughts, beliefs, and actions" (p. 5).

The thematic units in the library set the stage for students to discover important themes or significant truths about the human experience embedded in the selected literary texts. Although Moss had selected these texts because of important themes she had identified in each one, she encouraged the children to engage in thoughtful and imaginative exploration that produced new meanings, insights, interpretations, and discoveries of themes that she had not considered during the planning-selection process. Literary texts are rich reservoirs of truths about human nature and human relationships; therefore, literary exploration should be a journey of inquiry and discovery.

For each unit, Moss selected age-appropriate, meaningful, and relevant literary material to foster personal involvement. The children's interests, concerns, and experiential background influenced her selection process. To challenge the children to stretch their minds and imaginations, Moss chose narratives with complex events, multiple layers of meaning, and unfamiliar language and ideas. These texts provided the context for an in-depth study of single texts, as well as an intertextually rich environment to promote the comparative analysis of multiple texts. Another primary objective for the selection process was to identify the literature that invited reader engagement and inspired lively discussion.

The texts that Moss collected for each unit also exposed the children to diverse literary genres to help them discover the distinguishing features of each genre, what to expect of each genre, and the relationships between traditional and modern literature and between fiction and nonfiction. The traditional literature she chose introduced the children to stories that originated in other parts of the world. Moss also selected picture storybooks that allowed the children to explore the craft of the diverse authors and artists responsible for the aesthetic experiences featured in the literary sessions.

Fenster used similar criteria to select the shared books for the thematic units she developed in her classroom. However, these units were incorporated into her curriculum so her selections also were guided by her own objectives for the learning experiences in each discipline as well as the objectives of the children. Fenster introduced the children to the topic for each unit with two questions: (1) "What do you already know?" and (2) "What do you want to know?" The children responded to the second question with their own questions, and Fenster used the list of questions generated by the group of children to help her select nonfiction books that the children could consult to find answers to their own questions. Because one of her teaching goals was to help her students learn *how to learn*, she demonstrated a basic learning strategy in which learners formulate their own questions and then find answers to these questions (for specifics on this strategy, see following section titled "Using Questions as Tools for Teaching and Learning"). Fenster evaluated these nonfiction books for accuracy and authenticity and in terms of the diverse reading levels of her students. She also searched for read-aloud books that could be used as springboards for in-class discussion about the topic and for relevant research, writing, art, and drama projects that would extend the literary experiences in each classroom unit.

In addition to listening to shared texts in the read-aloud sessions in the library and in the classroom, the children selected books for independent reading from the classroom collection. Fenster set up three collections of books for independent reading in her classroom. One of these collections included books that were related to the focus of the thematic unit evolving in the library. During the Dog Tale Unit, for example, Fenster displayed a multigenre collection of books featuring dogs. This collection offered a range of readability levels and topics to meet the children's diverse needs and interests. Fenster talked to the children about the books in the collection to assist in the selection process. She also gave them opportunities to share their own experiences with these books, to add new titles to the collection, and to recommend favorite titles to classmates. During the literary discussions that were part of the read-aloud sessions in the library, Moss encouraged the children to search for connections between the shared texts and those texts from this collection that they had selected to read independently. The second collection of books for independent reading included books related to the focus of the thematic units integrated into the classroom curriculum. The children used some of these books as resources when they explored special areas of interest and searched for answers to their own questions, as well as to questions initiated by Fenster. The children also selected books in this collection for recreational reading and often chose to reread texts that Fenster had read aloud in a group session. The third collection of books in the classroom contained books for free choice. This collection was organized by genre and kept in a set of baskets that could be transported to the classroom reading corner.

The children helped Fenster organize and maintain this collection. For example, if a child noticed that a realism book had been returned to the fantasy basket, he or she made sure to place the book in the realism basket. The first two collections changed as new thematic units were introduced in the library and in the classroom; the free-choice collection changed each month in response to the children's changing interests and needs as growing readers. Each collection was easily accessible to the children, who were invited to participate in the selection and organization of the books in each collection.

As the children developed confidence and competence as independent readers over the course of the school year, they became more actively involved in sharing their responses to these self-selected books during the ongoing literary discussions in the library and in the classroom. They also responded to their independent reading selections in impromptu conversations with other students and with us and by drawing or writing about their selections. Through exposure to the wide variety of books in the three classroom collections, the children discovered new possibilities for pleasure and growth as independent readers. Thus, as their reading interests expanded, so did their motivation to engage in deeper exploration of the world of books.

Using Questions as Tools for Teaching and Learning

During the cumulative group sessions in the library, Moss introduced questions to demonstrate strategies for interacting with literary texts and generating meaning and to stimulate critical and creative thinking in response to these texts. Moss asked questions that called attention to narrative elements (characters; setting; problem, or conflict; viewpoint; and theme, or message), genres, author's craft, and new vocabulary and challenged students to explore multiple perspectives and layers of meaning in the meaning-making process. Teacher-initiated questions were used as *teaching tools*; that is, the ultimate goal was for students to generate their own questions as they listened to stories and engaged in independent reading and writing. Thus, student-initiated questions were used as *learning tools* to guide their literary explorations and as strategies to guide the reading-thinking process during their transactions with literary texts.

In many classrooms, questions are used primarily for assessment purposes and skills instruction, and answers to these questions usually require literal-level thinking and a single correct answer (see Beck, McKeown, McCaslin, & Burkes, 1979; Durkin, 1978/1979, 1981; Saul, 1995). However, investigators interested in the comprehension of written language have focused on the role of questioning in molding the quality of students' thinking as they read and listen to written discourse (for example, Ausubel, 1960; Carroll & Freedle, 1972; Frase, 1967; Pollack, 1988; Rothkopf, 1970). These studies have demonstrated that questioning can be used as a valuable tool to teach and guide the meaning-making process, to foster higher level thinking, and to encourage students to formulate questions that stimulate critical and creative thinking and that promote aesthetic response, analysis of literary texts and authors' craft, literary interpretation, shared inquiry, and metacognition (see Chambers, 1985; Noden & Vacca, 1994; Pearson & Johnson, 1978; Plecha, 1992; Probst, 1990; Sanders, 1966; Taba, 1965; Zarillo, 1991).

Taking this a step further, in her 2001 article in *School Library Journal*, Barbara Kiefer suggests that school librarians and classroom teachers can collaborate to help students develop as critical readers who love to read. According to Kiefer,

> The reports of the National Assessment for Educational Progress given every four years have long shown that most senior high school students are adequate at reading literal information—they can answer questions about material if it is stated explicitly on the page. But they do less well when it comes to critical reading—making inferences, analyzing or synthesizing information. In addition, there are many children who remain semiliterate if not illiterate, and many others who may be alliterate—they can read but choose not to, perhaps because they have never had an opportunity to get lost in a good book. (p. 50)

Our ultimate goal, therefore, was to develop a program in which the children would not only learn how to read and write, but also learn how to become critical readers who are motivated to read on their own for personal pleasure and growth. To this end, we designed literary/literacy experiences that would provide opportunities for children to read widely and deeply and to discover what it means to "get lost in a good book." The questions introduced in our program were designed to foster higher level thinking in the students and to promote their growth as critical readers and writers. We used open-ended questions to develop thoughtful transactions with literary texts and to encourage the children to engage in literary discussion, to articulate their own interpretations and perspectives, and to explore literary patterns and the craft of authors and artists.

For example, Moss used questions to demonstrate a "cover-to-cover" study of literary texts. Before reading aloud a new book, she asked the children to talk about the front and back covers, the dust jacket, endpapers, dedication and title pages, and the author's notes. According to Margaret Higgonnet (1990), French critics use the term *peritext* to refer to these peripheral features, as well as the illustrations that surround or enclose the verbal narrative. Moss showed the children how to use the peritext to make predictions, raise questions, and explore layers of meaning. After a number of these demonstrations in the group sessions in the library, the children—when reading independently or listening during the sessions—began to develop this habit of using the peritext in their own transactions with literary texts.

The teacher-initiated questions also invited the children to share their personal reactions to a story, to explore multiple meanings and interpretations, and to think beyond the story. These questions, however, always took them back to the text. In their introduction to *Transactions With Literature: A Fifty-Year Perspective* (1990), Edmund Farrell and James Squire highlight some of the significant points advanced by Rosenblatt (1982) in her reader response theory of literature. The first point they select is relevant here:

> Though students should be allowed to express freely their reactions to a selection in both writing and class discussion...the text must remain a constraint against total relativism and subjectivity. Nowhere does Rosenblatt suggest that all interpretations of literature are equally cogent. The dialectic of class discussions offers a means of modifying or correcting interpretations for which there is inadequate textual support. (p. x)

In the group sessions in the library, some of the children entered into the literary discussion by sharing personal experiences or background knowledge that was not related to the story. Moss always acknowledged students' contributions but then invited them to return to the text with responses such as "Let's go back to the story," or "What does the author tell us about that?" or "I'll read that part again so we can see what happens in the story." We expected the children to be able to provide textual support for their responses because according to Rosenblatt, text defines the validity of responses.

Recording the Children's Responses During Read-Aloud Sessions in the Library

While Moss introduced selected stories in the weekly 30- to 40-minute read-aloud sessions in the library and guided the literary discussions in these sessions, Fenster recorded the children's words and body language as they responded to the unfolding story, the illustrations, Moss's questions, and the other children's comments and questions. This written record enabled us to engage in an ongoing process of assessment. We monitored the children's attitudes, involvement, and contributions during the group discussions and looked for evidence of collaboration in meaning making during these discussions. We used our instructional objectives as the criteria for evaluating the children's responses. In our own running dialogue about the literary/literacy program, we used this information to assess the program's relative effectiveness and to make necessary changes to meet the needs of individual students and to improve the quality of the learning experiences offered in this program.

The Literacy Learning Curriculum in the Classroom

The Classroom Teacher's Theoretical Background

Fenster has been teaching since 1975. Prior to and throughout her career as a classroom teacher, she has studied the work of a variety of educational researchers and theorists, which has informed her teaching and her response to the students in her classroom. Over the years, she has developed learning experiences for her students by drawing from key individuals who have shaped the course of literacy instruction since the 1960s. For example, the work of Calkins (1994, 2001); Harwayne (1992); Harste and colleagues (1988); and Harste, Woodward, and Burke (1984) provided her with insights about the value of readers' and writers' workshops in promoting literacy development. This research also gave Fenster suggestions for adapting these models for use in her own classroom. In *Creating Classrooms for Authors: The Reading-Writing Connection*, Harste and colleagues (1988) emphasize the importance of reading aloud to children every day:

> Through read-aloud times...children experience book language, the patterns of stories, and different types of literature. They develop interest in books and

are introduced to quality literature that might be beyond their reading ability but not their comprehension. Read-aloud time encourages children to grow as readers and broadens the types of literature they choose to read.... Teachers [also] can use this time to offer invitations that will extend their experiences as writers as well as readers. (pp. 125–126)

Further, Hansen (1987) suggests that the library should be the center of the reading program and emphasizes the pivotal role of the school librarian. She states, "The reading process begins when a reader chooses a book" (p. 28). The work of Donald Graves (1983, 1984), along with Hansen's writings, offered Fenster further insights and ideas for creating a rich environment for literacy learning in her classroom. In *Writing: Teachers and Children at Work*, Graves (1983) invites teachers to brainstorm with their students about the students' interests and life experiences in preparation for making lists of possible writing topics. These lists are kept in the students' Author's Folder, and the students consult this list to select their own topics for daily writing. Drawing from Graves's work, Fenster encouraged the children to talk about their interests and experiences as preparation for generating lists of possible writing topics. Graves and Hansen introduced the concept of Author's Chair in which young readers sit to share either a self-authored text or a professionally authored text. Children and teachers come to the Author's Chair to read aloud and discuss with the group texts they are writing or reading. As part of the writers' workshop in her classroom, Fenster used the term *Author's Share* to designate the use of a special chair in which the children would sit to share their finished writing pieces with the group. The children would sit in a circle, listen attentively to each featured author, and respond to the author's writing with thoughtful comments, questions, and compliments. During readers' workshop, Fenster also invited children to share the books they were reading independently.

From Kenneth Goodman (1967, 1973, 1985), Fenster learned to use miscue analysis to discover the strategies individual children used to read texts. She then used this information to plan appropriate learning experiences to address each individual's strengths and weaknesses as a reader. Don Holdaway (1979) introduced the use of Big Books in a shared-book experience inspired by the bedtime story usually requiring a one-to-one relationship. Holdaway's Big Books are enlarged storybooks that the teacher can place on an easel, so all the children can see the print and the illustrations while he or she shares the books with the entire class. Also, these books often have predictable stories, and there is a clear association between the words on the page and the illustrations. Shared experiences with Big Books can be the basis for teaching beginning reading as children identify letters and words, build sight vocabulary, explore phonetic principles, use context clues to predict meanings of words, and predict events in the narrative. Therefore, Fenster used Big Books as part of the shared-book experiences she incorporated in readers' workshop. The shared texts that Fenster and Moss introduced in the read-aloud sessions during the thematic literary units in the classroom and library, respectively, are distinguished from the Big Books in that these shared texts were used as the basis for studying literature and developing literary awareness and appreciation.

In *Learning to Read Through Experience*, Dorris May Potter Lee and Roach Van Allen (1963) introduced the *language experience approach* in which children draw pictures and dictate stories about them. In this approach, the teacher records the children's language and immediate interests and experiences and uses these records as the core of their early involvement in reading and writing. Fenster used this approach at the beginning of the year with children who were in the early stages of reading development. Rosenblatt's transactional theory of reading (1978, 1982), discussed in depth earlier in this chapter, contributed significantly to Fenster's understanding of children's responses to literary texts and influenced her own responses to children as they experienced texts as listeners and readers.

Frank Smith's work (1982a, 1984, 1985, 1988), also discussed earlier, helped Fenster understand the nature of the reading process as an interaction between a reader and a text in which the reader actively generates meaning by bringing his or her prior knowledge and personal experience to the text. According to Smith (1982a), reading involves a combination of *visual information*, or the information that the brain receives from the print, and *nonvisual information*, or the prior knowledge the reader brings to the text. Smith's theories of reading have informed Fenster's work with individual students during reading conferences and with whole groups during read-aloud sessions. For example, whenever she introduced a book to an individual child or to a group, she explored with them the prior knowledge they would need to make sense of the book.

The Responsive Classroom approach to teaching and learning, which emphasizes the importance of creating classroom environments in which children feel comfortable, respected, and safe, has influenced Fenster's teaching as well. She has drawn from two books about this approach to develop the learning environment in her classroom: *Teaching Children to Care: Management in the Responsive Classroom* by Ruth Charney (1992) and *The First Six Weeks of School* by Paula Denton and Roxanne Kriete (2000). According to Denton and Kriete, who have elaborated on Charney's earlier work, the goal of this approach is to "help schools become caring communities in which social and academic learning are fully integrated throughout the school day, and in which students are nurtured to become strong and ethical thinkers" (p. 13). Fenster developed a thematic unit that was based on an idea for a "hopes and dreams project" (p. 45) first presented in Denton and Kriete's text (Fenster's unit is described in more depth later in the chapter).

Fenster's teaching also has been influenced by Moss's early writings about her own experiences as a classroom teacher and her use of literature to teach reading and writing (see Moss, 1972, 1975, 1983). In 1983, Moss and Sherri Oden wrote about a friendship unit that Moss developed in her own classroom to promote the children's literary and literacy learning, as well as social development. Moss's more recent texts about thematic literary units that she developed as a librarian/literature teacher (1996, 2000) also informed Fenster's practice as a classroom teacher.

Readers' and Writers' Workshops

Readers' and writers' workshops served as the center of Fenster's literacy instruction in the classroom. These workshops lasted from 60 to 90 minutes each morning and included

- independent reading and writing,
- sharing independent reading and writing,
- book talks before children selected titles for independent reading,

- informal dialogue during and after these independent reading experiences,
- conferring with Fenster or peers about writing in progress,
- group discussions about shared texts read aloud by Fenster,
- rereading and discussion of shared texts read aloud in the library, and
- guided reading lessons designed to focus on the skills and strategies used to make sense of texts.

Fenster opened each readers' workshop with a shared reading of a poem or story. This shared reading provided the basis for minilessons with whole or small groups or in individual reading conferences. For example, when Fenster used Big Books, she first invited the children to talk about the story and the illustrations and then focused on teaching the children decoding skills and reading strategies such as predicting, questioning, and using context clues in the text and illustrations to generate meaning. Whereas, when Fenster used library books, she first invited the children to talk about their personal responses to the story or poem and then focused on narrative elements, genre, new vocabulary and word phrases, and intertextual links. Extending the children's experiences in the library with Moss, Fenster also invited them to examine the peritext, engage in cover-to-cover exploration of books, and focus on the craft of the authors and artists. Depending on their reading needs, children read alone, with a peer partner, with an older student, or with Fenster. During reading conferences, Fenster responded to each child's unique needs as a beginning, developing, transitional, or independent reader and kept a running record of the child's reading miscues, strategies, strengths, and weaknesses. She used these records to guide her planning for individual children, as well as for group minilessons and parent-teacher conferences.

During writers' workshop, Fenster invited the children to become actively involved in writing their own texts so they could learn to see themselves as authors. Because the writing process begins with meaning making, Fenster encouraged the children to use invented or phonetic spellings so their limited knowledge of conventional spelling would not interfere with the free expression of their ideas. This risk-free environment enabled the children to enjoy writing and helped them become fluent composers. However, Fenster explained to the children that they would use these phonetic spellings only until they learned to spell the words "the way they are written in the dictionary."

Children gradually internalize conventional spelling patterns through wide reading and abundant writing. Mary Heller (1991) notes, "It is crucial to have numerous opportunities to read and write connected text *every day* for the children to internalize the many spelling patterns that govern written language" (p. 91). To that end, Fenster focused on composition first, inviting the children to practice writing to convey meaning. She encouraged them to read and reread what they wrote during the composing process so that they could monitor their word choice, sentence structure, and overall meaning. Because the children regularly shared what they wrote with others, either informally or as part of Author's Share, they developed a sense of audience. In their chapter "Reading With a Sense of Writer: Writing With a Sense of Reader," Suzanne Holt and JoAnne Vacca (1984) state, "Not only is our purpose clearer with a 'sense of reader' but our language is more precise and more coherent if we write so that our readers can comprehend" (p. 179). As the children became more aware of their audience or readers, they paid more attention to what the reader would need to know or what would be interesting or funny for the reader. Fenster also encouraged the children to talk *during* the composing process. When children are allowed to think aloud during writing, they help one another clarify meanings by asking questions, making suggestions, or offering explanations about ideas being presented (Cazden, 1981).

Even though Fenster emphasized meaning over standard writing conventions, she still maintained high standards for written work. She helped the children develop transcription skills such as handwriting, orthography, and punctuation. During the composing process, for example, the children reread what they had written, and Fenster helped them use periods, question marks, and exclamation points at the end of sentences and uppercase letters for sentence beginnings or proper nouns. She also helped them form their letters so other people could read what they wrote. As the children gained knowledge of phonics and expanded their sight vocabularies as readers and writers, they moved toward more conventional spelling. Fenster reminded them to think about their audience and explained that these conventions made it easier for others to read what they had composed.

The children practiced many different kinds of writing during writers' workshop: lists, how-to books, recipes, poems, letters, observations as part of science projects, weekend journal entries, research reports, memoir pieces, stories, cartoons, captions, advertisements, holiday cards, responses to favorite books, riddles and jokes, and many more. Fenster introduced selected authors as models for the children's writing, and the children also were inspired by stories introduced in the library sessions. For example, they experimented with speech and thought bubbles they had discovered in several animal fantasies read during the Dog Tale Unit, wrote memoir pieces after listening to examples of memoirs, and wrote poems after listening to selections from diverse poetry collections. Some of the texts introduced in the library read-aloud sessions even prompted the children to write a new ending or a sequel to a story that they did not think had a satisfying ending. After composing a number of original narratives, poems, and nonfiction, the children selected a piece of prose or poetry that they wanted to publish for an audience. The children learned to proofread their pieces as part of the editing process to prepare their writing for publication. Fenster developed an editing list that increased over the course of the school year as she introduced the children to transcription skills in a series of minilessons; for example, after a lesson about the use of capitalization for sentence beginnings and proper nouns, Fenster added these rules to the list. This list included other specific information such as, "All words must have at least one vowel," "Remember the silent *e* rule," "How do you end a sentence?" and "Make sure your letters sit on the line." Although Fenster helped the children correct their spellings and punctuation in their drafts, she did expect them to work on some of the corrections on their own. They also illustrated their stories or poems. After the stories or poems were published, Fenster displayed bound copies of these published pieces in the classroom so that others could select these books for independent reading.

Another integral component of writers' workshop was that each child had what Fenster called a Literary Notebook for recording responses to the selections read aloud in the library and the classroom and to those selected by the children for independent reading. Some entries in the notebooks were the children's personal responses to stories, whereas other entries were their responses to questions Moss introduced in the cumulative literature sessions in the library. These entries were in the form of drawings and text. Even though some children dictated their responses to Fenster at the beginning of the year, all the children eventually were ready to write their own texts using invented spelling. The children also used their notebooks to keep records of all the books they had read over the school year. From this list, the children selected their favorites, which they then reread and responded to through writing, drawing, or both. When recording their personal responses to books, the children often drew pictures of their favorite characters or scenes. Fenster also asked the children to write recommendations for their favorite books. For example, some recommendations were, "If you want to learn more about dog breeds, you would like this book," or "I would recommend this book to someone who likes animal fantasy." These recommendations were then shared with classmates and often prompted other children to select these favorite titles for their own independent reading. The notebooks were stored in the classroom until the end of the year when the children took them home.

Fenster kept running records during writing conferences with individual children to inform and guide her teaching of writing. Mainly, she was interested in the quality of the children's involvement, what they did on their own, and whether they took risks. For example, Fenster looked for the use of the language of literature in their own stories and for signs of children's willingness to experiment with different types of writing or new topics for their pieces. Although Fenster had emphasized the importance of meaning and looked for evidence in children's writing of meaning-making skills and their sense of audience, she also evaluated their use of writing conventions—conventional spelling, punctuation, letter formation, and increasing complexity in sentence structures. Further, she looked for evidence that the children were using the skills taught in readers' workshop in their writing. Fenster's goals for each child were determined by his or her individual strengths and learning needs; therefore, these records provided the information she needed to plan appropriate challenges for each child and to confirm or revise the expectations she had for each child.

Because reading and writing were taught as complementary and interdependent processes, the line between readers' and writers' workshops was less obvious in practice than in this description. Experiences in one workshop built on and enriched the experiences in the other workshop, and Fenster extended the literary experiences in the library into both workshops. As readers and writers, the children discovered inherent connections between reading and writing. For example, they learned to view favorite authors as mentors who can teach them about writing. They also learned to think about potential readers as they read and reread their own writing. Over the years, studies of literacy learning have demonstrated that reading and writing are similar processes of meaning construction. Smith (1984) writes that "[the child] must read like a writer, in order to learn how to write like a writer. There is no other way in which the intricate complexity of a writer's knowledge can be acquired" (p. 51). In their chapter titled "Toward a Composing Model of Reading," Robert Tierney and P. David Pearson (1984) articulate their view of reading and writing as acts of composing: "We see these acts of composing as involving continuous, recurring, and recursive transactions among readers and writers, their respective inner selves, and their perceptions of each other's goals and desires" (p. 43). Fenster's workshops helped the children develop the tools necessary to engage in thoughtful reading during their quiet reading time after lunch each day and in thoughtful involvement in the read-aloud and discussion sessions in the library and at the end of each day in the classroom. The workshops also provided a context in which the children became involved in the reading and writing experiences integrated into most of the activities across the curriculum throughout the day. Fenster used the literary sessions in the library to develop literary/literacy experiences in the classroom. She provided the children with many opportunities to listen to their favorite text selections again in the classroom, to continue their discussions about these texts, and to record their responses to these texts in their Literary Notebooks. Indeed, our literary/literacy program was grounded in the continuity between the learning experiences in the library and in the classroom. Examples of these library/classroom connections and the literary/literacy connections that evolved out of the thematic units developed in the library are included in chapters 2 through 6.

Overview of Thematic Units Used in the Literary/Literacy Program

The purpose of our collaboration was to record the library experience and to study its coordination with and integration into the classroom learning experience. Although only the two thematic units introduced in the library are discussed in depth throughout the book, Fenster developed other thematic units as part of her total curriculum. We describe these units only briefly in this section to suggest the nature of the children's immersion in literature throughout the school year and across disciplines.

The Dog Tale Unit, which we discuss in depth in chapters 2 through 4, was designed to provide the children with opportunities to explore a wide variety of stories, poems, and informational books about dogs. Moss originally selected the focus of this unit in response to the children's expressed special interest in dogs. As outlined in the original objectives for this program, Moss constructed the unit around a multigenre collection, which included traditional and modern tales, fantasy and realism, humorous and thought-provoking fiction, poetry, and nonfiction. In the context of the Dog Tale Unit, the children discovered distinguishing features of these genres and relationships between traditional and modern literature. This unit also provided a context for studying the craft of authors and artists and for exploring literary themes about the human experience and gaining insights about relationships between humans and animals. During this unit, Moss invited the children to explore connections between the diverse literary selections read aloud or independently in this unit and between literature and life.

The Transformation Tale Unit, which we discuss in depth in chapters 5 and 6, also was designed to expose the children to diverse literary genres and to invite them to read widely and deeply. This unit highlighted *transformation* as a common literary motif found in many traditional and modern tales. The central question that guided Moss's planning, implementation, and evaluation of this unit was, To what extent will the study of the literary motif of transformation enhance the quality of children's responses to more complex narratives that feature dynamic characters, whose transformation is associated with internal change and growth? A *dynamic character* matures emotionally; gains insights; and develops new traits, attitudes, and values in the course of the events in the story. During the first part of this unit, Moss introduced the children to stories about characters who experience external transformation. In many of these stories, human characters are transformed into animals or beasts through some type of magic or enchantment. During the second part of the unit, however, Moss introduced stories that featured dynamic characters. Following our original objective, she invited the children to engage in a comparative analysis of the characters in these diverse tales and to study the differences between external and internal transformation.

Throughout the Transformation Tale Unit, Moss also asked the children to study literary texts with a writer's eye in preparation for creating their own transformation tale. That is, they were invited to learn to "read like writers" (Smith, 1984, p. 51) to discover the knowledge that writers require. In his essay "Reading Like a Writer," Smith (1984) emphasizes that one "must read like a writer, in order to learn how to write like a writer" (p. 51). When children see themselves as writers, they may reread a passage in a text "because something in the passage was particularly well put, because [they] respond to the craftsman's touch. This is something [they] would like to be able to do themselves" (Smith, 1984, p. 52). As children learn about the craft of authors—their language, techniques, and style—their own writing experiences are enriched. According to JoAnn Portalupi (1999), "we build our knowledge of craft each time we engage in discussion of literature" (p. 5). In an earlier text, Smith (1982b) writes that "children also need to learn to write like readers" (p. 5). He further explains that the writer becomes a reader during the rewriting phase of the composing process; that is, "rewriting is the writer's own response to what has been written" (p. 127). Smith recommends that young writers need to become critical readers of their own writing from the viewpoint of their potential audience members. Because Fenster had incorporated the theories of Smith and Portalupi into her readers' and writers' workshops, she felt that the children would be well prepared for the writing project that concluded this unit.

Eight other thematic units were woven into the classroom curriculum during the school year. Moss helped Fenster select appropriate titles for her read-aloud sessions, as well as for the children's independent reading and to provide research opportunities for the children within several units. The first unit Fenster introduced in the classroom was the Hopes and Dreams Unit. As previously mentioned, the idea for this unit came from Denton and Kriete's *The First Six Weeks of School* (2000). After listening to a series of stories about the hopes and dreams of specific characters, the children discussed and dictated their own hopes and dreams for the school year. After all the children had an opportunity to illustrate and share their work, it was prominently displayed in the classroom.

This introductory unit was followed by a two-month study of bears, which Fenster integrated into her science curriculum and for which she used fiction and nonfiction books. The unit opened with a brainstorming session in which the children shared what they already knew about bears and what they wanted to know. According to Smith (1988), "the meaning that readers comprehend from text is always relative to what they already know and to what they want to know" (p. 154). Fenster recorded a list of what the children already knew on a wall chart, and a list of questions based on what they wanted to know was recorded on a second wall chart. Together, these lists guided the children's study of bears as they listened to texts in whole-group read-aloud sessions, responded to these texts as independent readers, and engaged in group research about bears. Each group, which contained three or four students, selected a particular kind of bear to study. Each group's research started with questions generated in the initial whole-group session; then they searched for answers to these questions in books, on websites, and in science magazines. Through these searches, the children also discovered new information that prompted new questions as they continued to listen to fiction and nonfiction texts in the regular read-aloud sessions with the whole group. Each group worked collaboratively to create a short written report and a diorama depicting the particular bear's habitat and lifestyle. Fenster also encouraged the children to choose books for independent reading from the classroom collection of books about bears, which included fiction, nonfiction, and poetry. The children brought their learning from this small-group research and independent reading to the whole-group read-aloud sessions. This learning enriched their responses to each new literary selection and prompted intertextual analyses and comments (for example, they found connections between fiction and nonfiction and discovered that authors and artists of storybooks use facts to create fiction). At the conclusion of this unit, Fenster returned to the list of questions on the second wall chart. Revisiting this list generated at the beginning of the unit enabled the children to reflect on what they had learned in the course of this unit. Fenster recorded their discoveries, as well as new skills, on a third wall chart, so they could see evidence of their own growth.

The next unit focused on the guest author, Eric Kimmel, who had been invited to the school for its annual book fair. During this unit, the children spent several weeks reading books that Kimmel had written and learning about his life and interests. They prepared questions for him, which reflected what they had been learning about literature in the cumulative literary discussions in the library, as well as what they had learned about him in the biographical material that Fenster had shared with them. The children enjoyed meeting Kimmel when the day of his visit arrived. Long after this special day, they continued to search for his books in both the school and local libraries and were delighted whenever Moss introduced a new literary selection by this author.

When Fenster introduced a social studies/literary unit featuring friendship stories, the children clearly were puzzled by this choice of topic and wondered what they could learn because "friendship is just something that happens to people." However, their initial concern soon faded as they engaged in a lively discussion of what the word *friendship* meant to them. For example, they talked about making new friends, their experiences with best friends, how good friends treat one another, problems with friends, long-distance friendships, intergenerational relationships, and how friendships can change. This unit helped the children expand their understanding of friendship as they entered into the lives of the fictional characters they encountered during read-aloud sessions and independent reading. The children compared and contrasted the different ways in which characters in these texts negotiated their friendships and solved their problems. Throughout the unit, they also explored literature-life connections as they compared the story world to their own worlds and looked for ways in which they could apply their new understandings about friendships, learned from their reading of fiction, to their own real-life friendships. At the end of this unit, the children made books with helpful tips for maintaining friendships, interviewed each other to discover common interests, and made friendship bracelets and small gifts for one another.

During the initial brainstorming session for the next unit, a science/literary study about color and light, the children generated a list of what they already knew about these topics, as well as a much longer list of questions about what they wanted to know. Fiction and nonfiction library books served as the springboard for inquiry and discovery and prompted the children's experiments with prisms, color wheels, and flashlights. The children loved the hands-on aspect of this unit, as well as the opportunities to conduct their own research.

Fenster and the children initiated the next unit, featuring caterpillars and butterflies, by unpacking a butterfly garden and opening a small canister of larvae, which had been mail ordered. Their study began with the usual brainstorming session in which they shared what they already knew about caterpillars and butterflies and what they wanted to know. They searched for answers in books (fiction, nonfiction, and poetry) and science magazines, as well as in their own daily observations of their caterpillars. The children recorded their observations and predictions about the caterpillars in their own special booklets; they sometimes had to revise entries on their lists as they gained new information. As they became immersed in this topic, the science table brimmed with books, paintings, sketches, clay models, and stuffed toys related to the unit's theme. They read about different types of butterflies and used the class globe to find where these butterflies were located. They compared real transformations that occurred in nature with the magical transformations that they had learned about in the stories introduced in the read-aloud sessions in the library. At the beginning of the unit, the children did not believe that metamorphoses would occur, but fortunately, they were in the classroom on the day that their painted lady butterflies shed their cocoons to emerge. Fenster set up a schedule so that each child would have a turn to feed the butterflies. To end this unit, Fenster and the children planned for a day when they would set their butterflies free. In preparation for this day, the children collected poems and wrote their own, baked cookies that were shaped like butterflies, and invited guests to join in on the celebration, which took place on the school lawn.

The idea for the next unit grew out of an annual schoolwide event called "Focus Week." The elementary school faculty selects a topic, and the classroom teachers work with all the children and the specialist teachers (art, music, literature, computer, foreign language, and physical education) to prepare for a full week of integrated study of this topic. Because the children in each grade level had begun to study the French language as part of the general curriculum, the faculty decided that France would be an appropriate topic for Focus Week this year. After listening to *Linnea in Monet's Garden* (Bjork & Anderson, 1987), Fenster's students decided to develop a new thematic unit around a study of the painter Claude Monet in preparation for this special week. Fenster and the children found art books, photographic slides, videos, postcards, prints, and biographies to help them better understand Monet and his work, and the art teacher planned a special field trip to the local art gallery so that they could see two of Monet's masterpieces. After their research and the field trip, the children were inspired to try to paint like Monet, and they took great pride in their own masterpieces. By the time Focus Week arrived, the school halls had been transformed into the city streets and countryside of France, and the children in Fenster's classroom joined in with all the other children in the elementary school in a week of discovery and sharing.

The final unit featured *memoir*, a literary genre the children studied and used as a springboard for their writing. After reading aloud such books as *The Relatives Came* (Rylant, 1985), *When I Was Young in the Mountains* (Rylant, 1982), *Hairs = Pelitos: A Story in English and Spanish* (Cisneros, 1994), *Bigmama's* (Crews, 1991), *Thank You, Mr. Falker* (Polacco, 1998), and *26 Fairmount Avenue* (dePaola, 1999), Fenster asked the children to work on their own memory pieces, or memoirs, for the final writing project. The children brought photographs from their homes that reminded them of special times in their lives. They then wrote about their memories of these special moments and read their pieces at the last Authors' Share of the year.

Concluding the Literary/Literacy Program

At the end of the school year, the children engaged in a collaborative writing project that allowed them to apply and reinforce the literary/literacy understandings that they had gained throughout the program. The children worked together to compose an original transformation tale. The process of composing this story was a natural extension of the cumulative experiences in the Transformation Tale Unit. To create this original story, Moss encouraged the children to draw from their growing knowledge of literary genres, narrative elements, and authors' craft and to experiment with the literary language, patterns, and themes that they had learned in this unit. (A description of this collaborative process and the full text of the "The Magic Library," which was the product of their collaborative effort, is in chapter 7.) Unlike this tangible result of their work, the collaborative process in which the children engaged yielded important intangible results. Of most significance was the strengthening of the bonds that connected the students to one another and to the teachers. These bonds emerged during the cumulative dialogue in the library and contributed to the classroom community that was an integral part of the literary/literacy program.

CHAPTER 2

The Dog Tale Unit:
A Shared Beginning

Over the course of the Dog Tale Unit, Moss introduced the children to several reading strategies for interacting with literary texts and encouraged them to use these strategies as they responded to the texts selected for the cumulative group sessions in the library. The strategies, which the children put to use throughout the literary/literacy program, are as follows:

- Engage in a cover-to-cover study of each new text to enrich the meaning-making process.

- Use knowledge of genre to respond to literary texts.

- Use prior knowledge (linguistic, literary, conceptual, and experiential) to make predictions about a new text and to generate meaning as the narrative unfolds.

- Use questions to guide the reading-thinking process.

- Use gap-filling strategies to generate meaning.

- Search for and use textual and visual clues to infer implied meanings and the inner thoughts and feelings of the story characters.

- Identify the craft of authors and artists to generate meaning.

- Engage in comparative analysis of multiple texts, and use intertextual links to expand understandings of these texts.

- Use context to figure out the meaning of unfamiliar words or phrases in order to make sense of the text and to enrich the meaning-making process.

- Integrate fiction and nonfiction to enrich the literary experience.

A review of Fenster's written record of the children's responses during this unit revealed that the children began to use these strategies on their own as they initiated the cover-to-cover study of new texts and spontaneously engaged in comparative analysis, intertextual talk, explorations of authors' and artists' craft, and genre study. As the children moved between the peritext and the text to generate meaning, they discovered "big ideas," or themes, and significant truths or issues woven into the stories. Fenster also noted that the children extended this type of exploration into the classroom: They initiated a cover-to-cover study of each book introduced during shared reading in the classroom and often initiated the type of literary analysis that had become an integral part of the discussions in the library sessions.

This chapter shows how Moss first introduced the Dog Tale Unit and these strategies. We also have included a complete listing of the literature used in the Dog Tale Unit (as well as several new titles that were not available then) at the end of chapter 4 (see pages 99–105).

Session One: Introduction to Literary Genres and the Library

Moss introduced the first graders to the concept of literary genre in the first session of the Dog Tale Unit. Sitting with the children and Fenster in the story circle in the school library, Moss asked them, "What kinds of books do you like?" Some of the children's responses follow:

"I like books about dinosaurs and reptiles."

"I like books where you look for a man in the crowd like the Waldo books."

"My favorite stories have princesses and unicorns."

"Dr. Seuss is the best."

"I like books about real kids my age."

"I like poetry."

"I like made-up stories."

All the children's personal reading interests were recorded on a chart, and Moss helped them formulate labels to identify the different kinds of books listed on the chart. In the course of this discussion, she introduced the children to terms such as *fiction* and *nonfiction, fantasy, realism,* and *poetry.* The children came up with their own term, *picture puzzle books,* to identify texts that invite readers to search for hidden pictures. Although the term *genre* was not used with the children, Moss gave them the language used to discuss literary genres. For example, in response to the child who expressed a preference for stories about princesses and unicorns, Moss explained, "The word *fantasy* is used to talk about stories with princesses and unicorns and other magical creatures." To reinforce this literary concept, she then wrote *fantasy* on a chart and asked the children to identify some examples of fantasy stories. Moss similarly introduced the concept of realism in response to the child who expressed his preference for books about real kids that were his age. After writing the word *realism* on a chart and inviting the children to name other examples of realism stories, she asked them to explain the difference between fantasy and realism. The children's responses, such as "Fantasy has magic, and realism doesn't," "Realism is about something in real life," and "Fantasy has things that you couldn't have in real life, like dragons and unicorns and animals that talk," suggested their initial understanding of the distinguishing features of these genres. When several children expressed interest in books with facts about snakes, horses, and space, Moss introduced the term *nonfiction.* This time, she recorded the term on the chart under the word *fiction* and asked the children to compare the two terms. They noticed that the words "looked sort of alike," but comparing the words in terms of their actual meaning was a challenge for them. Moss, therefore, showed the children several examples of each type of work to help them begin to understand the significant differences between fiction and nonfiction. Later, the children would discover more specific subgenres such as realistic folk tales. Moss's introduction of the literary concept of genre, as well as her introduction of specific genres, informed the children's response as readers, their discussion of literature, their selection of books for independent reading, and eventually, their experiences as writers.

After this discussion of personal reading interests, Moss took the children on a tour of the library to show them the organization of the library and where they could find different kinds of books. After each child had an opportunity to select a book to take home for a week, they returned to the story circle to share their selections and identify what kind of book they had chosen to borrow from the library. The library was a fitting setting for an introduction to our literary/literacy program.

Session Two: Introduction to the Dog Tale Unit

To acquaint the children with the Dog Tale Unit, Moss held up the book *Argo, You Lucky Dog* by Maggie Smith (1994). She then invited them to examine and talk about the front and back covers of this picture storybook, thus asking them to engage in the cover-to-cover study. Several children recognized Maggie Smith as the author of one of their favorite books, *There's a Witch Under the Stairs* (1991). Other children noted that the picture of the two people holding the dog on the front cover is in a frame hanging on a wall and that the wallpaper behind that picture has a paw-print design. Some noticed another picture frame on the back cover with the same paw-print wallpaper behind it. The teacher read aloud the words *DREAM ON LOTTERY*, which were on the ticket inside the frame on the back cover. One student, Nik (pseudonyms have been used in place of the children's real names to protect their identities), volunteered to explain the meaning of a lottery ticket to the other students. It was important for all the children to understand the concept of lottery before they listened to the story because this prior knowledge was necessary to make sense of the story (one of our original objectives was to promote the development of vocabulary, an important part of the knowledge base children need to become thoughtful readers and writers). Several children questioned the role of lottery in this story. In response, Moss asked them to look for the answer to this question as they listened to the story and to "try to figure out why Ms. Smith chose to place the framed picture of the lottery ticket on the back cover." Before turning to the first page of the book, Moss called attention to the book's genre by telling the children, "As you listen to the story, think about what *kind* of story this is." Then, she wrote the title of the book on a chart with the heading DOG TALES. Later, when the children decided what kind of story this was, Moss recorded the genre, fantasy, next to the title, thus fulfilling another objective by starting to expose the children to diverse literary genres.

On the first page of *Argo, You Lucky Dog*, there is a picture of Argo sleeping on a cushion. The "dream balloon" above the dog contains the book's title. Again, Moss invited the children to talk about this picture and to explain both the balloon above the dog and the *zzz*'s next to his head. The children had enough exposure to cartoons to realize that in the picture, Argo is dreaming and snoring. For example, Jonathan used the term *dream bubble* rather than *balloon* to talk about the picture. Clarissa seemed to like Jonathan's term and used it in her own comment about the picture. The two-page spread that follows this first page includes the publication data and the title page. Samantha observed, "Now the dog's cushion is empty, and the dog is on the bed waking up his owners." When asked to talk about the characters' feelings, Jonathan, who owns a dog, inferred that the dog is happy because his tail is wagging. The children did not make inferences about the humans in this picture, even though they seem to be smiling, and no one noted what Argo is doing to wake up his owners.

Moss asked the children to examine the book covers and the pages that lead up to the beginning of the narrative text in order to demonstrate the cover-to-cover study of literary texts and to acquaint them with basic reading, or text-processing, strategies such as making predictions, inferences, and interpretations. She also introduced to the children the strategy of using questions about the story and using relevant prior knowledge to guide the meaning-making process as the story unfolds, because "the meaning that readers comprehend from text is always relative to what they already know and to what they want to know" (Smith, 1978, p. 5). Readers' prior knowledge enables them to make predictions as they interact with a text. As Smith (1988) writes, "prediction means asking questions, and comprehension means being able to get some of the questions answered.... There is a *flow* to comprehension, with new questions constantly being generated from the answers that are sought" (p. 19). The goal of prestory discussions in these group sessions was to help the children learn how to read books from cover to cover in search of clues in the peritext, the narrative text, and the illustrations that would inform the meaning-making process and enrich their transaction with the story as whole. Moss encouraged the children to articulate their initial understandings after their first encounter with the text and then to extend or revise these understandings as they gained new information from the unfolding text. Before and during the reading, teacher-initiated questions prompted the children to use their literary histories, linguistic knowledge, and life experiences to explore possible meanings, perspectives, and interpretations; after the reading, teacher-initiated questions prompted them to reflect on their own understandings as they engaged in a collaborative study of the text with their peers. Thus, throughout each read-aloud session, Moss endeavored to provide the children with opportunities to develop these meaning-making strategies.

Argo, You Lucky Dog is the story of a dog whose owners, Bob and Glynis, leave him home when they go away for a five-day business trip. Home alone, Argo wonders what he will do with himself while they are gone and decides to read the newspaper. He sees the headline "Winning Lotto Ticket Still Missing!" and suddenly remembers the old lottery ticket that he had found in the street earlier that morning. He takes the ticket to the store mentioned in the newspaper article and is told that he has the winning ticket. The money from the lottery is delivered to Argo's home that afternoon and enables him to make his wildest dreams come true. When Bob and Glynis arrive home after their trip, they find new landscaping, a bone-shaped swimming pool, and a house newly decorated inside and out. All the changes, however, are canine-centric.

As this story unfolded, Moss invited the children to respond to specific illustrations that expanded on the text. For example, she held up the picture of Argo burying 17 sacks of money in the yard. However, the children did not respond until she introduced a *prompt question*—"What do dogs do when they get a treasure?"—which was designed to help them use their life experiences as relevant prior knowledge to explore meanings. And when Moss showed the children the two-page spread that depicts Argo dreaming of all the ways he can spend his money, the children did not respond until Moss prompted them with questions, such as "Why would he dream of having that pile of slippers?" Clarissa's response to this question, "Dogs like to chew on them," was as brief as the other children's responses to other prompt questions. The rationale behind these questions was to call attention to the notion that illustrations in picture storybooks often provide information that is not in the text and to encourage the children to focus on clues that pointed out the similarities between Argo and real-life dogs. By asking the children these questions, Moss was trying to teach them the reading strategy of searching for and using relevant clues to make inferences about a story.

After Moss finished reading the story, she asked the children to examine the two spreads that show Bob and Glynis returning from their trip and discovering Argo's renovations, as well as the final page in which Argo is sitting between Bob and Glynis on the new couch he has bought, which has a Dalmatian design on it. Again, the children responded to these illustrations only after Moss introduced another prompt question: "How do you think Glynis and Bob felt about these changes? Look at the pictures for clues." The children's brief comments follow:

Mason: She's wearing dog earrings.

Nik: They're smiling.

Riley: They [Glynis and Bob] even got bone-shaped pepperoni for the pizza!

The children did not use the details they identified as clues to make inferences about the characters' inner feelings or thoughts. Also, they directed their comments to Moss, which were, for the most part, responses to her questions. The children did not seem to be attending to the contributions of their peers.

To continue with the cover-to-cover reading, Moss next showed the photograph of the book's author and her real-life dog, which was on the back flap of the book. Nik noted that it reminded him of the photograph of author Steven Kellogg and his dog in the back of *Pinkerton, Behave!* (Kellogg, 1979). When Moss asked why these authors might have included their own dogs in these photographs, the children did not respond.

To close this session, Moss had the children reconsider the question about genre that she had posed at the beginning of this session. She asked them, "What *kind* of story is this? Is it fantasy or realism?" Jonathan responded, "This is a fantasy story because Argo can talk and read, and dogs in real life can't." The other children agreed with him, and Moss wrote *fantasy* next to the title of this book on the chart with the DOG TALES heading.

During these first two sessions, Moss introduced the literary concept of genre and meaning-making strategies. She was setting the stage for learning; her plan was to provide literary experiences in which children could further practice meaning-making strategies and make use of literary concepts to enhance their transactions with literary selections. After these first two sessions, we met to review Fenster's written record of the children's responses and noted that many of the children were not fully engaged in the story or the literary discussion. This record revealed that most of their responses were superficial and were simple responses to teacher-initiated questions; therefore, we realized that the children had not begun to engage in critical thinking or form a community of readers in accordance with our objectives. We concluded that the children were not used to the idea of literary study as a collaborative process of meaning making, and we hoped that further experience with this approach would enable them to become more active participants in the process. As the literary unit continued, and as we will show in the coming chapters, the nature of the literary discussion changed and the quality of the children's transactions with literary texts improved significantly.

Session Three: Introducing Comparative Analysis

Reinforcing the cover-to-cover reading strategy, Moss held up *Martha Speaks* by Susan Meddaugh (1992) and invited the children to examine the front and back covers. The front cover depicts a dog along with a "speech bubble" that contains the book's title. The frame around this picture has the letters of the alphabet. The back cover shows a picture of a bowl of soup, as well as letters that spell *GOOD DOG*. First the children focused on decoding the words, and then they offered their comments:

> Samantha: It says *Martha speaks*. She's saying *Ruff Ruff*.
>
> Jonathan: No, she's saying *Martha speaks*.
>
> Samantha: She'll talk to the owner, probably.

In order to encourage the children to engage in comparative analysis, Moss held up *Argo, You Lucky Dog* alongside *Martha Speaks*. After examining both covers, Jonathan noted that "*Argo* had dream bubbles instead of speech bubbles." Then, Moss focused on *Martha Speaks* and turned to the title page in which Martha is looking down at a bowl of soup with the letters *MARTHA SPEAKS* floating on top. Samantha identified the soup as "alphabet soup" and noted that the bowl on the back cover must contain alphabet soup, too. Nik brought the conversation back to the covers and pointed out the letters in the frame. At this point, Moss commented, "The author seems to want you to start thinking about alphabet soup!"

The story opens with the following lines: "The day Helen gave Martha dog her alphabet soup, something unusual happened. The letters in the soup went up to Martha's brain instead of down to her stomach. That evening Martha spoke. 'Isn't it time for my dinner?'" (n.p.). As the children responded in appropriate places in the story with laughter and surprise, it was obvious that they were becoming increasingly engaged with the story as it unfolded. However, teacher-initiated questions that required inferential thinking about characters' thoughts continued to be a challenge for them. For example, the children who owned dogs initiated comments about Martha based on their personal experiences, but for the most part, they waited for teacher-initiated questions to guide their responses.

At the end of the session, Moss held up *Martha Speaks* and *Argo, You Lucky Dog* once again and asked the children to compare the books. Jonathan commented that both stories have happy endings. In response, Moss displayed the last page of each book, which both have illustrations that show how happy the owners and their dogs are to be together, and explained that artists often *show* the way characters feel. Finally, to initiate a conversation about the literary concept of genre, she asked, "What *kind* of book is this?" Mason identified it as realism and supported his response by telling her, "Dogs *can* talk." Mason's comment prompted a discussion about the difference between human speech and the ways in which dogs communicate with humans in real life, and most of the children concluded that this was a fantasy story rather than realism. Samantha, for example, said, "It's not real. It's false...because dogs *can* eat alphabet soup, but it would go to their stomach *not* to their brain! So it's fantasy." However, when Moss told the children that "there are parts of this story that are real," they turned their attention to elements in the story that *could* happen in real life.

Riley: A dog *can* really scare off a burglar.

Nik: Dogs *can* guard a house like Martha did.

Tamara: Some people get a dog to be a watchdog.

Jonathan: My family didn't get a dog to scare off people. We just wanted to have a dog because we all wanted to have a pet.

Moss: Yes, a dog is often like a member of the family.

Because the exploration of the nature of literary genres was an integral part of our literary/literacy program, this discussion concluded with a focus on the complexity of fantasy stories and on the idea that fantasies can have real-life elements. Moss's comment about the realistic parts of this fantasy story had compelled the children to move beyond their preconceived notions of fantasy as being false or not real. Her comment also caused the children to look for not only imaginative and magical elements that make a story a fantasy, but also those elements that could occur in real life. At the end of the session, Moss wrote *fantasy* next to the book title on the chart.

Session Four: Using Inferential Thinking and Examining Author's Craft

When Moss presented *Martha Blah Blah* (Meddaugh, 1996) to the children, she asked them to look at the front and back covers, as well as the title page of this picture storybook. The following are the children's responses:

Tamara: The dog on the front cover looks sad. Her face looks sad.

Clarissa: It's Martha. She looks sad because her bowl is empty on that page [the title page].

Tamara: She's feeling hungry, and there's no food in her bowl. She looks sad.

Moss: Ms. Meddaugh gives clues to show you how Martha feels.

Nik: The cover of this book is like the other one [*Martha Speaks*]. It has the letters all around it.

Samantha: The back cover has the empty bowl and two alphabet-soup cans that are the same.

Mason: No...one says, "Every letter in every can," and the other one says, "Letters in every can."

Clarissa: It must be important in the story like in the other one.

Riley: So one can has 26 letters.

After listening to the children's comments, Moss showed the first two pages of the story, which show Martha carrying her empty bowl to Helen, her owner, to get her attention. The illustrations on these pages prompted the children to return to their earlier discussion about the ways in which dogs can communicate. This story opens with a revelation of what happened when Martha ate alphabet soup for the first time. The children were excited to discover this familiar scene and anticipated Martha's first words, "Isn't it time for my dinner?" (n.p.). The children also used clues in the illustrations on the front cover and on the first three pages that helped them figure out that Martha is depicted here *before* she is able to use human language. The children were beginning to read one text in light of previous texts, thus fulfilling our program objective of providing opportunities for the children to engage in comparative analysis. Jonathan noted that this story must be fantasy because "the dog speaks human language instead of dog language." The other children agreed with his interpretation and seemed to like his implied distinction between the language of humans and the language of dogs.

In *Martha Blah Blah*, Martha has her daily bowl of alphabet soup, but instead of saying actual words, she makes only strange sounds. For example, when she tries to say "Good soup" she can only utter "Goo oup" (n.p.). Martha discovers that the new owner of the soup company is trying to save money by putting only half the letters in the alphabet in each can, although she eventually convinces the new owner to put all the letters in each can so she is able to say all the words clearly again. At this point of the read-aloud, all the children spontaneously began singing the ABC's together. After Moss read the last page of the story, she asked them what they noticed about the last illustration. The children's responses, which follow, were richer than in previous sessions because they were engaging in comparative analysis and using clues to infer characters' thoughts, as they had not done in previous sessions.

Clarissa: The family is hugging Martha, so they're glad that she's home.

Mason: She left home because she couldn't speak some of the words anymore. She thought the family would feel like Martha wasn't so special anymore.

Tamara: She discovered that the family did care about her.

Samantha: And they didn't even know that she could speak again. She thought her family would think she was like all the other dogs.

Clarissa:	So they loved her even if she couldn't talk; they're hugging her *before* she shows them that she's got her words back again.
Nik:	It's like the end of *Argo*. They were hugging him, too.

At the conclusion of this read-aloud, Moss focused on the back cover again and asked a question that was designed to call attention to the craft of the author-artist:

Moss:	Why do you think Ms. Meddaugh chose to put these two cans on the back cover?
Clarissa:	Because the story is about alphabet soup, and in the end Martha has to go to the soup factory!
Riley:	One can has all the letters. The next one only had some of the letters.
Moss:	Why is this important?
Riley:	She [Meddaugh] put them there so people who read the story won't be surprised the soup was changed. That was the problem in the story.

At this point, Mason pulled another book about Martha from a shelf on which a number of dog tales were displayed near the story circle. He held up the front cover of *Martha Walks the Dog* (Meddaugh, 1998), and Moss asked, "Who's holding the leash?" Mason responded, "Martha!" Then, he held up the back cover and said, "A big dog is chasing her so that must be the problem." Again, the children could see that Meddaugh had chosen to feature the problem, or conflict, in the story on the back cover. In previous sessions, whenever Moss reached the conflict in each narrative, she noted, "This is the problem in the story." It was apparent that Riley and Mason had internalized the term we would be using to identify *conflict* as a basic narrative element.

As she shared *Martha Blah Blah* with the children, Moss called attention to the use of speech and thought bubbles and asked the children to talk about the differences between them. This is an important literary concept for readers to understand, because all authors use techniques to distinguish between what a character says out loud and what a character thinks or feels.

More experienced readers are expected to figure out the inner thoughts and feelings of characters with the use of subtle or implied clues. When the children returned to the classroom after the conclusion of this session, Fenster invited them to experiment with speech, thought, or dream bubbles in their own writing. See Figure 1 for samples of the children's experiments. In the first two samples, the children dictated their ideas to Fenster, who then transcribed them; in the third sample the child used invented spelling to write his own text. Most of the children created these first samples using a cartoon-like format. During these experiments, several children created new adventures for their favorite story characters, whereas others incorporated these bubbles into pictures of themselves and their family members. As the children worked on their pictures, they chatted with one another and sought opinions about their work. They also practiced drawing different types of speech and thought bubbles in their pictures. Later, during in-class "choice time," the children chose to create new stories that incorporated speech, thought, and dream bubbles. During daily choice time, Fenster invited the children to plan their own time by choosing one activity from a number of possibilities listed on a wall chart. For example, children could choose to work on an ongoing project such as bubble pictures; work on puzzles with a partner; play checkers or chess; respond to a math or language challenge introduced by Fenster; work on an art project; or use building materials such as Legos, Lincoln Logs, or blocks. Fenster recorded the children's choices to see how they used their time, note special patterns or interests, and guide them in new directions if necessary. Creating bubble pictures became such a popular activity with the children during choice time that it continued throughout the school year. Over time, their drawings became less cartoon-like, and their use of the bubbles became more complex as their language skills improved and as their knowledge of story ideas increased. The children were delighted whenever they found bubbles in other books and enjoyed sharing these discoveries with their classmates and teachers. Their shared delight contributed to a growing camaraderie and sparked student-initiated discussions about the craft of the authors and artists who used this particular technique. These discussions, similar to the more formal literary discussions that formed the core of the library sessions, further helped build a community of readers in the classroom and in the library.

FIGURE 1

● ● ●

Samples of Students' Experiments With Speech and Thought Bubbles

Assessment

As part of an ongoing process of assessment of the children's involvement, we reviewed Fenster's written record of these introductory sessions by using the objectives outlined in the Introduction. We noted that the quality of the children's involvement in the stories introduced in the Dog Tale Unit improved over the course of the first three sessions. By the third session, the children seemed to be more engaged in the story as it unfolded, and they had begun to internalize some of the literary concepts and meaning-making strategies that Moss had introduced in the first two sessions. For example, they began to use external clues to infer characters' inner thoughts and feelings, and they began to engage in inferential thinking to construct meaning. The quality of the children's contributions improved in terms of the length and complexity of their responses. They also initiated more comments about the story and relied less on the teacher-initiated questions, or prompts. For instance, some children were so eager to share their own ideas that they interrupted the child who was speaking (of course, Moss responded to these interruptions with reminders about appropriate and respectful behavior during group sessions). As the children became more active as participants in these discussions, they began to respond to each new story in light of previous texts and to use a few intertextual links to generate meaning. Through our assessment, we concluded that the children were making progress and using the reading strategies that Moss had introduced in these first few sessions.

Looking Ahead

In addition to listening to and discussing dog tales in the group sessions, the children also were selecting fiction and nonfiction texts featuring dogs for independent reading in class or at home. Chapter 3 focuses on the children's growing experiences with independent reading and diverse literary genres, as well as their deeper group involvement in the Dog Tale Unit.

The Dog Tale Unit: Exploring New Literary Paths

ndependent reading was a critical component of our literary/literacy program. Each week, the children selected a book from the school library to take home until the following week. Over the course of the first semester, the children became more involved as a community of readers during this 20-minute book-selection period: They suggested book titles or authors to one another, talked about favorite books, searched the shelves together, and read together from new selections. The children's selections generally reflected their personal reading interests as well as the influence of peer recommendations. As the children became engrossed in each thematic unit, their independent-reading selections often reflected new interests that had emerged because of their exposure to new titles, authors, artists, genres, and topics. For example, many of the children chose to reread stories introduced during the Dog Tale Unit and selected other stories about Martha or books written by Meddaugh. Other children requested "books about dogs" or "funny stories like *Argo*." One child wanted "another book with speech bubbles." The books that the children selected to take home usually were shared with their parents and siblings. When they shared books that had been featured in a thematic unit, they made the important home-school connection by extending their in-school literary experiences into the home setting. These shared reading experiences with parents and other family members enriched the children's literary experiences and provided them with the opportunity to share their joy of reading with their families. In our ongoing evaluation of the Dog Tale Unit, we observed that the children were discovering new possibilities for independent reading, as articulated in our original objectives.

Likewise, Fenster encouraged the children to select books from the three classroom collections for either independent reading during the quiet reading times scheduled daily or to read along with Fenster as part of her literacy instruction. As described in chapter 1, the classroom collections included a special display of books that were related to the thematic units developed in the library. Each title in these collections was selected to meet the diverse needs, abilities, and interests of the individual children in the class. The children had opportunities to practice reading meaningful texts and to use the reading strategies introduced in the sessions in the library and in Fenster's readers' workshops. For example, in their encounters with self-selected books, most of the children made use of the cover-to-cover approach, drew from their prior knowledge to make predictions as they read a story, searched for clues to infer characters' thoughts and feelings, and considered the craft of authors and artists. Also important, we prompted the children to make connections between the stories they read independently and the shared texts they listened to during the group sessions. Moss then invited the children to share these discoveries during the sessions.

Some of the children began to use their growing knowledge of genre to select books for independent reading. Throughout the sessions described in this chapter, Moss introduced the children to traditional and modern realistic tales featuring different kinds of dogs, the dogs' relationships with humans, and the dogs' connection to wolves. The children selected nonfiction texts from the library and the classroom collections in order to complement or extend their literary experiences in the library. For example, some children chose books about a specific breed of dogs, working dogs, or wolves and shared what they learned in group discussions. Other children looked for folk tales retold or illustrated by those people who had created the tales they particularly enjoyed hearing during the sessions in the library. Several children found other retellings of the Welsh legend of Gelert, introduced during the Dog Tale Unit, as well as other legends about dogs. Others selected poems and riddles about dogs, whereas some chose animal fantasies featuring dogs that behaved like humans or realistic fiction about dogs that behaved in ways true to their species. Thus, the exposure to diverse literary genres in the course of the Dog Tale Unit seemed to prepare the children to select books for independent reading to fit their individual interests. Most of the children's selections were prompted by interests that grew out of their experiences with the stories introduced in the library, and many of these selections provided the children with relevant knowledge to bring to subsequent transactions with literary texts. Although the material within the school library and classroom collections satisfied most of the children's reading interests and needs, many became regular patrons of their local public libraries as they developed the reading habit.

Session Five: Introducing the Folk Tale as a Literary Genre

Moss designed the introductory session of the literary/literacy program, described in chapter 2, to acquaint the children with the way books can be categorized and with some of the literary terms used to discuss different kinds of books. The stories selected for the first three sessions of the Dog Tale Unit were modern fantasies, which focused on animals and had cartoon-like illustrations. For this session, Moss selected a different genre to increase the children's exposure to diverse literary genres. *Sirko and the Wolf: A Ukrainian Tale*, adapted by Eric Kimmel (1997), is a realistic folk tale from the oral tradition. Moss presented this illustrated tale the day before Kimmel was scheduled to visit the school in connection with the annual book fair. Of course, all the children in the elementary school had been listening to or reading the numerous books by this storyteller who has retold stories from around the world. Fenster's students were delighted to discover another tale retold by the man they would meet the next day.

Moss introduced *Sirko and the Wolf* by writing the words *folk tale* next to the title of the book on the DOG TALE chart. She explained that this book was a *written* and *illustrated* retelling of a very old folk tale that was first *told* by storytellers in a country across the ocean. Moss also explained that for many years, this story was told and retold aloud to audiences who listened to the words but had to create their own pictures of the characters and settings in their minds. Then she held up the book and said, "But now we have Eric Kimmel's telling of this old tale in a new book with illustrations by Robert Sauber." In subsequent read-aloud sessions, the children would have opportunities to listen to other folk tales retold from the oral tradition and to build their understanding of the folk tale as a literary genre.

Following this introduction to a different kind of story, Moss displayed the front and back covers and asked, "What do you notice about the two animals on the front cover?" The children noted that one was a dog and one was a wolf. They then continued their discussion by identifying differences, as well as similarities, between the two and the possible relationship between them:

Nik: Wolves have long noses and bigger ears.

Jonathan: Some wolves are bigger, but they both have sharp teeth.

Samantha: I think wolves run faster.

Mason: They both howl at the moon at night.

Clarissa: In the picture they look like they're friends.

Jonathan: They're in the same family. I read that in a library book… *Amazing Wolves and Dogs and*…I'm not sure of the title.

As Jonathan struggled to remember the title, Moss pulled the book off the shelf. The book Jonathan referred to was titled *Amazing Wolves, Dogs, and Foxes* by Mary Ling (1991) and was part of the Eyewitness series. Moss suggested that this book would be a useful resource for the children to explore the relationship between wolves and dogs, as well as the differences between wild and tame animals. This prestory discussion was intended to highlight relevant information that would help the children construct meaning as they listened to the story. By this time, many of the children had begun to use prior knowledge to generate meaning, thus using a key reading strategy.

After examining the illustrations on the covers, as well as those on the first few pages of this book, several children noted differences between these illustrations and the ones used in the stories about Martha and Argo. Moss was excited by the children's initiation of comparative analysis, which follows:

Mason: It looks more real. The others were more like cartoons.

Nik: It looks more realistic because the dog's not talking and stuff.

Jonathan: There's sheep…. It's in the country, not the city. I've heard of a sheepdog.

Mason: It keeps the sheep together…from running away.

Moss then read the first few pages of *Sirko and the Wolf*, which introduce Sirko, a faithful sheepdog who has lived with a farmer and his wife and guarded their flocks for many years, "but the time came when faithful Sirko grew too old to guard anything" (n.p.). The farmer's wife decides it is "time to get rid of their old dog and get a new one" (n.p.). Moss showed the two-page spread that portrays the farmer and his wife discussing Sirko's fate and asked the children to talk about this picture:

Tamara: It's like he's not sure about this. [She mimes the facial expression and body language of the farmer in this picture to make her point.]

Nik: She [the farmer's wife] looks really angry because the dog's not doing the work and all that. All he does is eat, sleep, and all that. She thinks he's not good for anything!

Samantha: The husband is not that mad.... He looks sad to have to give him away. The dog is like a pet.

Clarissa: The wife just wants the dog to do the work.

Tamara: The dog is over there on the side [of the illustration] listening to them. Maybe he knows what they're saying.

The children's comments revealed their use of external clues to infer inner feelings and attitudes of the characters; however, they continued to direct their comments to Moss instead of one another.

In the next scene, the farmer takes Sirko away from the house and takes out his gun to shoot Sirko. The children reacted with shock when they discovered what was meant by "getting rid of the dog" (n.p.). They were relieved as they listened to the next lines of the story: "Three times the farmer raised the gun and three times he lowered it. At last he said, 'Sirko, my faithful friend, I cannot bring myself to end your life.... I give you your freedom'" (n.p.). After the farmer walks away, Sirko finds himself alone and facing starvation. When Sirko howls, a wolf responds by coming to him and asking, "Why do you howl so mournfully, Cousin?" (n.p.). This scene prompted a number of comments:

Mason: He says *cousin* because they're in the same family!

Jonathan: They're talking to each other, but it's dog language.

Mason: In the other stories, the animals used human language. [He points to the other titles on the DOG TALES chart.] That's why they're animal fantasy.

Jonathan:　And this one is realism.

At this point, Moss clarified that Kimmel translates what the animals are saying to each other so readers will be able to understand this animal language. This discovery led the children to add *realistic* in front of the word *folk tale* written next to this title on the DOG TALES chart.

The narrative continues as the dog and wolf carry out a secret plan developed by the wolf who says, "I will help you because we are cousins" (n.p.). The children tried to figure out their plan as Moss continued to read the story: The wolf snatches the farmer's baby and runs away; Sirko pretends to attack the wolf and returns to his master, the farmer, carrying the unharmed baby. At this point, the children spontaneously responded to the text, without Moss's prompting:

Nik:　　　So now they'll [the farmer and his wife] think he's a good dog!

Clarissa:　They were pretending...that was the plan!

Samantha: They'll be so happy, and they'll want Sirko back!

Tamara:　Now they know he's good for something!

Jonathan: The plan worked!

Once again, Moss invited the children to examine the illustrations and to look for nonverbal clues about the characters' inner thoughts and feelings. The children noted that when the wolf takes the baby, the farmer and his wife look worried and frightened, but when Sirko saves the baby, they "hug and kiss him and they're all smiling because they're so happy."

Later in the story, Sirko finds a way to repay the wolf's kindness when he hears the wolf howling during the first snowfall. Sirko carries out his own plan to help the wolf, which allows the wolf to enjoy some food from the farmer's harvest feast. At story's end, Sirko and the wolf vow to be friends forever, and the story's last lines note that "whenever dogs hear wolves howling...they howl, too. For they still remember that vow. And they still tell this story" (n.p.). The children's discussion at the conclusion of the story focused on the friendship between these different animals and the way they cared about and helped each other. In an attempt to draw the students' attention to one another's comments, Moss referred to an earlier comment made by Clarissa in response to the front cover: "They look like they're friends." She also mentioned Mason's previous comment that both dogs and wolves howl at the moon at night. In reply, several children noted that dogs howl at night when they hear other animals howling, and they wondered if early storytellers created this story to explain why dogs and wolves howl at night. During this discussion, Samantha observed that this story did not have any speech bubbles like the other stories had. Jonathan responded to Samantha's comment by noting, "And no thinking bubbles.... Speech bubbles make it funny." Clarissa then made the following comment: "*There's a Witch Under the Stairs* [Smith, 1991] has speech bubbles, too. That was a funny story." Because we encouraged the children to make connections between the stories they read independently and the shared texts they listened to during the group sessions, it is important to mention that with this comment, Clarissa made an intertextual link with a story that Jonathan had recommended to her for independent reading. More important, Clarissa's comment—not Moss's—took the discussion in a different direction:

Tamara: I read that, too. A witch story would be scary for the nurseries. On some pages it would be scary about the witch, but it wasn't scary for me. It was funny.

Moss: Was there anything scary in *Sirko and the Wolf*?

Tamara: Parts of the story were scary. The part when the man was going to shoot Sirko. That would be scary for the nurseries.

Although Tamara seemed to be reluctant to share her *own* feelings about this scene, it had been clear that most, if not all, of the children reacted with fear and shock when they saw the farmer preparing to shoot Sirko. Moss commented that this was a very scary part for her too and that she was relieved when the farmer put down his gun.

The previous excerpts revealed a small but important change in the nature of the children's involvement in this group experience. That is, this was the first time that any of the children responded to the comments of their peers and began to engage in a collaborative process of building meaning together and learning from one another. Several of the children directed their ideas to their classmates instead of to Moss. They seemed to have taken the first step toward developing a community of readers, thus fulfilling another of the literary/literacy program's original objectives.

At the end of this session, Moss turned to the last page of the book and read aloud the Author's Note, in which Kimmel explains that this story has personal meaning because his family originally came from a city in western Ukraine. Kimmel also articulates the theme of the story, which is that "Like dogs and wolves, people of different backgrounds can live together. They can even become good friends" (n.p.). After recalling Clarissa's observation about the picture on the book cover, Moss asked, "How can you tell that Sirko and the wolf are good friends?" This question was designed to encourage the use of textual and visual clues to make inferences about the story characters, as well as to recognize Clarissa's earlier contribution. The children's responses indicated to us that they were using inferential thinking to understand the relationship between Sirko and the wolf:

Robbie: They helped each other.

Samantha: Also, on one of the pages the wolf looked angry [she finds the page] when Sirko tells why he was sent away from home.

Jonathan: He's angry for the dog because he cares.

Nik: And he has a good plan to help the dog.... He has his tongue out because he's thinking so hard [points to picture].

Later in the semester, the children explored the nature of friendship in another thematic unit. *Sirko and the Wolf* was included among the literary selections that were introduced in the friendship unit, which provided the children with another opportunity to engage in comparative analysis and use intertextual links to generate meaning.

Session Six: Using Nonfiction to Study a Realistic Tale

Moss introduced *The Wolfhound*, written by Kristine Franklin and illustrated with oil paintings by Kris Waldherr (1996), as another "long ago, far away story" that featured a specific breed of dog. To provide the background knowledge necessary for meaning construction, Moss explained that long ago in Russia, the borzoi, or Russian wolfhound, was a very valuable dog and that only the tsar and nobles were allowed to own wolfhounds. She showed the children a picture of this dog in the book *Dog*, by Juliet Clutton-Brock (1991). Moss then told them that *Dog* is a nonfiction text, and to illustrate this, she read the following commentary next to the picture:

> The borzoi comes from Russia and used to be called the Russian wolfhound because it was used by the aristocracy for hunting and chasing wolves. The borzoi...were bred to look as aristocratic and beautiful as possible to match the noble aspirations of the Russian emperors. (p. 47)

After looking at the picture of the wolfhound in this book, the children wanted to find a picture of a sheepdog "like Sirko." Riley noted that both *Sirko and the Wolf* and *The Wolfhound* were about "kinds of dogs in real life and not like the cartoon dogs." Jonathan predicted that *The Wolfhound* would be "another realism tale." Moss expanded on their comments by telling them, "Yes. An artist who creates cartoons usually does not show a specific breed, but the artist who illustrates a realistic story often tries to make the picture of the dog look exactly like the actual breed." (At the end of this shared reading experience, the children agreed that *The Wolfhound* was a realism tale, which Moss indicated on the DOG TALES chart.)

Next, Moss held up the front cover of the book, which portrays a boy petting a wolfhound, who is standing eye to eye with the boy. Most of the children predicted that this must be the boy's pet. However, the double-page spread that is the backdrop for the title page shows a tsar and tsarina, with several nobles riding horses in the forest, and accompanied by the wolfhound. Light snow is falling. The wolfhound appears again in the next double-page spread, which also includes the dedication and publication data. This time, however, the wolfhound is alone and the falling snow is heavy. As the children examined these pages, they shared the following thoughts:

Charlene: Maybe the wolfhound is lost.

Riley: Maybe they abandoned the dog like in *Pole Dog* [Riley had selected Tres Seymour's 1993 book for independent reading].

Samantha: But we didn't get to look at the picture on the *back cover* yet!

Moss: Yes, the back cover is important. Thank you for reminding me about it. [Moss shows the children the back cover, which displays the same boy from the front cover. The boy is walking the wolfhound with a leash through a snow-covered forest.]

Samantha: It's the wolfhound and the boy again. We'll understand this picture better after we hear the story.

The children's prestory comments reflected their growing awareness of meaning-making strategies such as making predictions, using prior knowledge, and reading cover to cover as they responded to a new literary selection. For example, Samantha, not Moss, vocalized the importance of examining the back cover. The children's comments also revealed their expanding vocabularies, as they explored the literature for this unit. Riley, for example, had appropriately used the word *abandoned* in his intertextual comment about *Pole Dog*. Moss and the children originally discussed the meaning of this word after its introduction in *Sirko and the Wolf*. Riley apparently had internalized the meaning of this word and was able to incorporate it into his response to a new text. The children also used words such as *realistic* and *realism* to discuss these old tales. They spontaneously were using the language of literary analysis that Moss had introduced earlier in the initial focus on literary genres.

The Wolfhound opens as Pavel, the boy from the front cover, finds the wolfhound. After trudging through a snowstorm to milk the cows in the barn, Pavel hears a whimper and "plunged his arms into the snow. At the bottom of the drift...lay a half-frozen dog.... Pavel dragged the heavy animal into the barn" (n.p.). After rescuing and caring for the dog, Pavel asks his father if he can keep it. Because the dog is a wolfhound, Pavel's father tells him that the tsar will think he stole the dog and will send him to "prison or worse" (n.p.). Therefore, they must drive the dog away. But Pavel cannot let the dog die in the freezing night. Determined to return the dog to its royal master despite the danger, Pavel secretly takes the wolfhound through the tsar's private forest, which "besides the game keepers with their guns...was full of wild boars, bears, and wolves" (n.p.). Although Pavel does encounter wolves, which the wolfhound chases away, the most frightening moment is when Pavel meets the tsar himself. Fortunately for Pavel, the tsar seems to believe his story and is thankful that Pavel has saved the dog's life. In the spring, one of the tsar's messengers brings Pavel a basket that contains a puppy for him and a letter from Tatiana, the wolfhound he had saved. In the last lines of the story, the messenger from the tsar reads aloud Tatiana's letter to Pavel: Under an inky paw print are the words *Tatiana sends her love*.

At the conclusion of the story, Moss observed that there were no thought bubbles in this book. In order to engage the children in inferential thinking, she then asked, "How do you know what the boy was thinking?" The children identified clues in the words, as well as in the pictures. For example, after Pavel's father tells him to let the dog die, there is a picture of Pavel and the dog facing each other and "for an instant their eyes met" (n.p.). Nik noted that this picture also was on the front cover and that it showed the problem in the story because "he's thinking he doesn't want to kill it!" Nik's comment prompted the children to return to the picture on the back cover and look for this picture in the text as well. They found the same scene in a double-page spread and recognized that it portrayed Pavel's decision to take the dog into the tsar's private forest.

> Mason: It shows the boy is really being brave going into the forest with the wolves and bears.
>
> Nik: And the foxes.
>
> Jonathan: And the soldiers with guns!

A rereading of the text enabled the children to identify the following words that revealed Pavel's inner feelings when he entered the forest: "Pavel hesitated. His heart thundered in his chest" (n.p.).

> Mason: It shows he's afraid because they would shoot him—the soldiers.
>
> Riley: He's afraid of the beasts in the forest—the bears and wolves.

The children were impressed with Pavel's courage and enjoyed the contrary behavior of the wolfhound who pranced about wagging his tail. As they noted, "That shows the dog is happy, and he doesn't know the danger."

In a different scene, Pavel meets a man on horseback. The text for this scene tells the reader, "His father's words echoed in his head: 'Prison...or worse'" (n.p.). The children identified this as another way in which the author and artist revealed a character's inner thoughts and feelings without the use of thought bubbles.

At the end of the session, Moss held up the books *Sirko and the Wolf* and *The Wolfhound* and asked the children to compare these stories.

Clarissa: In the pictures [on the front covers] they're both together... like friends...Sirko and the wolf and Pavel and the wolfhound.

Riley: [pointing to each book] That one's in a forest, and that one's in a forest, too.

Nik: The wolf saves Sirko, and Sirko saves the wolf. The boy saves the wolfhound, and the dog saves him back.

Mason: They help each other in both stories. That's what friends do.

Tamara: They both have curvy letters for the titles. I can do that curvy one on the computer.

Moss: Authors often use a special font or form of lettering for long ago stories or for stories from different countries. It might be interesting to look at the different kinds of lettering used in the books you read, such as the kinds of letters used to show loud voices, whispers, or spooky noises.

This suggestion caused the children to attend to the lettering in the picture books they encountered after this session and to use this new awareness in their cover-to-cover reading of other texts. Some of the children even began to experiment with special lettering in their own writing, thus using their writers' eye.

According to Fenster's recorded observations during this session, "The children are fascinated and show a keen interest in the pictures and evolving story. They are listening more intently than in any of the previous sessions." This intense personal involvement was revealed in the children's detailed and thought-provoking comments.

Session Seven: Introducing the Legend as a Literary Genre

Before introducing *The Mightiest Heart* (Cullen, 1998), Moss recorded this title on the DOG TALES chart and wrote the word *legend* next to it. She provided a brief introduction about the legend as a literary genre and explained to the children that some legends are stories about people who actually lived long ago. To support her explanation, Moss read from the Author's Note, which contains information about three characters in *The Mightiest Heart*—Prince Llywelyn; his wife, Joan; and his loyal wolfhound, Gelert—who actually lived in Wales almost one thousand years ago. At the end of her note, however, Cullen also alerts readers that she does not know how *much* of this story about them is true. Moss also showed the children a collection of old tales, *Dogs of Myth: Tales From Around the World* (Hausman & Hausman, 1999). This collection includes *The Mightiest Heart* and the following comment about it: "The Gelert tale has been called 'the most famous dog story ever told'" (p. 44).

After this brief introduction, Moss asked the children to compare the covers of *The Mightiest Heart* and *The Wolfhound*. Several children noticed that both covers show a boy and a dog together. Using a map, Moss told them that although both dogs are wolfhounds, the story in *The Mightiest Heart* takes place in Wales, a part of the United Kingdom. Jonathan then recalled that the other story was from Russia. The children consulted the nonfiction text *Dog*, which includes pictures of the Russian wolfhound and the Irish wolfhound, as well as a reference to the Welsh legend about Gelert. They compared these pictures of wolfhounds with the pictures of the dog in *The Mightiest Heart* and decided that Gelert was probably an Irish wolfhound. Nik pointed to the back cover of *The Mightiest Heart* and said, "Let's talk about this later."

Next, Moss invited the children to talk about the words in the book's title. After figuring out that the word *mighty* meant *strong*, they translated the title as *The Strongest Heart*. Although the children knew the meanings of *warm heart* and *cold heart*, they were not ready to explain the meaning of the full title. Moss asked the children to think about how the title might describe the dog as they listened to the story. Her question was designed to narrow the children's focus as they tried to explain the meaning of the title. That is, she invited them to think of the title in terms of the dog and to search for visual and verbal clues about the nature of this central character, known for generations as a legendary hero. In the context of the cover-to-cover study of literary texts, Moss intended to call attention to the importance of story titles and to demonstrate how the title can be used to inform readers' response to the story as a whole. After the children had a chance to examine and discuss the pictures on the title page and the dedication page, Moss began reading the story of Prince Llywelyn and Gelert, who grew up together and were never apart. As the prince matured, however, he had less time for Gelert. When the prince married, his wife, the princess, pressured him to banish Gelert from their chamber. Moss stopped reading and asked the children to examine the picture of the wedding scene and the two-page spread that follows. She then introduced the following question to call attention to the craft of the artist and to encourage the children's use of nonverbal clues to infer the characters' inner thoughts and feelings:

Moss: How does the artist show the feelings and "inside thoughts" of the princess, the prince, and Gelert?

Nik: The dog is sitting very straight and proud in the wedding, but he has a sad look after he's banished from the palace.

Samantha: The princess looks mean in that picture, and the prince looks sad.

Jonathan: You can figure out how they feel inside without thought bubbles: He's feeling sad because he's thinking about the dog.

The responses demonstrated to Moss that the children were using the clues within the picture, such as the characters' facial expressions and body language, to infer inner thoughts and feelings of these characters.

Moss then continued reading the story and revealed that when the princess has a baby boy, she banishes Gelert from the nursery. But one day when the prince enters the nursery, he finds an empty crib and Gelert, "his jaws red with blood" (n.p.). The children expressed shock when they heard these words. For example, Tamara whispered, "Oh no! He hurt the baby!" Several children even predicted that the prince would accuse the dog. After accusing Gelert of murder, the prince "raised his sword over the cowering dog, ready to strike, when a cry came from beneath the cradle" (n.p.). After finding his baby unharmed, the prince sees a trail of blood on the windowsill and looking out, sees "the wolf lying in the snow, its throat stained with blood" (n.p.). Gelert, however, is gone. At this point, Moss asked, "What happened?" to prompt the children to fill in the gaps left by the storyteller.

Riley:	The prince knew he made a terrible mistake.
Nik:	Gelert...he was trying to *save* the baby!
Riley:	He might have attacked the wolf before he got the baby.
Nik:	But why was there blood in the cradle? Maybe the wolf went into the cradle to get the baby, and Gelert attacked him there. It's hard to tell. [During this session, he continued to look puzzled over the details of the attack.]
Clarissa:	Where's the princess? Isn't there a nurse?

Overall, the children's comments indicated that they were surprised that no one seemed to be with the baby during the attack. They also tried to figure out how the wolf got into the nursery, if the window had been wide open, and if Gelert had been watching the nursery window from outside and had followed the wolf after he jumped through the window. The children worked together in their attempt to fill in the gaps left by the storyteller (see chapter 5 for an in-depth description of gap-filling strategies), thus acting as a community of readers. Their emotional reactions as the narrative unfolded also made it clear that they had entered into the story world and had become immersed in the characters' lives.

Moss continued reading and now, the prince is in the forest after giving up his extended search for Gelert. A wolf attacks the prince "and all went black. When he awoke, his face was wet. A thin old dog stood over him, licking his cheek. On the other side of the brook a wolf lay dead" (n.p.). Without prompting from Moss, the children attempted to discover what had happened:

Nik:	Again, Gelert saved him! How did Gelert know it was his own prince?
Riley:	Because he knew him so long he would identify him by the way he looked even if he was a ghost.
Tamara:	Gelert is bleeding because he killed the wolf.

At the end of this scene, the prince has fallen asleep again and awakes a second time, but Gelert is gone. Unable to find his dog, the prince decides to create a mound out of stones in the place where Gelert had appeared. Again, the children tried to understand what had occurred:

Jonathan:	He thought he's dead. When someone dies, you put stones on them.
Nik:	Did he *see* Gelert dead? He marked the spot to remember him.
Tamara:	[looking at the picture of the prince sitting with his head in his hands in front of the pile of stones] He's feeling really sad because he's all curled up. [Note how Tamara uses the clues given by the artist to infer the prince's feelings.]
Nik:	Because he thinks he's dead, so the spot is a sacred spot.

The final scene in the story takes place years later when Dafydd, Llywelyn's son, comes into the Great Hall to show his father a pup he found in the woods "by that pile of stones" (n.p.). Llywelyn, who realizes that the pup looks exactly like Gelert, tells his son, "Treat him well. And mind you this—the mightiest heart can come in the humblest vessel" (n.p.). Once again, the children responded to this scene without Moss's intervention:

Tamara:	It's the baby! He grew up.
Charlene:	That's the son of the prince.
Nik:	[Remember that earlier, Nik pointed to the back cover and said, "Let's talk about this later."] Maybe that pup is a baby from Gelert because he had died. It [the text] said the pup was alone...by the stones.
Samantha:	The pup looks like the little dog on the dedication page.

Samantha's observation caused the children to reexamine the pictures on the front cover, dedication page, and back cover. They identified the dog on the front cover as Gelert and the dog on the back cover as Gelert's pup. The children were actively responding to one another and exploring the text together. Jonathan's observation that "At the end, it's just like the beginning.... Dafydd said he's the luckiest boy," is another example of how one child's observation prompted a discovery for all the students. His observation took the children back to the opening line of the story, "Prince Llywelyn was the luckiest lad in Wales" (n.p.). The children compared this line with the last page of the story, which includes Dafydd's response when his father says he can keep the pup, "Now I shall be the luckiest lad in Wales!" (n.p.). The children expressed interest in this discovery, and Moss explained that this technique was part of the storyteller's craft. When the children worked on their collaborative writing project, they decided to use this technique to develop the beginning and ending for their own story.

Moss then asked the children to reconsider the meaning of the title and returned to Llywelyn's appeal to his son on the final page, "And mind you this—the mightiest heart can come in the humblest vessel." Samantha responded, "Gelert had a strong heart. He was loyal." Nik added, "Gelert is like a brave hero." Although these children had found the clues that revealed Gelert's loyalty and courage, they did not elaborate, and the other children were apparently not ready to explore Llywelyn's statement further. Moss decided to return to this at a later time if the children showed signs of being ready to handle this type of figurative language. However, it was one of the children who returned to this statement weeks later during their study of transformation tales.

In an attempt to engage the students in comparative analysis, Moss asked the children to compare this story with the Russian and Ukrainian tales that they had heard in previous sessions. The children's responses follow:

Riley: The baby wolfhound was a special gift from the king's dog, Tatiana [in *The Wolfhound*]. And in this one, the boy got a pup from Gelert.

Mason: Gelert is a warm-hearted dog because he tries to be kind even when people don't treat him kind.... The princess yelled at him, and the prince started to kill him. But Gelert saves the baby.

Charlene: And he saves the prince, too.

Tamara: The wolf saved Sirko, and Sirko helped the wolf.... Pavel saved the king's dog, and then the dog saved Pavel from the wolves.

Jonathan: There are parts in [all] the stories that you have to figure out...like we don't know what really happened to Gelert.

Moss interjected the children's discussion with a reminder that *The Mightiest Heart* was about a real-life dog. She reread from the Author's Note that "in the mountains of Snowdonia there is an actual grave marking the resting place of Prince Llywelyn's loyal wolfhound, Gelert. Gelert's grave can be found to this day, near the town named after him, Beddgelert" (n.p.). This clue helped the children as they participated in the following comparative analysis:

Samantha: In *Sirko and the Wolf*, they called each other cousins and they helped each other...by pretending. [She was thoughtful at this point and clearly trying to figure out something. Nik picked up on what she seemed to want to articulate.]

Nik: This wolf [in *The Mightiest Heart*] didn't really talk or anything but he was like...it's hard to explain.... He just wanted to kill the baby because he was hungry.

Jonathan: And Gelert attacked it to save the baby, and the other wolfhound chased the wolves to save Pavel [in *The Wolfhound*]. That's what the book [the nonfiction text *Dog*] said that wolfhounds do.

Tamara: So those dogs are more real in those stories?

Samantha: And the wolves are more real.

Jonathan: Gelert was real.... There's a grave for him!

Nik: In the *Sirko* story, the wolf was a character in the story...but not in the others.

Samantha: So the wolf in the Gelert story was not really a character.... It was a real wolf like in the Pavel story.

The children built on Samantha's initial comment by turning their attention to the different portrayals of the wolfhounds and wolves in each of these stories. Nik's comment helped them discover the difference between *Sirko and the Wolf*, in which the wolf is a well-developed character, and *The Mightiest Heart* and *The Wolfhound*, in which the wolves were not really characters. By the end of their discussion, the children recognized that the wolfhounds and wolves in the last two tales Moss had read were more realistically portrayed than the sheepdog and wolf in *Sirko and the Wolf*. The children's dialogue in this session demonstrated their growing ability to work together as a community of readers to explore subtle meanings in these complex tales.

Session Eight: Exploring the Language of Literature

Moss introduced *Jojofu* (Waite, 1996) as a retelling of an old folk tale that had been told in Japan for over a thousand years. By presenting a Japanese folk tale, along with the Ukrainian folk tale and the Welsh legend, she was able to fulfill the objective of exposing the children to traditional literature from different parts of the world. According to a note above the publication data for this book, "*Jojofu* is based on a Japanese folk tale taken from the ancient Ima Mukashi scrolls, today known as the Ages Ago Stories.... The name, Jojofu, means 'heroine'" (n.p.). Moss showed the students the front and back covers. The children were excited to see the picture of a large white dog that extends from the front cover to the back cover. Riley commented that the dog looked like a Samoyed. In response, Moss showed the children the nonfiction text *The Samoyed* by Charlotte Wilcox (1999b), which was one of the books available for the children's independent reading. The group agreed that the dog on the front cover of this nonfiction text looked like the picture of Jojofu, the dog on the front and back covers of the Japanese folk tale, and Riley looked pleased to have this confirmation of his prior knowledge of dogs. Moss then called attention to the picture on the title page, which depicts a scroll tied with a red silk cord. On the next page, the scroll has been opened to reveal publication data, a note about the story, and a dedication. Moss showed the rest of the illustrated story, which has been made to look like it is recorded on this scroll (for example, the end of the scroll and the remaining red cord are on the last page of the book). The following discussion indicated the children's interest in this background information and their interest in how the artist had designed the story to reflect its origins in ancient scrolls:

Jonathan: The title is written up and down [vertically]. Languages like Chinese and Japanese are written like that.

Nik: The Ages Ago Stories are probably like a long, long ago story or a "Once upon a time" story.

Nik had figured out the meaning of the Ages Ago Stories from the brief note about the story that Moss had read previously. The other children nodded in agreement when he shared his interpretation of a term we had not discussed. At this point, Nik and Jonathan explained to the new student, Tom, about the Dog Tale Unit and the different kinds of stories that had been read aloud in the group sessions in the library. It seemed important to them that Tom have this prior knowledge before listening to the story. Also, notice in the following dialogue the quality of the children's explanations:

Nik: We're reading all kinds of stories about dogs. Some of the stories we read are funny, and some are serious. Some are fantasy, and some are realism. But sometimes, a fantasy story has realism in it.

Jonathan: And some are old stories, and some are new. We read an old Ukrainian folk tale and an old legend from Wales. And we have nonfiction books to get information about the dogs in the stories.

Riley and the other students continued to examine the title page. Their insights indicated that they were paying attention to the craft of the artist:

Riley: It looks like a diploma.

Nik: That's the scroll with the stories.

Clarissa: [looking at the next page] Now they untied the ribbon. They opened the scroll.

Samantha: The story is going to be written on a scroll!

Tamara: The writing on the rolled up scroll is up and down. It's Japanese writing.

The story opens with the following lines: "Ages ago, in the province of Mutsu, there lived a young hunter named Takumi" (n.p.). On hearing these lines, Nik was pleased to have his theory about the Ages Ago Stories confirmed. As the students listened to the story, they learned that Takumi has 30 hunting dogs, but his favorite is Jojofu, "the bravest and smartest hunting dog in the land" (n.p.). Moss told the students that Jojofu was a "working dog," not a pet. To help the children bring their prior knowledge to their transaction with *this* text, she asked them to identify other working dogs from previously read texts.

Samantha: Sirko worked as a sheepdog.

Riley: People who are blind have Seeing Eye dogs.

Jonathan:	The wolfhounds in the other stories were hunting dogs, too. Takumi loved his dogs like the prince loved Gelert.
Nik:	There's a book about working dogs on the shelf. [He points to one of the books available for independent reading, titled *Dogs With a Job* (Patten, 1996a).]

As the story continues, Takumi takes 10 of his dogs on a hunting trip. During this trip, Jojofu senses danger. She leaves the path, ignoring Takumi's angry shouts that this is not the right way, and "a moment later, a violent landslide of rock and gravel buried the path where Takumi stood only moments before" (n.p.). Takumi tells his dog, "Forgive me for losing my trust in you" (n.p.). At this point, Moss asked the children what Takumi meant with this statement. The purpose of her question was to encourage the children to use context to figure out the meaning of unfamiliar words or phrases in order to make sense of the text and to enrich the meaning-making process.

Samantha:	He felt bad that he didn't *believe* Jojofu. He just thought she was leading them all the wrong way...into the forest.
Tom:	Dogs can hear things better than humans. He [Jojofu] probably heard the rocks falling before the landslide came. So now he [Takumi] realizes he should have believed him.

Because the children were not familiar with the formal language patterns Takumi uses, phrases such as "forgive me" and "losing my trust in you" would have been difficult for them to understand without the textual and visual context surrounding these phrases. The children's comments revealed their successful use of context clues to generate meaning, a reading strategy that we had demonstrated, reinforced, and practiced throughout the literary experiences in both the library and the classroom.

After this brief discussion, Moss continued reading. In the next scene, Jojofu saves her master again when she stops Takumi from walking off a jagged cliff that Takumi does not see. Takumi says to Jojofu, "I will never lose faith in you, no matter what you do!" (n.p.). But later, Jojofu's behavior is so puzzling and frightening to Takumi that he draws his sword and is prepared to kill her—until he remembers his promise. Then, Jojofu attacks the large snake that has been lurking behind Takumi and causing her strange behavior. The children's responses to this scene revealed the intensity of their involvement as readers. For example, they seemed to hold their breath when Takumi takes out his sword. Conversely, when Takumi remembers his promise and jumps from the tree to the ground, the children responded animatedly with "Oh no," "He shouldn't do that," "That dog's mad," and "She's going to kill Takumi!"

At the end of this scene, the children examined the two spreads that feature the beginning and end of Jojofu's battle with the snake. The children then spontaneously compared *Jojofu* with *The Mightiest Heart*:

> Tamara: That part where Takumi took out his sword and was about to kill Jojofu was just like the part when the prince raised *his* sword to kill Gelert!
>
> Jonathan: He [the prince] thought the dog killed the baby. He lost trust in his dog just like when Takumi *lost his trust* in his dog. [Notice how Jonathan internalizes the literary language from *Jojofu*, which we had discussed previously.]
>
> Nik: But it's different here. Takumi got a second chance! He told Jojofu he was sorry, and they were always together after that. But Gelert never came back home to the prince.
>
> Samantha: The prince was sad the rest of the time, and Takumi was happy. It was a happy ending for Takumi and Jojofu.
>
> Riley: It was a sad ending for the prince and Gelert. The prince didn't get a second chance to be together with Gelert. He didn't even know where he was.

The children's discussion and their ability to find these intertextual links enabled them to engage in further meaning making, thus fulfilling one of our objectives. In addition, the children were actively using the reading strategies that Moss had introduced and encouraged throughout these sessions.

Assessment

A review of Fenster's record of the sessions described in this chapter enabled us to evaluate the nature of the children's involvement in the literary experiences in the library and their use of the reading strategies. We noticed that the quality of the children's participation continued to improve, and we were pleased to see the children begin to respond to the comments of their peers and enter into a collaborative process of constructing meaning together. According to Fenster's notes, the children's body language changed as well. For example, they tended to lean forward as they listened to each story unfold and turned toward one another during discussions instead of directing their attention to Moss alone. Spontaneous comments also became more frequent in the discussions. The children often initiated the cover-to-cover study of new texts, intertextual comments, and comparative analysis, and it was often a child's comment, rather than Moss's, that changed the direction of the discussion or led the children back to the text. The children used their prior knowledge to make predictions and generate meaning, and they asked questions as they attempted to make sense of the text. They needed fewer prompts from Moss to use context clues to figure out unfamiliar words or phrases in order to generate meaning in their transactions with texts. Many children began to incorporate new words or literary terms into their contributions to group discussions. As evidenced throughout this chapter, the children began to internalize new vocabulary and concepts they had learned in the course of the literary experiences in the library. The children became increasingly comfortable searching for and using textual and visual clues to infer characters' inner thoughts and feelings and exploring implied meanings in stories.

We also observed that as the children delved into the exploration of the four realistic tales introduced in these sessions, they discovered that they could use nonfiction to inform their study of these realistic tales. This growing awareness of genre was evident as the children talked about books they had selected for independent reading and as they responded to the shared texts in the library and the classroom, respectively. Throughout these sessions, we found that only a few children identified the craft of authors and artists and used this as a meaning-making strategy. Because an awareness of this craft significantly contributes to the quality of children's experiences as readers and writers, we realized that this was an area that needed further attention. Also, we realized that some of the children continued to be reluctant to enter into the ongoing dialogue that had become a central part of the sessions in the library. Therefore, we discussed ways to provide the support these children seemed to need in order to become more willing to share their ideas in the group discussions. For the most part, however, we were pleased with the children's progress as they became more active and thoughtful students of literature and members of a community of readers.

Looking Ahead

Chapter 4 will focus on the realistic fiction and nonfiction narratives about working dogs that Moss introduced in the shared reading sessions in the library and that the children selected for independent reading. The concluding sessions of the Dog Tale Unit show how the students continued to develop personal reading interests and became more involved in independent reading and writing.

The Dog Tale Unit: Introducing Nonfiction, Fiction, and Book Classification

The beginning sessions of the Dog Tale Unit introduced the children to diverse literary genres—modern animal fantasies, traditional folk tales from Ukraine and Russia, a modern folk tale from Russia, and a legend from Wales. Moss also used several nonfiction texts to provide the children with background information necessary to their understanding of the afore-mentioned tales. Over the course of these cumulative sessions, the children gradually developed an awareness of genre. That is, they learned what to expect from different kinds of literary texts and used their knowledge of genre to generate meaning. The sessions presented in this chapter illustrate how the focus of the Dog Tale Unit shifted from an emphasis on fantasy and folklore to nonfiction and realistic fiction. Through these sessions, Moss also was able to introduce the classification system in the library, as well as more complex literary terms to strengthen the children's literary analysis. The chapter ends with an assessment of the Dog Tale Unit as a whole, as well as a section titled "Literature in the Dog Tale Thematic Unit Collection," which provides an easy reference for the texts used in this unit.

Session Nine: Focusing on Nonfiction and Book Classification

When Moss held up *The Bravest Dog Ever: The True Story of Balto* by Natalie Standiford (1989), she asked, "What kind of story is this?" Nik read aloud the title and responded that "this is realism because it says it's *true*, and the picture looks real." Moss then identified the book as *nonfiction* and explained that nonfiction provides information, or facts, about something that actually happened and about real people and animals. After describing *The Bravest Dog Ever* as a "nonfiction story about sled dogs," Moss showed the children pictures of sled dogs (including Siberian huskies) in other nonfiction texts such as *Dog* (Clutton-Brock, 1991), *Dogs With a Job* (Patten, 1996a), and *Dogs: Evolution, History, Breeds, Behavior, Care* (O'Neill, 1999). Seeing these pictures allowed the children to share their prior knowledge about sled dogs.

Next, Moss explained the significance of the numbers on the spine of these nonfiction books and pointed to the 599 books (about mammals) and the 636 books (about dogs, cats, horses, etc.), located in the nonfiction section of the library. She told the children that this three-number classification system was called the Dewey Decimal System, which is used for book classification in most school and public libraries. Moss's discussion was integral to the development of the children's independent reading because it informed their selection of material for personal reading experiences. The children referred to it as the "number system" and over time, discovered its value in assisting in their book searches.

Following this discussion, Moss asked the children if they had ever heard of Balto, the sled dog featured in *The Bravest Dog Ever*.

Nik: I saw the movie!

Jonathan: I saw a statue of Balto. I can't remember where it was.

Moss: As you listen to the story, you will find out.

Samantha: I think Balto is part wolf and part dog. Wolves and dogs are related...like Sirko and the wolf.

Riley: Is that the one that the children got sick and the dog got the medicine?

Moss: Yes!

Nik: How did they get the disease?

Nik's question prompted further prestory discussion about contagious diseases and about immunizations that are available now but were not during the time of the events recounted in the story. As the story was read aloud, the children drew from this background information to make sense of the text.

The Bravest Dog Ever, which is part of the Step Into Reading series, focuses on Balto, the lead dog for a team of sled dogs in Nome, Alaska, USA, in 1925. (An updated and longer version of this story, *Balto and the Great Race* by Elizabeth Kimmel, was published in 1999 as a Stepping Stone book.) Balto's heroism occurred when a diphtheria epidemic threatened the people of Nome. The medicine to treat this epidemic was train-bound for Nome, but the train got stuck in snow 700 miles away from its destination. Then, a blizzard halted a dog-sled relay organized to transport the medicine. Balto, however, managed to carry the medicine through the snowstorm to save the people of Nome. Newspapers informed people all over the world about Balto's heroism, and in New York City, a statue of Balto was erected in Central Park.

As this read-aloud unfolded, the children asked questions about the nature of the dog-sled relay and consulted the map included in the book to better understand how each team of dogs traveled from town to town en route to Nome. At a crucial point in the narrative, Balto refuses to move across a frozen river with his dog-sled team despite the driver's insistence. When Moss finished reading the story, she asked the children to explain this scene because she believed that their prior literary experiences would enable them to construct meaning.

Jonathan: Balto noticed a crack in the ice, but Gunnar [the driver] couldn't see it.

Nik: They all would fall into the water and drown.... They would die. It's probably a pretty deep river.

Riley: Dogs see better and hear better. Like in the story of Jojofu. He stopped, too...before the rock slide. And Gunnar told Balto to go on just like Jojofu's owner said to go on.

Mason: And Balto helped Gunnar go on the trail. Gunnar couldn't do it without Balto.

Samantha: Gunnar couldn't find the trail, and Balto led them.

Charlene: So they got to Nome in time so everybody got the medicine in time.

Mason: Balto was a hero.... He saved them from the crack in the ice, and he led them through the blizzard.... He just kept going.

Samantha: And there's a statue in New York City.

Jonathan: Now I remember! That's where I saw it.

The children's literary experience with the story of Jojofu provided them with relevant information about dogs' keen vision, hearing, and sense of direction. The children's comments in the preceding dialogue suggested that they saw a parallel between Jojofu and Takumi and Balto and Gunnar. After this discussion, the children participated in a different kind of comparative analysis in which those students who had seen the movie about Balto compared it with the narrative in this book. Moss then told the children about other related nonfiction books that they could select for independent reading. These books and a brief explanation of their content follows:

- *Animals Who Have Won Our Hearts* (George, 1994)—a collection of stories that begins with "Balto: Indomitable Sled Dog"

- *Adventure in Alaska: An Amazing True Story of the World's Longest, Toughest Dog Sled Race* (Kramer, 1993)—a true story of Libby Riddles who, in 1985, crossed 1,200 miles of Alaskan wilderness with her dog team to become the first woman to win the Iditarod, the longest and most difficult dog sled race in the world

- *Iditarod Dream: Dusty and His Sled Dogs Compete in Alaska's Jr. Iditarod* (Wood, 1996)—a story of a 15-year-old Alaskan boy and his dogs as they prepare for and run the 158-mile course of the Junior Iditarod

- *Dogteam* (Paulsen, 1993)—an illustrated prose poem about a team of dogs pulling a sled on a beautiful moonlit winter night, written by an author who has raced in the Iditarod twice

In an attempt to reinforce the importance of the library's classification system—as well as the children's understanding of this concept—Moss asked, "What *kind* of books are these?"

Riley: Realism.... They're about things that really happen.

Moss: Yes, but look at the spine of each book.

Tom:	It's nonfiction! They have numbers. The one about Balto is 636. The one about the dogs and wolves and foxes is 599, for mammal books. *Dogteam* doesn't have a number.... It's fiction.
Samantha:	How come Balto isn't 599, too?

In response to this question, Moss provided further clarification about how these numbers are used to classify a wide variety of subjects covered in nonfiction books. Then, she showed the children three examples of realistic fiction about sled dogs: a picture book, *A Sled Dog for Moshi* (Bushey, 1994), and two chapter books, *Silver* (Whelan, 1988) and *Stone Fox* (Gardiner, 1980). Moss encouraged them to borrow these books for independent reading and to share them at home with their families, thus fulfilling the original objectives to provide the children with opportunities to discover new reading interests and a context for studying texts about the human experience.

To emphasize the nature of the classification of nonfiction and fiction, Moss asked the children to look at the books that they had selected from the library earlier. After noting that some books had numbers on the spine and some had letters, the children entered into a lively discussion in which they attempted to determine what these numbers and letters meant, how this classification system worked, and how to distinguish between nonfiction and realistic fiction. This discussion allowed them to make important discoveries about the great diversity of nonfiction books, as well as the differences between fiction and nonfiction and between traditional tales (classified under 398) and modern fiction (arranged alphabetically by author).

Session 10: Focusing on Realistic Fiction and Using Book Classification

To invite the children to predict what kind of story they would read next, Moss asked them to look at the front and back covers of *Emma and the Night Dogs* by Susan Aller (1997).

Nik:	It's realism. The dogs look real, and the girl looks like a real person.

Jonathan: It doesn't have a number on the spine, so it's not nonfiction.

Tom: What are night dogs?

Moss suggested that they search for the answer to this question as they listened to the story. That is, as part of their cover-to-cover study of this new text, she invited them to use a basic reading strategy: using questions to guide the reading-thinking process.

Before reading the story, Moss made sure to read the page of background information (just prior to the first page of the actual story), which began with the following sentence: "This story was inspired by a group of dogs and handlers belonging to Connecticut Canine Search and Rescue, Inc." (n.p.). Aller provides general background information about the dog handlers and search dogs, as well as more specific information about the Newfoundland breed of dog. Moss had displayed several nonfiction texts about the Newfoundland and about rescue dogs near the story circle for the children to choose for independent reading. By now, the children were familiar with the integration of fiction and nonfiction as a natural part of the process of literary study.

After a prestory discussion about this background information, Moss turned to the spread that set the stage for the opening lines: "A long time after he lost them the boy called out, 'Mommy! Daddy! I'm over here!' Now his throat was tight, and he plunged farther into the damp woods" (n.p.). Before reading the accompanying text, Moss asked the children to talk about the picture, which shows a small boy alone in the woods as night approaches. Her goal was to have the children use the picture's visual clues to infer how the boy was feeling.

Clarissa: He's probably lost. He's scared and he's looking all around.

[Nik uses body language to show what the boy in the picture is doing and how he feels.]

Tom: It's getting dark, so it's scary.

Charlene: He's so little.

When Moss read the text, the children were able to confirm the inferences they had made.

The next page of text faces a picture of a girl in bed, holding a teddy bear, and talking with her mother. The text reveals that the girl, Emma, is asking her mother about Aunt Alice, a handler, and the search dogs who are looking for the lost boy. Moss stopped reading and introduced a literary term—setting—in order to give the children the language to talk about the unfamiliar plot pattern in this story. Introducing this term also allowed Moss to carry out another objective—to provide the children with the language of literary analysis. She told the children, "The artist shows another *setting* here, so this story has two settings." The children then identified the woods and the cottage as the two settings in the story; Moss explained that the artist and the author would continue to switch from one setting to the other as the story unfolded. This brief preparation enabled the children to make sense of the complex narrative and parallel plots, with alternating settings that reveal the perspectives of the lost boy and the perspectives of the searchers and Emma.

The next picture, which also faces a page of text, that Moss showed the children depicts a search dog in the woods. The children responded to this picture using the literary language that Moss had just given them:

Clarissa: The *setting* is changed again. That's the woods where the boy is.

Nik: The search dogs are in the woods. That dog has the orange vest with the cross on it. [The author had included this in her background information.] It looks like a Red Cross sign...but it's white.

Mason: It's Juno, the Newfoundland dog.

When Moss read the accompanying text, the children discovered that the picture portrays Emma's thoughts as she imagines the scene taking place in the woods where the handlers and dogs are searching for the boy. The next scene is also in the woods, but this time, the text is in italics and reveals the boy's perspective. The children immediately picked up on this difference:

Samantha: The print is different. It's like the first page.

[Moss returns to the first page of the story, and the children note that the print was, indeed, the same.]

Jonathan: So on *this* page, the setting is the woods again, but it tells what the boy is thinking.

Charlene: He must be scared...and cold. He's shivering.

Mason: So Emma and her mother are in the cottage, and the boy is in the woods.

Jonathan: But in that one picture, Emma is at the cottage, but she's *thinking* about the woods so that's the picture in her head...like a thought bubble.

Clarissa: She's worried about the lost boy.

The children seemed to be helping one another build an understanding of the alternating settings and the alternating perspectives of the boy and Emma.

The setting then shifts to the cottage as the handlers and the search dogs arrive late at night to get food and sleep. The text reveals that Emma "only thought about the boy somewhere in the dark woods. She closed her eyes tight to hold back the tears" (n.p.). The next scene shifts to the woods, and the print is italicized. The children recognized this shift and that the spread shows the woods and the boy's perspective rather than the cottage and Emma's perspective. When the setting moves once more to the cottage, readers follow Emma as she quietly leaves the cottage and enters the woods with the dogs to look for the boy (Emma is familiar with the commands to use with the search dogs). Eventually, they find the boy and bring him back to the cottage. Tom observed, "So that's why the title is *Emma and the Night Dogs*." His question about the night dogs at the beginning of his reading experience guided his reading-thinking process and obviously, he was pleased to have found the answer to his question.

After the children expressed their content with the story's ending, they compared the search and rescue dogs with some of the other dogs they had encountered throughout the Dog Tale Unit:

Riley: Balto delivered medicine and saved the people; Juno saved the lost boy.

Clarissa: Jojofu saved his master.

Samantha: So did Gelert.

In the discussion that followed this segment, the children explored literature-life connections as they focused on the behavior of the lost boy:

Charlene: The boy was four. If he was six, he'd know to stay there.

Jonathan: If you're lost, stay in one place.

Tom: Don't wander off so your parents can find you...like in a grocery store or the mall.

Tamara: That's a safety rule.

Charlene: But he didn't know. He was only four.

Jonathan: If your parents don't know where you are, the dogs could smell you...but you should stay there. [Moss reinforces their comments about safety issues.]

After the children compared Juno with Balto, Jojofu, and Gelert, Moss asked them to review different kinds of "working dogs" that they had encountered in these stories. They identified the search and rescue dogs in *Emma and the Night Dogs*; the hunting dogs in *The Mightiest Heart* (Cullen, 1998), *The Wolfhound* (Franklin, 1996), and *Jojofu* (Waite, 1996); the sheepdog in *Sirko and the Wolf: A Ukrainian Tale* (Kimmel, 1997); and the sled dogs in the story *The Bravest Dog Ever: The True Story of Balto*. Moss then called attention to the numbers on the spine of each of those books. The children classified *Emma and the Night Dogs* as fiction because it had the first two letters of the author's name, but no numbers, on the spine. They also classified it as realism because "there are real-life search and rescue dogs, and this story could've happened in real life." The children classified *The Bravest Dog Ever: The True Story of Balto* as nonfiction "because of the number [636.7] and because it's about dogs that are trained to work with humans." Because *Sirko and the Wolf* and *Jojofu* each have 398 on the spine, the children noted that "they're old, old tales...from different countries. But they're part of nonfiction...because of the numbers." The children noticed that *The Wolfhound* was similar to a folk tale but noted that it was not an "old, old tale" because "it doesn't have 398 on the spine."

When the children returned to the classroom, Fenster displayed nonfiction books about working dogs and invited them to select one for independent reading. Because teachers may want to use these books with their own students, a list of these books and a description of their content follows:

- *Rosie: A Visiting Dog's Story* (Calmenson, 1994)—the story of a dog who works in hospitals and nursing homes to cheer up people who are sick or lonely
- *My Buddy* (Osofsky, 1992)—a story about a golden retriever who serves as "arms" and "legs" for a boy with muscular dystrophy
- *A Guide Dog Puppy Grows Up* (Arnold, 1991) and *Mom's Best Friend* (Alexander, 1992)—provide information about the process of training dogs to become guides for people who are blind
- *Hugger to the Rescue* (Patent, 1994)—a story about Newfoundland dogs who are trained for search-and-rescue work (as in the fictional story *Emma and the Night Dogs*)
- *Maggie: A Sheep Dog* (Patent, 1986)—describes the work of the Hungarian sheepdog, or kuvasz
- *Jake: A Labrador Puppy at Work and Play* (Jones, 1992)—observes Jake in his first year and shows how he is trained to become a hunting dog
- *Dogs Working for People* (Foster, 1972)—provides an overview of different types of work for which dogs have been trained—from Seeing Eye dogs to police dogs to circus dogs to television stars such as Lassie
- *A Dog Came, Too: A True Story* (Manson, 1993)—an account of the first European and the first dog to cross North America based on explorer Alexander Mackenzie's journals
- *Sammy, Dog Detective* (Bare, 1998)—a story about a dog who is part of the K-9 team of a police department

Other nonfiction titles that Fenster displayed—*The Newfoundland* (Wilcox, 1999a) and *The Samoyed* (Wilcox, 1999b), *The Terrier Breeds* (Patten, 1996b) and *The World's Smallest Dogs* (Patten, 1996c)—featured specific kinds of dogs. This wide variety of texts helped provide the children with many opportunities to engage in independent reading and possibly would lead them to develop new reading interests.

Session 11: Using Fiction to Focus on Setting and Plot

For the final read-aloud session in the Dog Tale Unit, Moss selected a fantasy tale to reinforce the concept of setting, which she had introduced in the previous session. Moss believed that *Trouble With Trolls* by Jan Brett (1992) would reinforce this literary concept because it is another example of a story with two settings. In this story, Treva sets out with her dog, Tuffi, on a journey across Mount Baldy to visit her cousin. The mountain setting dominates each page, but Brett also portrays on each page a setting that takes place underground. Treva is unaware that the trolls who live in this underground world long for a dog and plan to dognap Tuffi. The reader, however, is able to see the trolls' underground home, as well as their preparations for a dog of their own. That is, illustrations of the trolls' underground home reveal an empty dog basket in front of the fireplace, a water dish, and dog pictures covering the dirt walls.

Next, by examining the title and the pictures on the front and back covers of *Trouble With Trolls*, the children engaged in a cover-to-cover study. When Moss first showed the book to the children, they recognized the author, Jan Brett, and identified other books by Brett that they had read: *Annie and the Wild Animals* (1985), *The Mitten: A Ukrainian Folktale* (1989b), *The Hat* (1997), and *Goldilocks and the Three Bears* (1987). Riley observed that this would be a fantasy because trolls are make-believe. The other children agreed, and several supported their claims by pointing out the letters on the spine, which identified this book as fiction.

When Moss turned to the title page, the children counted the five trolls walking in the snow across the page and again counted the trolls when they first saw them in the underground setting, which occurs as Treva begins her journey up the mountain. Fenster observed in her notes that the children were intrigued with the details in each illustration and the way Brett portrays the underground and above-ground settings on each page throughout the book. The children held a running commentary about each page's details, including what they noticed in each setting, how the story unfolded in each setting, and the connection between the parallel stories.

At one point in the narrative, one detail in particular caught the children's attention: They discovered a small animal entering the trolls' home, which Tamara identified as a hedgehog. Although some children argued about this detail, Tamara held her ground and used an important reading strategy to back up her claims. Using her experiential background to support her response, Tamara told the others, "I *know* it's a hedgehog because I was a hedgehog in the play last year, and I looked it up, and I saw a picture of it, and that's what a hedgehog looks like!" The appearance of the hedgehog in the trolls' home while the trolls were above ground trying to capture the dog also prompted the children to focus their attention on a *third* story:

Jonathan: Is he a guest?

Tom: No...an intruder.

Tamara: It's like *Goldilocks and the Three Bears*.

Nik: He ate all the fish! He's making a mess.

Tom: He knocked the water over.

Mason: Now he's putting on the collar...that was for the dog.

Nik: Now he's in the bed with the collar on.

Tamara: Just like in *Goldilocks and the Three Bears*!... She ended up in the bed, too.

While the children were following the hedgehog story, they also were following the trolls' story and Treva's story. Unlike the alternating settings in *Emma and the Night Dogs*, *Trouble With Trolls* begins with two settings and parallel plots that Brett goes on to reveal on each page, as the parallel plots unfold and intersect. Instead of using the term *plot* with the children, Moss continued to use the word *problem* to call attention to the conflict that drives the plot. For example, she asked the children to identify the "trolls' problem" and "Treva's problem." In response, one child suggested that the hedgehog had a problem, too, because "he wanted a home. That's the third story." The children became intensely involved in this more complex narrative: They frequently revisited previously read pages to reexamine the text and illustrations in order to clarify what was happening in each page and in each setting.

The children's discussion of this book and their comparative analysis revealed their growing awareness of literary elements and the craft of authors and artists. For example, their attention to the detail of the hedgehog story demonstrated that they were more adept at analyzing character development and the plot structure. Also, the children noted that much of the story was told with pictures, not text, and they expressed their appreciation for Brett's skill as an artist. They then stated that the book is really about Treva and the trolls because the dog is not well developed as a character. To back up this idea, Tom compared Tuffi with other dogs Moss had introduced during the Dog Tale Unit: "The author doesn't tell you as much about Tuffi, and we don't get to know him much...not like all the other dogs in the other stories." Samantha compared Tuffi to the wolves in *The Wolfhound* and *The Mightiest Heart* because "they weren't really characters you get to know either." Adding to Samantha's comment, Jonathan noted that the dogs in the other stories were more interesting than Tuffi. His comment led to a group discussion in which the children reflected about what was interesting about these other dogs. Their review of the dogs featured in the diverse fiction and nonfiction texts during this thematic unit set the stage for their final projects in the unit, which would take place in the classroom.

Final Projects

Because of the children's investment in the Dog Tale Unit, Fenster decided to have a culminating project that would showcase their interests, new knowledge, and hard work. She asked the children to choose their favorite book and use it as a starting point for their projects. In preparation, Fenster invited the children to look through the collection of dog tales, think about the books they had especially enjoyed listening to or independently reading, and talk about the titles of these books in a group session and reread favorite sections in these books. The children spent several days talking to one another as they revisited these books and conferencing with Fenster as they engaged in the selection process. Once they made their individual choices, the children met as a group to brainstorm about possibilities for projects that could be developed to extend these books. The children generated a list of suggestions that Fenster recorded on a wall chart to help them get started on their projects. Their suggestions included the following:

- Paint a picture of the main characters or something that happened in the story and write about the picture,

- Make a shoe-box diorama,

- Make puppets for a puppet show,

- Make a poster to advertise the book,

- With other children, make an illustrated dictionary of dogs,

- Write a fiction story about a dog,

- Write a poem about a dog, and

- Research to learn more about a specific kind of dog, and create a non-fiction book about what you learn.

Fenster helped each child write a plan for his or her project. When the children were ready to get started, they worked on their projects during readers' workshop time each day for two weeks. The children worked independently or with partners on their final projects. One child, for example, read and wrote about Newfoundland dogs and created a Newfoundland habitat, using a shoebox, clay, and paint. Another child used Kristine George's *Little Dog Poems* (1999) as a springboard for writing her own poems about her dog. George's poem "Morning Nap," an example of concrete poetry, inspired this child to create her own concrete poems. Two other children worked together to study sled dogs and the Iditarod.

Throughout the children's work on these projects, Fenster helped them gather materials they would need, and Moss helped them find resources to supplement the books in the classroom collections. The children became so involved in their projects that they decided to use choice time to work on them. They enjoyed working together on individual projects and used one another as guides and coaches to translate their plans into a finished product. According to Fenster, the children formed a happy, hardworking community as they sought advice from one another and shared discoveries. She noted that she had not expected the children to become so involved and committed to this project and that it seemed to take on a life of its own as it extended beyond the week she originally had set aside for these final projects.

Assessment of the Dog Tale Unit: Revisiting Our Objectives

Personal Enjoyment and Growth

We observed the children's enjoyment as they entered into the story worlds that Moss introduced in the read-aloud sessions and explored the story ideas together. According to Fenster's written records of the children's responses to the literary texts, as described throughout these chapters, they showed increased involvement as active and enthusiastic participants. By the third session, for example, the children began to respond spontaneously to the stories and unlike earlier sessions, very few children tuned out during these discussions. According to Fenster's notes, the children's body language also revealed their growing involvement as they actively responded to stories with facial expressions that reflected their feelings and spontaneous utterances that reflected their engagement in a lived-through experience. For example, in *The Mightiest Heart*, when the prince is in the forest after giving up his search for Gelert and encounters a "thin old dog" (n.p.), several children whispered in delight, "It's Gelert!"

Fenster's notes also revealed that the children's involvement deepened when Moss introduced them to the realistic tales about Sirko and the wolf, Pavel and the wolfhound, Tokumi and Jojofu, Emma and Juno, and Balto. These stories of the human experience had the power to touch the minds and hearts of the children as they entered into the lives of the literary characters. At the end of the unit, *Trouble With Trolls* seemed to be a source of great enjoyment for the children because of the intellectual challenge involved in following the three stories in the text and the illustrations and trying to figure out the complex narrative as it unfolded. Because Moss introduced them to the literary technique of the dual setting, the children were prepared to take on this challenge on their own.

In the classroom, Fenster observed that the children became more connected to the library experience: They looked forward to the library sessions and often counted the days until it was their day in the library. In addition, individual children often asked Fenster for permission to make special trips to the library to show Moss some of their writing, to read a favorite passage in a book, or to recommend a new title to add to the library collection. As the children engaged in their classroom activities, they often made comments such as "I think Mrs. Moss would like this poem," or "Let's take our clay dogs to show Mrs. Moss." They also asked Fenster to reread books that Moss had read aloud in the library. When they noticed new details in the pictures or text of these books, they knew "Mrs. Moss would be interested in this!" Their love of the Argo and Martha series of books was apparent as they reread these books on their own. Fenster's observations from the classroom suggested that the children were creating their own bridge between the library and the classroom.

Student-Initiated Book Exploration, Inquiry, and Discovery

In order to meet this objective, Moss introduced the cover-to-cover study of literary texts during the sessions in the library. Moss first modeled this approach and then invited the children to follow suit. Over time, she observed that the children began on their own to examine front and back covers, book titles, title pages, dedication pages, and other relevant material before and after she read aloud the story. They also studied the illustrations and learned that illustrations are an integral part of each story, revealing information that is not given in the text. This cover-to-cover approach also allowed the students to use the many reading strategies that Moss had demonstrated. For example, they used questions prompted by the material in the peritext to respond to the unfolding stories. Or, they confirmed or revised initial predictions, from their examinations of the peritext, as the text unfolded.

Fenster also observed the children's growing involvement as independent readers in the classroom. She noted that most of the children were using the cover-to-cover approach in their transactions with self-selected stories. In addition to selecting stories about dogs from the classroom collection, the children used nonfiction texts for research. That is, they used nonfiction to find answers to questions raised as they read fiction or to pursue special interests that they developed as they became immersed in the study of dog tales. The children learned to actively engage in inquiry and discovery as motivated and thoughtful readers and writers.

Critical Thinking

As the children gradually internalized the reading strategies and used them to explore literary texts, they began to think critically. For example, many of the children used the *why* questions that Moss had introduced in the library sessions to discover the motivation behind a particular character's behavior or to explain the choices made by an author or artist. Some of their student-initiated questions included the following:

- "Why does the farmer look so sad in this picture?" (This question was in response to seeing a two-page spread in *Sirko and the Wolf* that portrays the farmer and his wife discussing the fate of their sheepdog.)
- "Why didn't the author tell what happened to Gelert after the prince accused him of hurting the baby?"
- "Why did the prince create a mound out of stones in the place where he saw Gelert?" (This was not an actual question but was implied in the children's spontaneous responses to this scene as they tried to imagine how the prince felt and why he created the mound of stones.)

Many questions like these, which were recorded by Fenster, proved to us that the students were stretching their minds and imaginations to understand the stories' details, as well as the authors' intentions.

Community of Readers

We observed not only the children's literary learning during this unit, but also their social growth in the context of these cumulative literary sessions. In the first few sessions, there was no student dialogue. When Moss invited the children to share their personal responses to the book covers, the illustrations, or the text, only a few responded. Often, the text or illustrations triggered children's personal associations or memories that had little, if anything, to do with the story. Although a few children replied to Moss's questions, their comments were brief and directed only to Moss. In addition, when a child did speak, the others did not listen or verbally reflect on what that child said. In these early sessions, a few children even needed frequent reminders about inappropriate behavior. The children seemed to enjoy listening to the stories but had difficulty sustaining their attention during discussions about stories.

Because we were concerned about the children's apparent lack of involvement, we decided to give them more time to familiarize themselves with the idea that talk was an important part of the read-aloud sessions. We thought they needed more time to discover the pleasure inherent in working together to explore and build meanings before, during, and after the read-aloud. In addition, we realized that the children probably needed more time both to learn and to understand the reading strategies that Moss demonstrated as she explored story ideas with them.

We observed that, with more time and experience, the children adjusted to the idea of responding to each new story. In the context of the cumulative sessions, the children's confidence as participants in these group sessions increased. As their literary background grew, they had more to contribute to the ongoing dialogue, and they no longer waited for teacher-initiated questions to respond to the stories. More children began to contribute thoughtful and relevant comments, and their contributions increased in length. As they became actively engaged in exploring and building meanings together, the children began to listen to one another and to direct their comments to one another. Not long after this, the children began to reflect on, respond to, and build on the ideas expressed by the other children. By the end of this unit, each child seemed to have gained enough confidence to articulate his or her ideas, interpretations, and questions in this group setting. Most of the children were even willing to support or defend an idea that others challenged. The children were learning how to work together—building on the ideas of others and learning from one another—and in the process, were becoming a community of readers.

Exposure to and Awareness of Diverse Literary Genres

The children's growing understanding of the concept of genre or *kinds* of stories was apparent as they began to identify the various dog tales as fantasy, realism, folk tales, or legends. They learned to distinguish between the "long, long ago" stories, which were told by ancient storytellers, and the modern stories, which were written by authors they recognized. The children noticed that the dogs in fantasies often were similar to humans in their behavior, language, interests, and goals. Conversely, they discerned that dogs in realistic fiction generally acted like dogs. The children also discovered that many authors blur the lines of genre; that is, some realistic stories have fantasy elements embedded in them, and most fantasy stories reveal important truths about life. They also discovered that some folk tales were realistic, or "true to life," and "did not have magic."

The children compared the illustrations of humorous tales with those from more serious or realistic stories to survey the craft of artists working in various genres. They found that they could often use the cover-to-cover study, specifically examining the title and the picture on the front cover, to predict the kind of story they were about to hear. And, as the story unfolded, they could confirm or revise these predictions.

The children also learned to distinguish between nonfiction and fiction and to use the Dewey Decimal System to locate different types of nonfiction in the school library. For example, the children who had especially enjoyed the folk tales introduced in this unit discovered that the 398 section in the library housed a rich selection of books for them to read independently in the classroom or take home for family read-aloud experiences. Knowing this classification system allowed the children to locate these traditional tales more easily. Other children who wanted to find out how to take care of their own dogs or do research on working dogs like Sirko and Juno were delighted to be able to locate appropriate books on their own. Some children specifically asked Moss for fiction. One child, for example, requested a "fiction story about a Great Dane." When Moss showed her how she could use the computer in the library to search for fiction by subject or keyword, the child found Steven Kellogg's books about the dog Pinkerton. After reading all four of the Pinkerton books in the library collection (1979, 1981, 1982, 1987), she asked Moss if she could take the books and add them to the classroom collection. Following her immersion in the Pinkerton stories, this child decided to look for nonfiction books about Great Danes. Because she had a clear idea of what she wanted to read, was able to use the classification system in the library, and had a knowledge of genres, she found these nonfiction books with little adult assistance. Moss observed that most of the children were becoming more independent as library patrons and often seemed self-sufficient in the process of selecting books for independent reading.

Exposure to Literary Heritage

In order to expose the children to their literary heritage, Moss selected traditional tales from different parts of the world to include throughout the unit. For example, she read aloud *The Mightiest Heart*, a Welsh legend; *Sirko and the Wolf*, a Ukrainian tale; and *Jojofu*, a Japanese tale. Moss also introduced the children to other traditional tales that they could select for independent reading in the classroom or at home, such as *Kashtanka—A Russian Tale* (Chekhov, 1995); *Dream Wolf* (Goble, 1990), a Plains Indian tale; *Good Morning, Grannie Rose: An Arkansas Folktale* (Ludwig, 1990); and *Dogs of Myth: Tales From Around the World* (Hausman & Hausman, 1999). An awareness of these tales from other cultures provided the children with opportunities to develop a global perspective as they encountered characters from various parts of the world and learned to view cultural differences as a natural part of the human experience. When Moss first introduced these tales during the Dog Tale Unit, the children had many questions about external differences between themselves and the characters such as clothing, hairstyles, food, and homes. However, as they entered into the lives of these characters, the children discovered how much they shared with them in terms of the range of human emotion.

Independent Reading and Personal Reading Interests

Although Moss concluded the Dog Tale Unit after the final projects in the classroom, the children returned to their favorite titles from this unit for independent reading. In fact, a year later, most of the children who participated in the literary/literacy program were still talking about the stories featured in this unit. Because Moss worked regularly with all the children in kindergarten through grade four, she still had contact with and observed many of these students after their first-grade year. (Specific examples of these observations are included in chapter 8.) Moss noted that although they often returned to these old favorites, the children also searched for new or more challenging dog tales. Some of the new titles they enjoyed reading are listed at the end of the chapter under the sections titled "Longer Fiction for More Experienced Readers" and "Suggested Reading."

The Dog Tale Unit provided a context in which the children discovered new possibilities for personal reading and developed the motivation to read for personal pleasure and growth. For them, the learning that began in this unit did not end: They continued to explore familiar literary paths, but they also embarked on new journeys on their own. Indeed, this thematic unit set the stage for their experience as independent readers.

The Human Experience and Literature-Life Connections

The children discovered connections between literature and life as they discussed the dog tales introduced in the read-aloud sessions and selected for independent reading. For example, they noticed that most of the realistic stories portrayed close bonds between humans and dogs. The children who had dogs of their own talked about their close bonds with their dogs, thus confirming the literature-life connections. Similarly, when the children pointed out examples of the ways dogs in the realistic stories communicated their feelings and desires to humans, the children who owned dogs offered firsthand experiences regarding their dogs' abilities to express themselves and to comprehend the language of humans. These dog owners also identified and confirmed characteristics of different breeds of dogs in particular stories because of their life experiences.

The children read nonfiction texts to learn more about the different kinds of dogs introduced in this unit, especially working dogs, their training, and the traits that qualify these dogs for particular jobs. Through this research, the children discovered that authors use factual information to create fiction—another literature-life connection. For example, the sheepdog in *Sirko and the Wolf* also is described in nonfiction texts about working dogs. The relationship between the dog and the wolf in this particular story is based on real-life relationships between dogs and wolves depicted in nonfiction texts such as *Amazing Wolves, Dogs, and Foxes* (Ling, 1991) and *Dogs: The Wolf Within* (Patent, 1993).

The children also learned that many authors use their own life experiences to write a story or to develop a character. For example, in *Martha and Skits* (Meddaugh, 2000), a new puppy, Skits, is added to the household. As the children engaged in the cover-to-cover study, they noticed that the front flap of the book shows a photograph of "Susan Meddaugh and Skits." The back flap of Kellogg's *Tallyho, Pinkerton!* (1982) displays a photograph of the author and a Great Dane, "the *real* Pinkerton." Four photographs of Kellogg playing with and hugging "the *real* Pinkerton" also are on the back flap of *Pinkerton, Behave!* (Kellogg, 1979).

Moss also highlighted the study of literary themes about the human experience in the context of exploring these literature-life connections. For example, *Emma and the Night Dogs* portrays the courage and commitment of rescue workers, who spend countless hours searching for people who are lost or in danger. The children identified with Emma, whose deep concern for the lost boy prompted her to set out with the dogs into the dark woods in the middle of the night: They expressed their own feelings about the lost boy and the empathy they felt for him as he wandered alone in the woods. As they examined the relationships between humans and dogs featured in many of the stories in this unit, the children also related to the recurring themes of trust, loyalty, and betrayal. For instance, they noticed that although the human characters in *The Mightiest Heart* and *Jojofu* lost their trust in their beloved dogs at critical moments, these dogs remained loyal to their masters. The children identified the conflicting emotions experienced by the farmer in *Sirko and the Wolf* and Pavel in *The Wolfhound*. The farmer knows that Sirko is too old to do the work required of a sheepdog, but as the children observed, he is "sad to have to give him away. The dog is like a pet." When the farmer decides not to shoot his dog, the children expressed their own relief that he had resolved his conflict in this way. Pavel, too, is conflicted— terrified of the dangers involved in taking the wolfhound through the tsar's private forest, but unable to let the dog die in the cold. The children identified with these characters' inner struggles and shared struggles and dilemmas they had experienced in their own lives.

The best example of the children's growing knowledge of literary themes occurred in response to *Sirko and the Wolf*. Several children identified a thematic connection between this folk tale and other traditional tales. That is, when one child noted that Sirko decided to repay the wolf for helping him win the respect and affection of his owners, several of the children repeated the moral of the fable *The Lion and the Mouse* (Jones, 1997), which Moss had introduced and read to them a year earlier: "One good deed deserves another." The children's knowledge of this connection showed us not only their understanding of literary themes, but also their growing ability to make intertextual connections.

Literature, Literary Analysis, and the Craft of Authors and Artists

We observed that the children were becoming attentive to the craft of authors and artists as they learned to distinguish between characters' external speech, internal thoughts, and dreams. In her stories about Martha, for example, Meddaugh uses thought and dream bubbles to convey the inner thoughts and feelings of characters, whereas she places speech bubbles around characters' words to convey external speech. When Moss introduced the children to more complex narratives that did not have these bubbles, the children were then able to "imagine the bubbles" in order to identify the difference between characters' internal and external language. Conversely, the image of a speech or thought bubble helped them use textual and visual clues to infer implied meanings about the inner thoughts and feelings of the characters. For example, the illustration on the cover of *Martha Blah Blah* (Meddaugh, 1996), which shows a dog with a sad face sitting in front of an empty bowl, prompted the children to infer that "the dog is sad because she's hungry and there's no food in her bowl." At each successive session, the children focused on each character to figure out his or her thoughts, feelings, and intentions and to support their conclusions with clues from the text or illustrations. The children's responses to *Emma and the Night Dogs* revealed their ability to apply their learning about the inner life of characters: They discovered what Emma was thinking and recognized that one of the illustrations portrayed "the picture in her head." Further, they were able to understand the connection between the alternating perspectives of the boy and Emma. As readers, the children used this literary learning to explore layers of meaning in the literary texts. This is important because most authors assume that their audiences will be able to distinguish between what a character says and what he or she thinks, feels, or dreams.

We also wanted to make available to the children the language of literary analysis, which would enable them to talk about narrative elements. For example, Moss introduced the term *setting* during the read-aloud of *Emma and the Night Dogs* because the story has two settings, which the author alternates throughout the narrative. The story introduced in the next group session, *Trouble With Trolls*, also has two settings. Moss specifically used this story to reinforce the concept of setting and the craft of authors and artists who choose to develop these dual settings. In the course of the discussion about *Trouble With Trolls*, many children used the term *setting* in their own responses. The children further revealed that they had begun to internalize this literary concept as they continued to use this term appropriately in their discussions of other stories later in the semester.

Fenster augmented the children's learning of the language of literary analysis in the classroom. For example, when she read aloud to the children, she focused on genre by asking, "What kind of book is this?" One child responded to this question by identifying the book *Canines: Predators* (Stone, 1993) as nonfiction by pointing to the number on the spine and explaining, "It tells true facts and information about real dogs and wolves and foxes and other animals in the dog family." Another child replied to this question about the book *Burnt Toast on Davenport Street* (Egan, 1997) by noting that it was an animal fantasy "because dogs can't talk in real life, and they [dogs in the story] wore clothes and acted like humans act." After Fenster read aloud a new book, she recorded on a wall chart the title, author, and genre of each book. She encouraged the children to identify the genre of the books they were reading independently. Fenster invited the children to engage in the cover-to-cover study of read-aloud selections, as well as the books they selected for independent reading. For example, before she read aloud *Officer Buckle and Gloria* (Rathmann, 1995), she showed the children the front and back covers and used literary language to ask, "Who do you think are the main characters in this book?" After reading *Officer Buckle and Gloria*, Fenster asked, "Is there a helper character in the story?" It was clear that the children understood this literary language because they identified Officer Buckle's dog, Gloria, as the helper character "because she helped Officer Buckle feel important again." Fenster also encouraged the children to describe the setting of the stories they listened to or read independently. They then had opportunities to describe the settings orally in group sessions or during a reading conference with Fenster, to write a description of the settings in their Literary Notebooks, and to draw pictures to depict the settings. Thus, during her read-aloud sessions in the classroom and her reading conferences with individual children, Fenster was able to reinforce the language of literary analysis introduced by Moss in the library.

Comparative Analysis and Intertextual Links

Guided by this objective, Moss demonstrated ways to explore connections between characters, settings, plot patterns, and themes in the texts introduced during the Dog Tale Unit. As the unit progressed, the children began to initiate a comparative analysis of multiple texts and to engage in intertextual talk in response to the literary texts read aloud in the group sessions and those read independently. For example, they linked *Sirko and the Wolf* with other stories in which characters help one another. The children likened *Sirko* to *The Wolfhound* "because Pavel saved the wolfhound when he was buried in the snow, and the wolfhound saved Pavel from the wolves," and they found similarities between the reciprocity in *Sirko* and the reciprocity in *The Lion and the Mouse* (Jones, 1997) and *The Hungry Otter* (Ezra, 1996). They compared Jojofu to Balto because both dogs save the lives of humans because of their abilities to sense danger before the humans were aware it. The children also contrasted these two stories with *Trouble With Trolls*: They noted that in the latter tale, the human saves the dog from the trolls. They also found connections between specific scenes in *The Mightiest Heart* and *Jojofu*, in which each dog's owner wrongly accuses him of a terrible deed. Over the course of this cumulative experience, these responses and many more demonstrated that the children were learning to respond to each new story in light of previous ones and to use intertextual links to make predictions, inferences, and interpretations and more important, to generate meaning.

Opportunities to Study
Literature With a Writer's Eye

In order to prepare the children to create original narratives, Moss provided opportunities for them to study literature with a writer's eye. The children explored the craft of authors and artists by examining the words and pictures in each story in order to discover how stories were created. Moss intended for these experiences to set the stage for the Transformation Tale Unit, which would conclude with a collaborative writing project in which the children would create an original narrative. Thus, during the Transformation Tale Unit, we intended to use this final objective as the children's guide for studying the transformation tales as models of writing and the tales' storytellers as mentors in preparation for this writing project.

Our assessment of the children's progress by the end of the Dog Tale Unit suggested that most of the children had taken the important first steps toward realizing the goals we had established for them as literary/literacy learners. We decided our next step was to reinforce and build on the understandings and strategies the children had begun to develop and to provide special support and guidance to those children who had not become active participants in the community of readers that was emerging in the library and the classroom. Our review of Fenster's written records also convinced us that the children seemed to enjoy the increasingly complex stories that Moss introduced after the third session of the Dog Tale Unit. This discovery influenced our selection of stories we would introduce in the library and the classroom during the second semester.

Literature in the Dog Tale Thematic Unit Collection

Traditional Tales

Chekov, A., & Spirin, G. (1995). *Kashtanka—A Russian tale* (R. Meyer, Adapt.). New York: Harcourt Brace.

Cullen, L. (Retell.). (1998). *The mightiest heart*. Ill. L. Long. New York: Dial.

Goble, P. (Retell.). (1990). *Dream wolf*. New York: Bradbury Press.

Hausman, G., & Hausman, L. (Retell.). (1999). *Dogs of myth: Tales from around the world*. Ill. B. Moser. New York: Simon & Schuster.

Kimmel, E. (Adapt.). (1997). *Sirko and the wolf: A Ukrainian tale*. Ill. R. Sauber. New York: Holiday House.

Ludwig, W. (Retell.). (1990). *Good morning, Grannie Rose: An Arkansas folktale*. New York: Putnam.

Waite, M.P. (1996). *Jojofu*. Ill. Y. Ito. New York: Lothrop, Lee & Shepard.

Fiction

Aller, S.B. (1997). *Emma and the night dogs*. Ill. M. Backer. Morton Grove, IL: Albert Whitman.

Baker, B. (1998). *Digby and Kate and the beautiful day*. Ill. M. Winborn. New York: Dutton.

Bechtold, L. (1999). *Buster, the very shy dog*. Boston: Houghton Mifflin.

Brett, J. (1992). *Trouble with trolls*. New York: Putnam.

Brett, J. (1999). *The first dog*. San Diego: Harcourt Brace.

Bridwell, N. (1985). *Clifford, the big red dog*. New York: Scholastic.

Bridwell, N. (1985). *Clifford, the small red puppy*. New York: Scholastic.

Brodkin, A.M. (1998). *The lonely only dog*. Ill. L. Di Fiori. New York: Scholastic.

Brown, M.T. (1993). *Arthur's new puppy*. Boston: Little, Brown.

Burningham, J. (1994). *Courtney*. New York: Crown.

Bushey, J. (1994). *A sled dog for Moshi*. Ill. G. Arnaktauyok. New York: Hyperion.

Cebulash, M. (1993). *Willie's wonderful pet*. Ill. G. Ford. New York: Scholastic.

Day, A. (1991). *Carl's afternoon in the park*. New York: Farrar, Straus & Giroux.

Day, A., & Edens, C. (2000). *Darby: The special-order pup*. New York: Dial.

Egan, T. (1997). *Burnt toast on Davenport Street*. Boston: Houghton Mifflin.

Ernst, L.C. (1990). *Ginger jumps*. New York: Bradbury Press.

Feiffer, J. (1999). *Bark, George*. New York: HarperCollins.

Franklin, K.L. (1996). *The wolfhound*. Ill. K. Waldherr. New York: Lothrop, Lee & Shepard.

Gackenbach, D. (1989). *Dog for a day*. New York: Clarion.

Gackenbach, D. (1990). *Beauty, brave and beautiful*. New York: Clarion.

Harper, I. (1994). *My dog Rosie*. Ill. B. Moser. New York: Blue Sky Press.

Hendry, D. (1995). *Dog Donovan*. Ill. M. Chamberlain. Cambridge, MA: Candlewick.

Herriot, J. (1985). *Only one woof*. Ill. P. Barrett. New York: St. Martin's.

Hesse, K. (1993). *Lester's dog*. Ill. N. Carpenter. New York: Crown.

Hewett, J. (1987). *Rosalie*. Ill. D. Carrick. New York: Lothrop, Lee & Shepard.

Kellogg, S. (1979). *Pinkerton, behave!* New York: Dial.

Kellogg, S. (1981). *A rose for Pinkerton*. New York: Dial.

Kellogg, S. (1982). *Tallyho, Pinkerton!* New York: Dial.

Kellogg, S. (1987). *Prehistoric Pinkerton*. New York: Dial.

Killilea, M. (1992). *Newf*. Ill. I. Schoenherr. New York: Philomel.

McNeal, T., & McNeal, L. (1996). *The dog who lost his Bob*. Ill. J. Sandford. Morton Grove, IL: Albert Whitman.

Meddaugh, S. (1992). *Martha speaks*. Boston: Houghton Mifflin.

Meddaugh, S. (1994). *Martha calling*. Boston: Houghton Mifflin.

Meddaugh, S. (1996). *Martha blah blah*. Boston: Houghton Mifflin.

Meddaugh, S. (1998). *Martha walks the dog*. Boston: Houghton Mifflin.

Meddaugh, S. (2000). *Martha and Skits*. Boston: Houghton Mifflin.

Paterson, K. (1998). *Celia and the sweet, sweet water*. Ill. V. Vagin. Boston: Houghton Mifflin.

Pomerantz, C. (1993). *The outside dog*. Ill. J. Plecas. New York: HarperCollins.

Rand, G. (1998). *A home for Spooky*. Ill. T. Rand. New York: Henry Holt.

Rathmann, P. (1995). *Officer Buckle and Gloria*. New York: Putnam.

Robertus, P. (1988). *The dog who had kittens*. Ill. J. Stevens. New York: Holiday House.

Rossiter, N.P. (1997). *Rugby and Rosie*. New York: Dutton.

Rylant, C. (1987). *Henry and Mudge in puddle trouble*. Ill. S. Stevenson. New York: Bradbury Press.

Seymour, T. (1993). *Pole dog*. Ill. D. Soman. New York: Orchard.

Smith, J. (1994). *Wizard and Wart*. Ill. P. Meisel. New York: HarperCollins.

Smith, M. (1991). *There's a witch under the stairs*. New York: Lothrop, Lee & Shepard.

Smith, M. (1994). *Argo, you lucky dog*. New York: Lothrop, Lee & Shepard.

Steig, W. (1977). *Caleb and Kate*. New York: Farrar, Straus & Giroux.

Thomas, A. (1994). *Lily*. New York: Henry Holt.

Thompson, C. (2000). *Unknown*. Ill. A. Pignataro. New York: Walker.

Weller, F.W. (1990). *Riptide*. Ill. R.J. Blake. New York: Philomel.

Wells, R. (1997). *McDuff and the baby*. Ill. S. Jeffers. New York: Hyperion.

Wells, R. (1997). *McDuff moves in*. Ill. S. Jeffers. New York: Hyperion.

Zion, G. (1960). *Harry and the lady next door*. Ill. M.B. Graham. New York: Harper Trophy.

Nonfiction

Alexander, S.H. (1992). *Mom's best friend*. Ill. G. Ancona. New York: Macmillan.

Arnold, C. (1991). *A guide dog puppy grows up*. New York: Harcourt Brace Jovanovich.

Bare, C.S. (1998). *Sammy, dog detective*. New York: Cobblehill Books.

Calmenson, S. (1994). *Rosie: A visiting dog's story*. Ill. J. Sutcliffe. New York: Clarion.

Calmenson, S. (1998). *Shaggy, waggy dogs (and others)*. Ill. J. Sutcliffe. New York: Clarion.

Clutton-Brock, J. (1991). *Dog*. New York: Knopf.

Crisman, R. (1993). *Racing the Iditarod trail*. New York: Dillon Press.

Darling, K. (1997). *ABC dogs*. Ill. T. Darling. New York: Walker.

deBourgoing, P. (1999). *Dogs*. Ill. H. Galeron. New York: Scholastic.

Evans, M. (1992). *Puppy: A practical guide to caring for your puppy*. New York: Dorling Kindersley.

Foster, J. (1972). *Dogs working for people*. Ill. J. Stanfield. Washington, DC: National Geographic Society.

George, J.C. (1994). *Animals who have won our hearts*. Ill. C.H. Merrill. New York: HarperCollins.

George, J.C. (2000). *How to talk to your dog*. Ill. S. Truesdele. New York: HarperCollins.

Gibbons, G. (1996). *Dogs*. New York: Holiday House.

Jones, R. (1992). *Jake: A Labrador puppy at work and play*. Ill. B. Eppridge. New York: Farrar, Straus & Giroux.

Kehret, P. (1999). *Shelter dogs: Amazing stories of adopted strays*. Photo. G. Farrar. Morton Grove, IL: Albert Whitman.

Kimmel, E.C. (1999). *Balto and the great race*. Ill. N. Koerber. New York: Random House.

Kramer, S.A. (1993). *Adventure in Alaska: An amazing true story of the world's longest, toughest dog sled race*. Ill. K. Meyer. New York: Random House.

Ling, M. (1991). *Amazing wolves, dogs, and foxes*. Photo. J. Young. New York: Knopf.

Manson, A. (1993). *A dog came, too: A true story*. New York: Macmillan.

O'Neill, A. (1999). *Dogs: Evolution, history, breeds, behavior, care*. New York: Kingfisher.

Osofsky, A. (1992). *My buddy*. Ill. T. Rand. New York: Henry Holt.

Patent, D.H. (1986). *Maggie: A sheep dog*. Ill. W. Muñoz. New York: Dodd, Mead.

Patent, D.H. (1993). *Dogs: The wolf within*. Photo. W. Muñoz. Minneapolis: Carolrhoda.

Patent, D.H. (1994). *Hugger to the rescue*. Photo. W. Muñoz. New York: Cobblehill Books/Dutton.

Patten, B. (1996). *Canine companions*. Vero Beach, FL: Rourke.

Patten, B. (1996). *Dogs with a job*. Vero Beach, FL: Rourke.

Patten, B. (1996). *The terrier breeds*. Vero Beach, FL: Rourke.

Patten, B. (1996). *The world's smallest dogs*. Vero Beach, FL: Rourke.

Radlauer, E. (1974). *Dogs*. Glendale, CA: Bowmar.

Rinard, J. (1982). *Puppies*. Ill. J.H. Bailey. Washington, DC: National Geographic Society.

Smith, E. (1987). *A guide dog goes to school: The story of a dog trained to lead the blind*. Ill. B. Dodson. New York: Morrow.

Smith, E. (1988). *A service dog goes to school: The story of a dog trained to help the disabled*. Ill. S. Petruccio. New York: Morrow.

Standiford, N. (1989). *The bravest dog ever: The true story of Balto*. Ill. D. Cook. New York: Random House.

Stone, L. (1993). *Canines: Predators*. Vero Beach, FL: Rourke.

Wilcox, C. (1999). *The Newfoundland*. Mankato, MN: Capstone High/Low Books.

Wilcox, C. (1999). *The Samoyed*. Mankato, MN: Capstone High/Low Books.

Wood, T. (1996). *Iditarod dream: Dusty and his sled dogs compete in Alaska's Jr. Iditarod*. New York: Walker.

Wratten, P., & Smart, T. (1978). *Dogs*. New York: Crescent Books.

Poems and Riddles

Baylor, B. (1999). *Amigo*. Ill. G. Williams. Topeka, KS: Econo-Clad Books.

Cole, J., & Calmenson, S. (1996). *Give a dog a bone: Stories, poems, jokes, and riddles about dogs*. Ill. J. Speirs. New York: Scholastic.

Cole, W. (Sel.). (1981). *Good dog poems*. New York: Scribner.

George, K. (1999). *Little dog poems*. Ill. J. Otani. New York: Clarion.

Hall, K., & Eisenberg, L. (1998). *Puppy riddles*. Ill. T. Wickstrom. New York: Dial.

Hopkins, L.B. (Sel.). (1983). *A dog's life*. Ill. L.R. Richards. New York: Harcourt Brace.

Kuskin, K. (1994). *City dog*. New York: Clarion.

Livingston, M.C. (1990). *Dog poems*. Ill. L. Morrill. New York: Holiday House.

Paulsen, G. (1993). *Dogteam*. Ill. R.W. Paulsen. New York: Delacorte.

Longer Fiction for More Experienced Readers

Armstrong, W. (1979). *The tale of Tawny and Dingo*. Ill. C. Mikolaycak. New York: Harper & Row.

Auch, M. (1994). *The latchkey dog*. Ill. C.B. Smith. Boston: Little, Brown.

Bauer, M. (1997). *Alison's puppy*. Ill. L. Spencer. New York: Hyperion.

Bechtold, L. (1999). *Buster, the very shy dog*. Boston: Houghton Mifflin

Carrick, C. (1974). *Lost in the storm*. Ill. D. Carrick. New York: Clarion.

Carrick, C. (1976). *The accident*. Ill. D. Carrick. New York: Seabury Press.

Carrick, C. (1977). *The foundling*. Ill. D. Carrick. New York: Seabury Press.

Carrick, C. (1984). *Dark and full of secrets*. Ill. D. Carrick. New York: Clarion.

Christopher, M. (1988). *The dog that pitched a no-hitter*. Ill. D. Vasconcellos. Boston: Little, Brown.

Christopher, M. (1993). *The dog that stole home*. Ill. D. Vasconcellos. Boston: Little, Brown.

Cleary, B. (1964). *Ribsy*. Ill. L. Darling. New York: Morrow.

Cleary, B. (1989). *Henry Huggins*. Ill. L. Darling. Santa Barbara, CA: Cornerstone Books.

Duffey, B. (1991). *A boy in the doghouse*. Ill. L. Morrill. New York: Simon & Schuster.

Duffey, B. (1992). *Lucky in left field*. Ill. L. Morrill. New York: Simon & Schuster.

Gardiner, J. (1980). *Stone fox*. Ill. M. Sewall. New York: Crowell.

Hanel, W. (1996). *Abby* (R. Lanning, Trans.). Ill. A. Marks. New York: North-South Books.

Hanel, W. (1999). *Rescue at sea!* (R. Lanning, Trans.). Ill. U. Heyne. New York: North-South Books.

Hesse, H. (1994). *Sable*. Ill. M. Sewall. New York: Holt.

Hickman, J. (1981). *The thunder-pup*. New York: Macmillan.

Hooper, M. (2000). *Dogs' night*. Ills. A. Curless & M. Burgess. Brookfield, CT: Millbrook Press.

Howe, J. (1990). *Hot fudge*. New York: Avon.

Hurwitz, J. (1990). *Aldo Peanut Butter*. Ill. D. DeGroat. New York: Morrow Junior Books.

Knight, E. (1971). *Lassie come-home*. (D. Bolognese, Ed.). New York: Holt, Rinehart and Winston. (Original work published 1940)

Labatt, M. (1999). *The ghost of Captain Briggs*. Buffalo, NY: Kids Can Press.

Levy, E. (1973). *Something queer is going on (a mystery)*. Ill. M. Gerstein. New York: Delacorte.

Lexau, J. (1994). *Trouble will find you*. Ill. M. Chesworth. Boston: Houghton Mifflin.

Little, J. (1985). *Lost and found*. Ill. L. O'Young. Markham, Ontario, Canada: Viking Kestrel.

Lowry, L. (1997). *STAY! Keeper's story*. Ill. T. Kelley. Boston: Houghton Mifflin.

Newman, N. (1983). *That dog!* Ill. M. Hafner. New York: Crowell.

Rodowsky, C. (1999). *Not my dog*. Ill. T. Yezerski. New York: Farrar, Straus & Giroux.

Rounds, G. (1969). *Stolen pony*. New York: Holiday House.

Ruch, S.B. (1990). *Junkyard dog*. Ill. M. Wunsch. New York: Orchard.

Sharmat, M. (1974). *Morris Brookside is missing*. Ill. R. Himler. New York: Holiday House.

Shortall, L. (1968). *Andy the dog walker*. New York: Morrow.

Vincent, G. (1999). *A day, a dog*. Asheville, NC: Front Street.

Voigt, C. (1986). *Stories about Rosie*. Ill. D. Kendrick. New York: Atheneum.

Whelan, G. (1988). *Silver*. Ill. S. Marchesi. New York: Random House.

Suggested Reading

Note: The following titles were not included in the original Dog Tale Unit but could be included in a newly created Dog Tale Unit.

Auch, M. (2001). *I was a third grade spy*. Ill. H. Auch. New York: Holiday House.

Crisp, M. (2000). *My dog, Cat*. Ill. T. Kelley. New York: Holiday House.

Desimini, L. (2001). *Dot the fire dog*. New York: Blue Sky Press.

DiCamillo, K. (2000). *Because of Winn-Dixie*. Cambridge, MA: Candlewick.

Dickson, L. (2001). *Lu and Clancy's secret languages*. Ill. P. Cupples. Buffalo, NY: Kids Can Press.

George, J. (2001). *Nutik and Amaroq play ball*. Ill. T. Rand. New York: HarperCollins.

George, J. (2001). *Nutik, the wolf pup*. Ill. T. Rand. New York: HarperCollins.

Graham, B. (2001). *"Let's get a pup!" said Kate*. Cambridge, MA: Candlewick.

Hall, L. (1992). *Barry, the bravest Saint Bernard*. Ill. A. Castro. New York: Random House.

Holub, J. (2001). *Why do dogs bark?* Ill. A. DiVito. New York: Puffin.

Kellogg, S. (2001). *A penguin pup for Pinkerton*. New York: Dial.

Lang, G. (2001). *Looking out for Sarah*. Watertown, MA: Charlesbridge.

L'Engle, M. (2001). *The other dog*. Ill. C. Davenier. New York: SeaStar Books.

McFarland, L.R. (2001). *Widget*. Ill. J. McFarland. New York: Farrar, Straus & Giroux.

Meister, C. (2001). *Tiny the snow dog*. Ill. R. Davis. New York: Viking.

Perrow, A. (2000). *Lighthouse dog to the rescue*. Camden, ME: Down East.

Rylant, C. (2001). *The great Gracie chase: Stop that dog!* Ill. M. Teaque. New York: Blue Sky Press.

Sharmat, M.W. (2000). *Dirty tricks*. Ill. V. Jones. New York: Random House.

Simont, M. (2001). *The stray dog*. New York: HarperCollins.

Smith, C.R., Jr. (2001). *Loki and Alex: The adventures of a dog and his best friend*. New York: Dutton Children's Books.

CHAPTER 5

The Transformation Tale Unit: Introducing a Literary Motif

A t the beginning of the second semester, Moss introduced the children to a new unit featuring transformation tales. By this time, the children viewed stories as invitations to respond to and participate in literary analysis. They were developing the habit of using reading strategies such as engaging in cover-to-cover study, identifying genre, asking questions and making predictions (and confirming or revising these predictions), using textual and visual clues to make inferences, appreciating the craft of authors and artists, searching for intertextual links, figuring out unfamiliar words, and integrating the use of fiction and nonfiction. More important, the children were forming a community of readers as they used these strategies to further the meaning-making process during the read-aloud sessions and independent reading.

At the same time, the children also were becoming active participants in the world of the story, as we noted in their comments and reactions to stories such as Cullen's *The Mightiest Heart* (Cullen, 1998; see pages 63–64). Recall that the text confirmed one child's prediction, as the prince raises his sword over Gelert. At this point, the children wanted to stop the prince and addressed the prince directly: "No. Don't! Don't do it!" Lawrence Sipe (2002) identifies this type of expressive engagement as "talking back to the story or characters" and notes that "talking back to the story and addressing the characters directly begins to blur the distinction between the story world and the children's world. For a moment the two worlds become superimposed—one transparent over the other" (p. 477; see also Sipe, 2000a, 2000b). Further, responses that reveal this expressive engagement with stories are "*deeply pleasurable* for children" (Sipe, 2002, p. 479). For example, when Moss continued reading and revealed that the prince does not harm Gelert, the children heaved a collective sigh of relief.

Because the first objective we identified as we developed our literary/literacy program was to provide opportunities for the children to experience personal enjoyment through literature, we noted this increasing frequency of active, expressive engagement as the children entered into each new story during the first semester. As Moss introduced the transformation tales in this unit, she looked for further evidence that suggested the children's responses to the literary experiences in this new unit were deeply pleasurable for them.

This chapter shows how Moss first introduced the literary motif of transformation. Lukens (1999) defines the term *motif* as "a recurring element in a literary work, often found in traditional literature" (p. 261). Magical objects, long sleeps, supernatural beings, three wishes, and transformation are typical motifs in folk tales. Because transformation is such a common motif in folklore, as well as in modern fantasy, Moss decided that her literature program in the library should include a study of stories that feature this motif. One of her goals for this unit was to expose the children to this common literary motif; another goal was to use the study of this motif in traditional tales to prepare the children for more complex narratives featuring dynamic characters. A complete listing of the literature used in the Transformation Tale Unit is included at the end of chapter 6 (see pages 164–166).

Session One: Introducing Transformation as a Literary Motif

When the children settled in the story circle in the library, Moss asked them to look at the chart by the story circle and try to read the new heading, Transformation Tales. Because Moss introduced this unit during the second semester, most of the children were able to decode the words in the heading but were unable to give the meaning of the word *transformation*. Then Moss asked, "Who knows the meaning of the word *transformer*?" Those children who were familiar with the Transformer, a toy, explained that "it changed from a super jet or a race car or a space shuttle to a robot." Using this prior knowledge, they were able to figure out that "transformation has something to do with changing from one thing to another." Moss then asked the children to identify the transformation in each tale read aloud during this unit.

Moss selected *The Boy Who Knew the Language of the Birds* (Wetterer, 1991), an Irish fairy tale, to read aloud. This story focuses on Colum, a boy who has the ability to understand the language of birds and therefore, learns the stories they bring from all over the world. When Colum shares these stories and when news of his fame as a storyteller reaches the king, he is summoned to the castle to tell stories to the royal family. Here, Colum learns about the mysterious disappearance of the king and queen's newborn sons. In a strange turn of events, Colum is transformed into a dog, and it is in this form that he is able to rescue the missing princes.

As soon as Moss held up the book and read the title to engage the children in a prestory discussion, they predicted that this would be a fantasy. Moss explained that this was a fairy tale set in Ireland, where storytellers have been telling fairy tales for hundreds of years. She then asked the children to look at the picture on the front cover (there is no picture on the back cover), which shows the back of a young boy, standing on a hilltop, and reaching upward to five large birds who seem to be looking directly at him. The children responded as follows:

Clarissa: He's talking to the birds.

Nik: He's *listening* to the birds because he understands them.

Jonathan: The sky is very dark—that could mean something.

Moss's goal was for the children to use these predictions and observations to generate meaning as the story unfolded. Indeed, as she read aloud the story, the children spontaneously responded with more observations and predictions. For example, Nik made the following comment about the scene in which Colum's mother warns him not to tell anyone about his special gift: "He shouldn't tell about his magic because it could be bad luck." When Moss read the scene in which Colum is telling stories to the royal family, the children examined the corresponding illustration of Colum and the royal family in which the characters from Colum's stories are on the wall behind them:

Sean: [a student who arrived in January] It looks like a scratching on the wall behind them.

Clarissa: I think it's the stories Colum is telling...in the background. It's like thought bubbles.

Samantha: So, they're thinking of the pictures in their minds.

In a later scene, Colum tries to entertain the princess, who is feeling neglected after the arrival of a new baby. He learns from two birds that the branch on which they are sitting can grant three wishes, and he gives the branch to the princess. When he explains to the princess that he heard what the birds said, there was an immediate response from the children that revealed their involvement in the story world: "Oops!" "Uh-oh!" "Oh no!" "He *told*!" "He forgot the warning!"

In the next scene, the princess makes the wish, "I wish you were a dog" (p. 17), even though she does not believe the stick is magic. Suddenly, Colum is transformed into a hound dog. The children expressed shock and carefully examined the illustration of Colum's transformation. It was clear from their discussion that the children had remembered Moss's request to identify the transformation in each tale.

Charlene: She didn't believe him, and she didn't know it would really happen. But he knew it would really happen because he believed the birds. Look...he's turning into a dog!

Moss: Yes.... He is transforming.

Samantha: [pointing to the chart] So transformation does mean *changing*!

Riley: Yes! This is the transformation.

Sean: [looking at the picture] Pretty soon he'll be all dog and not a boy.

As the story progressed, the children also began to engage in comparative analysis by linking the dog element in Colum's transformation with the texts in the Dog Tale Unit. For example, Colum, as a dog, saves the new baby from capture by the fairy queen; Tom linked Colum's heroic deed to the heroic deeds of Gelert and Jojofu. The children made another intertextual link when, later in the story, Colum (still a dog) guards the baby in the nursery and a large red hand reaches down the chimney to snatch the baby. Colum bites the hand, but another hand grabs the baby. When the servants wake up, they see that the dog's mouth is covered with blood and accuse him of attacking the baby. Several children noticed a connection between this scene and the nursery scene in *The Mightiest Heart*. However, they also noticed a significant difference because "In this story we know Colum is innocent, but in the other one we didn't *know* he was innocent when the prince accused him." By noticing this difference, the children also were attending to the craft of the authors in these stories.

When Moss continued reading, she revealed that Colum uses the second wish to escape from the king's guards and manages to locate the fairy fort in which the princes are held captive. Colum now has a choice: He can either use the last wish to save the three princes from the evil fairy queen or use it to become human again. We observed that the children were immersed deeply in the story world, as they reacted emotionally to Colum's terrible dilemma:

Nik:	If he uses the wish to save them, he'll always be a dog!
Clarissa:	He'd use up his last wish! Don't do it! [Note how Clarissa talks back to Colum, blurring the distinction between the story world and her world.]
Jonathan:	If he uses the magic stick, he has to decide if he wants to be a dog or a human. Maybe there's another way to save them.
Moss:	[reading from the text] Colum says, "I wish we were back at the castle" (p. 41).

Jonathan shook his head sadly and held up three fingers as Moss read these words, which indicated that he understood Colum's dilemma and that Colum had decided to use his last wish to save the princes. The children wondered aloud what would become of Colum.

The children's question was answered as Moss continued to read. The fairy queen finds Colum to punish him and takes all his magic away from him. The following discussion demonstrated how the children worked together to answer one another's questions and build meanings (also, notice that there was only one teacher-initiated question):

Tom:	So now he'll be able to turn back into a boy because it was the *magic* that turned him into a dog.
Tamara:	She [the fairy queen] didn't know it would *help* him instead of punishing him.

Charlene:	[looking at the picture] Now he's a boy!
Samantha:	But he won't be able to understand the bird language anymore.
Sean:	That's right…because that's magic, too. That's so sad.
Samantha:	But he'll still be able to remember all those stories he got from them, so he can still be a storyteller. So it'll be OK, Sean.
Moss:	Why did the fairy queen take away Colum's magic?
Nik:	The queen stopped his magic so he couldn't understand the language of the birds so he couldn't stop her from stealing babies.
Sean:	She was mad because he wrecked all her plans with his magic. She knew he had magic because he escaped from the fairy fort!
Tom:	Maybe she didn't even know that he knew the bird language.
Charlene:	But it's good he got changed back into a boy!

At the end of this session, the children reflected on their experience with this story. They marveled at Colum's willingness to use his last wish to save the princes. They also found connections—three wishes, ignored or forgotten warnings, human transformation into animals—with other fairy tales in general. To conclude the session and to highlight the literary motif of transformation, Moss pointed to the heading on the chart and asked them to talk about the transformation in this story. The children recognized that the boy had been transformed into a dog and that the princess had caused the transformation, but they agreed that it was "sort of an accident, and the princess didn't *plan* to change him into a dog." In response, Moss invited the children to identify the transformations in the stories they would hear in later sessions and to think about three questions: (1) *Who* caused the transformation? (2) *Why* was the character transformed? and (3) *How* was the spell broken?

Session Two: Concentrating on Character Development

Moss presented *The Six Swans* (San Souci, 1988), which is a retelling of an old tale recorded by the Grimm brothers, who collected and recorded in writing fairy tales that had been passed orally through generations. This tale is about a princess who rescues her six brothers who have been transformed into swans by their evil stepmother because of her jealousy about their close relationship with the king. The children first talked about the front and back covers of this picture book, making many predictions:

Samantha: The old lady on the back cover is a witch. She's probably going to be a mean witch because of the look on her face.

Clarissa: The girl on the front cover could be a princess.... You can see the castle. And there are six swans flying by.

Nik: So the title is about those six swans.

Moss then opened the book and showed the children the picture on the first title page, which shows a boy transforming into a swan. This picture prompted a discussion of the possible transformation in the story:

Sean: He's changing like in the other story.

Jonathan: So is this another *transformation* story...about a human changing into something?

Nik: The swans on the front cover could be *boys*.

Tamara: So transformation is changing into animals?

Nik: Or into birds...and changing back to humans like Colum.

Then Moss turned to the next page (the major title page), which includes portraits of the central characters. These portraits prompted the children to make inferences to identify each of the characters:

Nik: There's the witch from the back cover and the girl on the front cover.

Tom: So it's fantasy, because of the witch.

Riley: That swan has a crown on it!

Tamara: And now that girl from the front cover has a crown so she probably is a princess. She didn't have it on in that first picture. Hmmm. I wonder what that means.

Tom:	It's probably a fairy tale.... It has a witch, and a princess, and a transformation.
Samantha:	The girl with the black hair has a mean look. The other girl looks nice.

After Moss read the first two pages, the children returned to these portraits to identify the characters they had first missed. For example, they found the portrait of the witch's daughter by using the clue in the text that she "was beautiful, but her eyes glittered like a spider's" (n.p.). They then used this information to predict what might happen as the text unfolded:

Clarissa:	The king sees that her eyes are like a spider.... He doesn't like her. But he has to marry her, or the witch won't let him out of the forest.
Nik:	I think of spiders as witches.
Sean:	But witches don't make webs or curl up their prey in a web.
Nik:	But you think of spiders as bad insects.... Sometimes witches eat spiders in a brew.
Sean:	Some spiders are good...like Charlotte.
Nik:	Anyway, witches aren't really real. They're in stories. I think that girl with the black hair...the witch's daughter.... I think she used to be a spider or something.
Jonathan:	I think she's trapping the king! Sometimes spiders are poisonous.
Nik:	Maybe she'll poison the king when they get married.
Clarissa:	I think she might be transformed at the end of the story and that she might be a witch like her mom.
Nik:	I think Clarissa, and Jonathan, and my ideas are all connected.
Jonathan:	[turns to Clarissa] Maybe at the end, she *does* turn into a spider, Clarissa. And maybe the king dies because of the poison.
Riley:	Maybe when that king followed the stag into the forest, it was really the witch and she transformed *herself* into a stag so he would get lost and then he would have to marry her daughter.

Nik: That's right, because when the stag disappeared, the witch was there!

When the children concluded their speculations about each of the characters, Moss returned to reading. The children paid close attention to each character. As the story unfolded, the new queen, who is jealous of the king's seven children, uses her magical powers to transform the six boys into swans. The boys' sister then sets out on a quest to rescue them. In the course of her six-year quest, she marries a king and has three babies. At this point, Tamara observed, "So that's why she had on the crown in that other picture. Now she's a queen." When the witch steals each of her babies, the children's faces revealed their anger at the witch, and some even shook their fists at the picture of the witch carrying away one of the babies.

At the end of the story, the sister breaks the spell. Her brothers are transformed into boys and her three babies are returned to her. The wicked witch changes into a blackbird, which the king then shoots with his crossbow. Several children remembered seeing a blackbird in an earlier picture and wondered if the witch sometimes transformed herself into a bird "to spy on people." When the wicked queen (the witch's daughter) sees "that her magic had been undone, she became so angry she turned into the ogress she really was, and ran howling into the woods, never to be seen again" (n.p.). At this point, Samantha realized "that's the daughter of the wicked witch. There are a lot of transformations in this story!" Nik, however, questioned why the queen has spidery eyes and noted, "This is the only thing we don't know." In answer, Moss reread the first part of the story in which the witch's daughter is described, "her eyes glittered like a spider's" (n.p.).

Nik: I think we forgot about the part that says *glitter*. It doesn't mean she really is a spider.

Tamara: It's like an *expression* like someone's eyes glitter like a cat.

Nik: Oh, so she isn't a spider.... She was really an ogress and was transformed into a beautiful girl to get the king. But she's still an ogress inside. Ogres are sort of ugly, but they're not really real. It looks a little scary, though. [He is looking at the last picture in the story, in which the ogress is running into the wood, but only her back can be seen.] Her face would be ugly if we could see it.

These excerpts capture only a fraction of the ideas and comments triggered by their study of the text and the illustrations. The children engaged in prediction, imagining, and critical thinking as they struggled to understand the complexities of this tale and the transformations.

Throughout the discussions in this session, the children listened to and addressed their comments to one another. They built on the insights and interpretations of others to study the characters' development, as well as plot and literary themes of good and evil, courage, and selflessness. When the children returned to the classroom after this session, Fenster invited them to draw and write about a favorite scene from *The Boy Who Knew the Language of the Birds* or *The Six Swans*. See Figure 2 for examples of the students' work, which demonstrate both their engagement with and personal enjoyment of these texts.

Session Three: Using Gap-Filling Strategies

Literary texts have gaps, or holes, that readers must fill in as they read. Readers need to figure out important information that the author does not include in the text (Iser, 1978). Consequently, readers must construct interpretations, form hypotheses, and make inferences to fill in these gaps. Lea McGee (1995) suggests that "the more enticing the gap, the harder readers and listeners will work to fill it" (p. 109). McGee also recommends that stories and poems selected for discussion should have the kind of gaps that leave room for readers' speculation and that stimulate rich conversations (pp. 109–110). The stories selected for all the thematic units challenged the children to use these gap-filling strategies in their transactions with each text and in their collaborative explorations during each session. Moss specifically chose the story in this session, however, to encourage the children to use gap-filling strategies to study the motivation behind the main characters' behavior and words.

The Glass Mountain, a Grimm brothers' tale retold and illustrated by Nonny Hogrogian (1985), is the story of a princess who has been changed into

THE BOY WHOW KNEW
THE LANGOAGE
OF THE
BIRDS

MY favorite Part was.
When THE HAND Got the
BABY BeCause iT Was
cool AND spooky At THE same
Time.

THE BOY WOY KBOVTHE LOINGUAG
OF THO Bird2

MY FAVR't PRTWAS
WAN THE HAND KAMD
OWN

THE SIX SWANS
I Like the Part
Wen the King
married the Princess

My favrite Part was when the girl.
Saved her Brothers cause it looked like
She cared about Her Brothers. She sa
veD them cause She DiDN't want them
toBe swans forever.

a raven and the young man who manages to release her from this enchantment. After Moss showed the children the front and back covers, they had much to comment about and made predictions about what might happen in the story:

Mason: It's another Grimm tale...like *The Six Swans*.

Riley: The man on the front cover looks sad...the way he's sitting.

Tamara: The bird on the back cover could be the man transformed.

Jonathan: We can figure out from the story why he's so sad and why there's a bird on the back cover.

Sean: The words on the back cover are backwards. It's a glass mountain, so that's what words look like when they're printed on glass and you see them from the back!

Tamara: The raven must be important because it's on the back cover. Maybe it's the problem in the story.

Next, Moss read aloud the note on the title page, which explains that the tale was originally titled *The Raven*. As she read the first page of the story, she revealed to the students that the queen's new baby is restless, and

> the Queen grew very impatient.... She looked at her daughter and cried, "If only you were a raven, you could fly away, and I would have some peace!" As these words came out of the Queen's mouth, the child turned into a raven...and flew from the arms of her mother. (n.p.)

After listening to this first page, the children shared their personal responses to this scene and then compared the queen's actions to real life (thus making a literature-life connection), as they tried to figure out the motivation behind her words and why the baby turned into a raven:

Mason: A baby cries and cries, and you can really get annoyed.

Clarissa: But she didn't really *mean* it. She didn't really want her words to come true!

Sean: You can get impatient or frustrated and say stuff you don't mean.

Jonathan: But how come the words came true? Who did that?

Nik: Maybe it tells in the story.

Moss continued reading and revealed that years later, a young man encounters the raven in the forest, and the raven asks him to lift the enchantment. The raven explains the conditions for breaking the spell: He must stay awake and wait for her for three days behind the house of an old woman. The raven also warns him not to take the food or drink that the old woman will offer him. The man agrees to lift the enchantment, but each day he succumbs to the old woman's offering to take a sip of wine and consequently, falls into a deep sleep. After failing this first test, the young man sets out on a quest to find the raven at the "golden castle of the Glass Mountain" (n.p.). After encountering two giants and three scoundrels, the young man finally climbs the Glass Mountain and frees the raven from her enchantment.

Throughout Moss's reading, the children searched for clues in the illustrations to fill in gaps in the text. When the story ended, they commented on their initial predictions, the transformation in the story, the characters, and the man's quest. Then, they turned their attention to what was *not* in the text:

Tamara: It never *says* who did the transformation. I think it was the old woman who might be the one who made the mother's wish come true, and she didn't want the man to break the spell so that's why she keeps giving him the food.

Clarissa: She's probably a witch because the food was magic and made him sleep.

Nik and
Jonathan: She did it! It was the witch!

Nik: And she probably didn't know he could break the spell by going to the golden castle.

Mason: The queen didn't know the witch could make her words come true.

Riley: It's like *The Six Swans*. They all turned into birds.

Mason: The queen caused the transformation in that one, too. She hated the children and changed them to swans.

Riley: But that queen was the stepmother...and an ogre...and she *wanted* to get rid of them. But in *The Glass Mountain*, it

Tom: was her own baby, and she loved her, and she didn't really *want* her to change into a raven.

Tom: Remember the dog one...with the fairies? The princess just said the words and POOF—the boy turned into a dog, and she didn't really think it would happen. She was just bored and wanted to do something different. That one was an accident.

Clarissa: The mom [in *The Glass Mountain*] just wanted some quiet. I don't see that the princess got to see the mom.

Jonathan: I think we have to make up that part of the story, Clarissa. [Notice here, how Jonathan uses different terminology but basically tells Clarissa that they must use gap-filling strategies to build meaning.] Either she does or doesn't find her mom and dad. I think she does, but you have to make it up and decide what is or isn't true.

Sean: I think she didn't because at the end, it says she just got married.

The children continued to discuss the "things the storyteller didn't tell us." Like Jonathan, most of the children assumed the story would have a happy ending that included a family reunion after the wedding. They drew from their prior literary experiences and the clues in the text and illustrations to fill in the gaps; that is, they figured out characters' motivations and imagined what happened in those parts left out by the storyteller. This gap filling allowed the children to stretch their minds and imaginations, thus fulfilling another original objective. (Only Sean had a hard time stretching his imagination beyond the actual words in the text. As Fenster observed in her written records, "Sean is very, very literal in all that he approaches in the classroom. This may be due to a limited exposure to good literature. He is improving, I think.")

At the end of the session, the children returned to the pictures on the front and back covers and attached meanings to details they had pondered during the original prestory discussion:

Tom: The man on the front cover is sad because that's when he didn't break the spell because he drank the wine. You can see the castle on the Glass Mountain in the background. He's going to get another chance to break the spell.

Samantha: The raven on the back cover is when she's in the dark forest [points to the picture of the forest scene in the book], and she sees the young man who's going to try to help her.

Tamara: So it's the princess that was transformed, not the man on the front cover. I *knew* it must be important because it was on the back cover. It was the problem!

Mason: I think they should have kept the old title, *The Raven*, because that's what the transformation was, and that's the whole story.

Tom: I agree. Anyway, there's another story called "The Glass Mountain," and it's different.... It's like Cinderella. So it would be better to have different names.

Nik: If they used *The Raven* title, they would put the picture of the raven on the front cover. But the man is the hero in the story because he's the one who did the quest.

Moss had used the literary term *hero* in context during the first-semester literary sessions. Nik apparently had internalized this term and used it appropriately in his analysis of this story. Because of our original objective, we were pleased at this successful use of the *language* of literary analysis.

The children also used gap-filling strategies to respond to the question, "Who caused the transformation?" Before they listened to the entire story, they had used literature-life connections to figure out why the queen made the wish that resulted in her daughter's transformation. After the story ended, they contrasted the mother in this story with the stepmother in *The Six Swans* to discover the motivation behind their deeds. For example, the children identified the stepmother as the *cause* of the transformation of the princes into swans because "she *wanted* to get rid of them. But in *The Glass Mountain*, it was her own baby, and she loved her, and she *didn't want* her to change into a raven." The children agreed that the mother in this story *did not cause* the transformation. Although they all seemed to understand why she uttered the words that brought about the transformation, most of them thought she should not have said these words. By the end of the story, the children concluded that the old woman in the cottage was a witch who had the power to use the mother's words to cause the transformation. Although most agreed that the old woman was the cause of the transformation, they did not come up with a possible motivation behind her deed.

When the children returned to the classroom, Fenster once again asked them to draw and write about the transformation in this tale. These creations, recorded in the Literary Notebooks, revealed the children's further attempts to fill in the gaps in this narrative (see Figure 3).

Session Four: Introducing Fable as a Literary Genre

In this session, Moss presented *The Brave Little Parrot*, a Jataka tale from India retold by Rafe Martin (1998). Jataka tales are ancient fables or moral tales told by the Buddha to his followers over 2000 years ago. Well-known storytellers such as Aesop and La Fontaine have adapted Buddha's teachings. Moss told the children that this story was a fable told long ago to teach an important lesson. Some children were familiar with Aesop's fables and mentioned examples of this traditional genre. The cultural origin of this tale was of special interest to the new student, Usha, because of her Indian heritage. Because this was Usha's first day at our school, Riley explained to her the nature of the literary program in the library and more specifically, this literary unit and the meaning of *transformation*.

The illustration on the front cover of this picture book extends to the back cover and shows a gray-and-white bird flying over a raging forest fire. After Moss showed the children the covers, several children predicted that the bird would escape from the fire. Jonathan said he thought the parrot had been transformed from a person. When Moss turned to the title page featuring a portrait of the gray-white parrot, the children observed that this did not look like a parrot because it was not colorful. As she had done in the Dog Tale Unit, Moss showed a nonfiction book to help the children in their study of fiction. This nonfiction book, *Let's Look at Birds* (Meadway, 1990), which included pictures of parrots, reinforced the contrast between this "colorless" parrot and the typical parrot with colorful feathers. Then, Moss pointed to the single red-and-green feather on the front flap of *The Brave Little Parrot*. Several

FIGURE 3

•••

Examples of Students' Written and Illustrated Creations to Fill in the Gaps

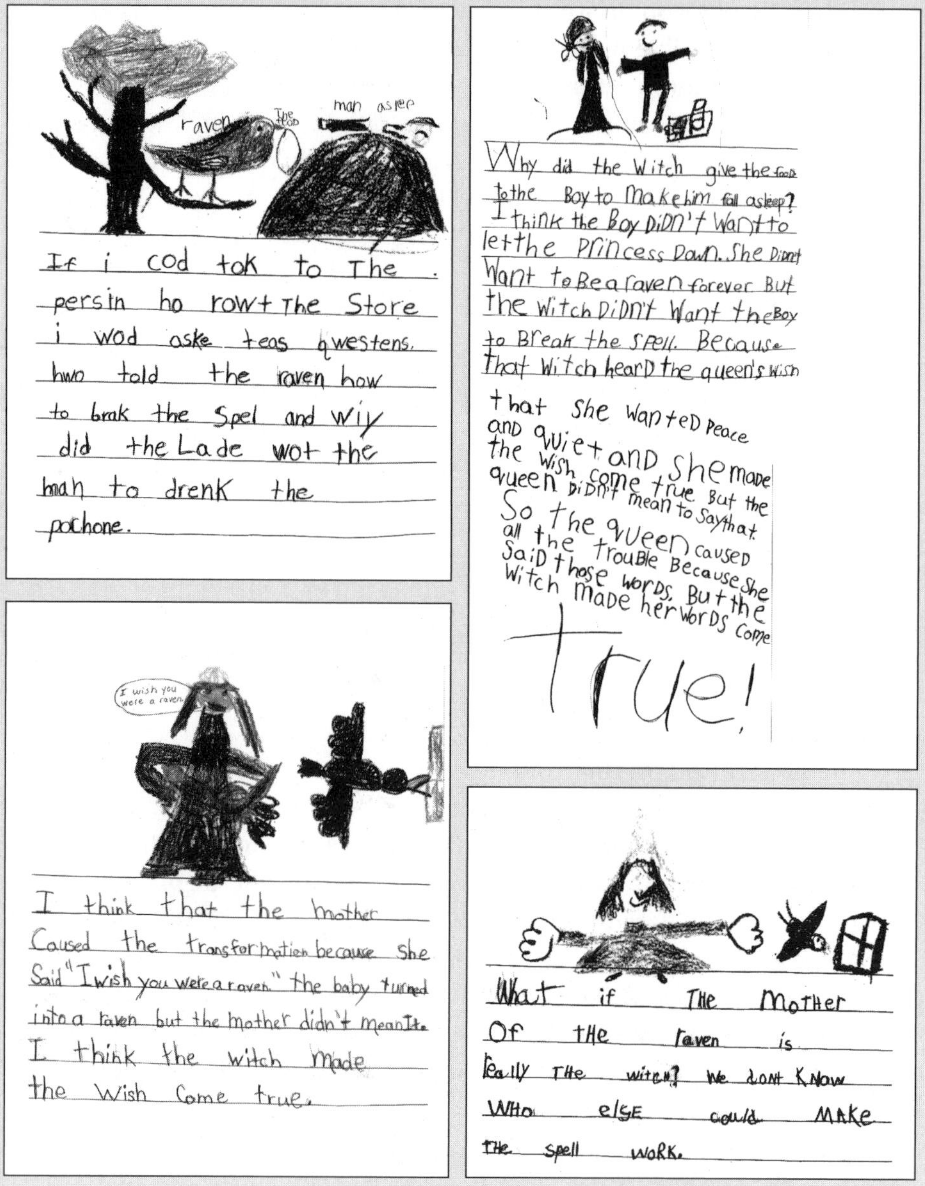
raven
The food
man aslep
If i cod tok to The persin ho rowt The Store i wod aske teas qwestens. hwo told the raven how to brak the Spel and wiy did the Lade wot the man to drenk the pochone.
Why did the Witch give the food to the Boy to Make him fall asleep? I think the Boy DiDn't Want to let the Princess Down. She Didn't Want to Be a raven forever But the Witch DiDn't Want the Boy to Break the Spell. Because That Witch hearD the queen's wish that She WanteD Peace and quiet and She maDe the Wish come true. But the queen DiDn't mean to Say that. So the queen caused all the trouble Because She Said those worDs. But the Witch MaDe her WorDs Come True!
I wish you were a raven.
I think that the mother Caused the transformation because She Said "I wish you were a raven." the baby turned into a raven but the mother didn't mean It. I think the witch made the Wish Come true.
What if The Mother Of the raven is really the witch? We dont Know Who else could Make the spell work.

children predicted that the bird would get colorful feathers, and most agreed that this would be the transformation in the story.

Next, Moss began reading the story, which opens with the following words: "Once a little parrot lived in a green forest" (n.p.). When lightning ignites a forest fire, the larger animals escape to the river, leaving the smaller animals trapped by the fire. The little parrot asks the larger animals to help her put out the fire in order to save the smaller animals, but they refuse. The little parrot devises another plan to save the smaller animals and "after soaking her feathers in the cool water and filling a cupped leaf, she flew back over the burning forest" (n.p.). She returns to the river repeatedly and each time flies back over the fire in a brave attempt to fight the flames, drop by drop. At this point, the children interjected and demonstrated their involvement in the story world:

Sean:	She's carrying it in a leaf!
Nik:	I don't think she'll be able to do it. I don't.
Tom:	It's important to try. Maybe the transformation will be the little drops of water get [*sic*] bigger and bigger.
Clarissa:	Oh no! Look! She's going to get burned!

While the little parrot is flying back and forth from the river to the fire in her attempt to save the small animals,

> some carefree goddesses and gods happened to drift by high overhead.... One of the gods happened to notice the little parrot flying far below.... "Just look at that foolish bird trying to put out a forest fire with a few sprinkles of water!" (n.p.)

This god takes the shape of a golden eagle and flies down to tell the parrot, "Stop now and save yourself." As this part of the text unfolded, several children expressed their anger toward the gods and goddesses, who were laughing at the little parrot, and "talked back" (Sipe, 2002) to these characters. For example, one student yelled, "Why don't you just help her instead of laughing at her!"

When the parrot refuses to stop carrying water, the god feels ashamed and begins to weep. These tears cause the fire to go out, and "new life burst forth!.... New feathers now grew on the little parrot, too—feathers red as flame, green as leaves, yellow as sunlight, and blue as a river!" (n.p.). The children listened intently to this tale but were anxious to share their thoughts at its conclusion, especially their thoughts about the transformation:

Usha:	The first transformation was the god changing into the eagle [points to the illustration portraying this transformation].
Moss:	Why did the god change his shape?
Tom:	He wanted to tell the parrot to stop so it wouldn't get hurt. But he didn't listen because he didn't know it was a god.
Sean:	I don't think she would have listened even if she *knew* it was a god.
Usha:	The next transformation was the parrot turned into a bright-colored parrot.
Sean:	Because the eagle cried.
Mason:	He cried because the parrot wanted to help the small animals get out of the fire.
Sean:	He cried because he was ashamed.
Clarissa:	The parrot was happy at the end because the fire was out and the trees came back and he got new colors.
Riley:	Maybe he was happy because the whole jungle got back together again.... She cared about all the others, not herself. She was a nice parrot.

Most of the children used *he* to refer to the parrot until this moment in their dialogue. Riley shifted the parrot's gender in the middle of his comment, and the children continued to refer to the parrot as *she* for the rest of the dialogue. In the book, the parrot is female. Riley's observation and his discussion of it contributed to the others' understanding.

With the goal of enriching the children's meaning-making process, Moss next introduced a question to prompt the children to focus on the characters in terms of their inner qualities:

Moss:	What does the word *selfish* mean?
Tamara:	Like not sharing your toys.

Charlene:	The big animals in the story were selfish. They didn't want to help the parrot save the other animals.
Mason:	The gods were selfish, too.
Clarissa:	The parrot was the only one who was *not* selfish. She didn't even seem to notice her new feathers. She was just so happy the fire was out and the animals were safe.
Sean:	But the parrot didn't save the animals. The god did.
Riley:	The parrot.... The parrot should get the credit. She worked hard, and the god just felt sad and ashamed and then he cried and that helped her.
Nik:	The god wouldn't have cried the special tears without the parrot. She made him feel ashamed because he told her to just stop and not help the other animals.
Clarissa:	He was ashamed because he knew the gods and goddesses were all being so selfish, and the little parrot was trying so hard to save the animals.
Tom:	[points to the list of transformation tales on the chart] This one is totally different. It had all animals and no people.
Charlene:	And gods.
Tom:	And in the other ones, the people changed to animals and back to people. In this one the colors changed...and stayed. The transformation was a *reward*.
Usha:	This is a different kind of transformation.
Moss:	Why do you think the storytellers chose to tell this story long ago?
Riley:	To teach a lesson. You shouldn't be selfish. You should help others like the parrot did.
Moss:	A fable is a special kind of story that teaches a lesson. Usually the characters in the old fables were animals, as Tom noticed about this story.

Moss chose this particular story for the Transformation Tale Unit for two reasons: (1) She wanted the children to discover a different kind of transformation, and (2) she wanted to introduce the fable as a literary genre. By the end of this session, Tom and Usha observed that this transformation tale was "totally different," and Riley was able to articulate the lesson, or moral, of this fable. Moss simply restated the distinguishing features of this literary genre for the benefit of the other children.

When the children returned to the classroom after this session, Fenster asked them to write and draw in their notebooks "about the main characters in this fable" (see Figure 4). Most of the children identified the parrot and the eagle as the main characters and wrote about one or both of these characters. Their illustrations also included additional details about the story.

Session Five: Further Study of the Possible Causes of Transformations

In this session, Moss read aloud *The Canary Prince*, an old Turinese tale translated and retold by Eric Nones (1991). When the children examined the title and the front and back covers of this picture book, a number of them predicted that this story would be like *The Frog Prince, or Iron Henry* (Grimm & Grimm, 1989). *The Frog Prince* is an old story about a prince who is transformed when a wicked witch casts a spell on him, "a spell that only the loveliest princess could break" (n.p.). The children used their prior knowledge of this old tale to make their predictions about *The Canary Prince*. The first pages of the story introduce a new stepmother-queen who is jealous of the king's daughter and arranges to have her imprisoned in a tower deep in the woods. At this point in the read-aloud, some children compared this to the story of Rapunzel, whereas others compared this evil stepmother-queen to the one in *The Six Swans*. They then examined the paintings in this book and used clues from the characters' facial expressions and body language to determine their feelings. For example, in the scene in which the stepmother-queen visits the princess in the tower, the queen sees how unhappy the princess is but says to her, "I can see that you are perfectly content" (n.p.). The children noted the difference between the queen's words and her inner thoughts.

The plot begins when a prince discovers the princess in the tower and through the power of a magical book provided by a good witch, manages to transform into a canary in order to reach the princess's room in the tower.

FIGURE 4

● ● ●

Examples of Students' Written and Illustrated Creations About Main Characters
From The Brave Little Parrot

the Parrot is helpful and very brave. because She tried SO hard. to Save the animals. from the fire. the bigger animals would not help her. the eagle was a god. He didn't care but then he felt ashamed.

this is about the parrot. On. his insides. he had a kind heart. He was never Selfish. the eagle changed because the parrot needed help. At first the eagle was selfish.

The eagle was KIND OF NICE because he WORRIED about the PARROT. THE eagle was KIND OF MEAN because he wasnt CARING About THE OTHER animals.

How did the eagle's tears stop the fire with his small tears? The gods tears were small. But now that the god is magicial the tears got Big enough to stop the fire.

When the queen discovers the prince's visits, she attempts to get rid of him and causes him serious injury. The princess then devises a plan to escape from her room and sets out on a quest to find the prince and a cure that will restore him to health. In the end, the prince and the princess get married, the truth about the queen's evil deeds is revealed, and the queen is sent to the dungeon.

After Moss finished reading the story, the children initiated a comparative analysis of the transformation tales introduced in this unit thus far, which also were listed on the chart. They began their analysis with a focus on the characters who had caused the transformations and the motives of the characters involved in the transformations:

Mason: The prince wished for wings so he could be with the princess, and a good witch helped make his wish come true. So she *caused* the transformation to help him. In the other stories they didn't *want* to be changed.

Tom: And this one was different because it didn't last long. She just had to turn the pages of that book to change him back to a prince.

Clarissa: The queen [in *The Glass Mountain*] didn't *want* her wish to come true, but that evil witch used her words to cause the transformation. The prince *wanted* his wish to come true. This canary story is different in a lot of ways.

Riley: The transformation was from prince to canary and back to a man so he could get up to the tower. In the other stories [he pointed to the relevant titles on the chart], mean characters like the evil queen in *The Six Swans* or the spoiled princess in *The Boy Who Knew the Language of the Birds* caused the transformations.

Clarissa: In *The Brave Little Parrot*, the god changed into a bird to get to the parrot...like in this story. But he did it for a different reason.

Mason: Even though they're all transformation tales, they're all different. It's mostly because the *reasons* for the transformations are different.

As the comparative analysis continued, the children shifted their focus from the transformations to the magic objects found in these tales. For example, they identified the magic ball of thread and the little shirts in *The Six Swans*; the "wishing stick" in *The Boy Who Knew the Language of the Birds*; the bread "that will replenish itself" and the magic horse, cloak, and stick in *The Glass Mountain*; and the magical book in *The Canary Prince*. In the course of their discussion of this recurring motif, the children concluded that all the magic objects in these stories had played a role in initiating the transformation or quest to break the spell or reverse the magic. This prompted a more complex comparative analysis of different kinds of magic objects that other storytellers had woven into their stories. This discussion demonstrated the children's ability to initiate extensive comparative analysis, in which they identified subtle differences among the transformation tales as well as similarities that connected them. The children also identified magical objects as a recurring motif that linked these tales. When they expanded their comparative analysis to explore intertextual links to other "magic object tales" that Moss did not include in this unit, such as *The Tale of Aladdin and the Wonderful Lamp: A Story From the Arabian Nights* (Kimmel, 1992) and *Strega Nona* (dePaola, 1975), the children provided a transition into the sixth session in which Moss planned to focus on the use of intertextual links as a meaning-making strategy.

Session Six: Using Intertextual Links to Discover Recurring Patterns and Hidden Meanings

When Moss introduced the children to the Grimm brothers' *The Seven Ravens*, adapted by Laura Geringer (1994), they first noted that this was "another Grimm tale." Several children made predictions based on another Grimm tale, *The Donkey Prince* (Craig, 1977), that they had selected to read at home for independent reading. The title of this new tale, *The Seven Ravens*, prompted speculation that this story would be similar to *The Six Swans* and set the stage for the children's use of intertextual linking as a meaning-making strategy.

Following this initial prediction, the children focused on the items featured on the front cover, the front flap, and the pages prior to the story text and used to decorate the first letter of the story: a jug, a loaf of bread, a wooden stool, a baby's rattle, and a raven. Because they were familiar enough with artist's craft, the children recognized this repetition as a device that the illustrator of this story, Edward Gazsi, had used to call attention to items that would be important in the story.

The first page of the story introduces a beautiful little girl whose parents are unhappy. In response to the story's opening lines, several children drew from their prior literary experience to predict that "the transformation is from humans into ravens." As the story continues, the girl finds seven boxes with seven shirts, "delicately sewn in colors of the rainbow with patterns of the sun, moon and stars" (p. 6). When she shows the shirts to her parents, her mother explains,

> Soon after you were born, you fell ill.... We asked [your seven brothers] to be very quiet when they came near your cradle, but they forgot our warnings. One day, while playing, they woke you from a sound sleep. "I wish you'd all turn into ravens and fly away!" cried your father in a rage. (p. 8)

The girl's mother tells her that after her father cried these words, the seven brothers were transformed into ravens, and before they flew away, "the largest one dipped down, [and] plucked the rattle from your hand" (p. 9). The next day the girl sets out on a quest to find her brothers, "taking only a loaf of bread, a jug of water, and a wooden stool. Over her blouse she wore her brothers' seven shirts" (p. 12).

Charlene: It's just like in *The Glass Mountain*!

Usha: Yes, but in that story the queen wanted peace and quiet for herself, and in *this* story the father was worried about the sick baby and wanted quiet so she could get better.

Clarissa: And she *found* the seven shirts.... In *The Six Swans*, the sister had to *make* them. She's going to look for her brothers like the sister in that story, and it's a hard journey. Maybe she'll put the shirts on them to break the spell.

Nik: [points to the illustrations] That's the rattle in all the pictures...and the bread and jug and stool!

Tom: So we were right about the artist. He wanted us to know those things were important.

Mason: And we were right about the transformation, too. And it is like *The Six Swans*, but it's also different.

The children listened intently as the story of the sister's quest unfolded. Her travels take her to the sun, moon, and stars and finally to a dwarf who commends her for being so "brave and faithful" (p. 22) and gives her a glass bone. The dwarf also tells her that her brothers live in the Glass Mountain "at the end of the world" (p. 22). At these words, the children's eyes lit up with recognition and together, they uttered: "Ah, the Glass Mountain!" This discovery prompted further discussion:

Nik: The glass bone is probably another magic object. Maybe she'll use it to break the spell.

Clarissa: So the dwarf is a helper. That was a surprise. The other ones were so mean to her. In *The Glass Mountain*, the giants were helpers. That was a surprise, too.

Usha: Where *is* the end of the world?!

Sean: It'll probably tell later on in the story, Usha.

As the story continues, the dwarf helps the girl reach the Glass Mountain, where she finds herself in a room lined with mirrors with "seven chairs and a crystal table set for seven...and a dusty baby's rattle hanging on the door" (p. 24).

Usha: It's the seven chairs!

Tamara: That baby rattle is *hers*!

Six ravens come into the room, put on the shirts, and change back into boys. Then the eldest raven, dragging his wings, limps into the room.

Sean: She's still holding his shirt. It may not work because it's all torn up.

Nik: It's like it's connected to him.... That sleeve is torn like the wing, and the other one is burned.

Samantha: Like the youngest brother in *The Six Swans*! His arm was still a wing because she [the sister] didn't get to finish the sleeve.

The girl gives the raven the water from the jug and the bread, and she uses the glass bone to mend the sleeves of her brother's shirt. When the raven is strong again, he takes his brothers and his sister on his back and flies them to their village. At their return to the village, "the eldest brother put on his rainbow shirt and turned into a boy.... 'We are eight now,' he said, smiling. And, together at last, they walked out of the shadows toward home" (p. 32).

The children's active discussion of this story was shaped by their discoveries of the intertextual links with the other transformation stories in this unit. Each time they identified a new link, their excitement grew and they searched more deeply in the text and the illustrations to uncover hidden meanings. As they engaged in this comparative analysis of all the transformation tales, the children's comments reflected their growing understanding of the recurring patterns found in traditional literature, which in turn, helped them to generate meaning. This was apparent as they began to identify the role of magic objects, helper characters, and the quest-journeys in these stories, as well as the nature of transformation as a literary motif.

Assessment

During the first part of the Transformation Tale Unit, the children became acquainted with the six transformation tales introduced in the group sessions, as well as others that they selected from the collection of transformation tales for independent reading. When we reviewed the children's discussions of these stories to find evidence of literary learning, we observed that they gradually became familiar enough with the concept of transformation to identify this literary motif in each new tale and to engage in comparative analyses and interpretive dialogue on their own. At the end of the first session, Moss had introduced three questions: (1) *Who* caused the transformation? (2) *Why* was the character transformed? and (3) *How* was the spell broken? In subsequent sessions, the children used these questions to guide their study of the nature of the transformation and its role in each story. They recognized the significant differences among the transformations in these tales and discovered that the cause of or reason for the transformation was not always articulated within the story. In response, they learned to use gap-filling strategies to generate meaning in their transactions with those literary texts that left room for speculation and interpretation. The children identified the villains, the helper characters, and the heroes or heroines. They used literature-life connections to study the motivation behind the behavior and words of central characters. For example, they discovered the power of words uttered in anger or frustration in stories such as *The Glass Mountain* and *The Seven Ravens*. And they engaged in intertextual talk as they explored recurring patterns such as magic objects, wishes, warnings, and quests.

As independent readers, the children examined each new book from cover to cover, searched for clues to infer meaning, predicted their way through each unfolding narrative, and filled in gaps left by the storyteller or author. They drew from their growing literary backgrounds to identify recurring patterns and intertextual links. The stories the children selected for independent reading were included in the discussions during the group sessions in the library and enriched the comparative analyses that the children initiated in each of these sessions.

Looking Ahead

Moss carefully selected the first six transformation tales to introduce the children to a literary motif found in diverse traditional tales as well as modern tales. She designed the first phase of this unit to prepare them for the next phase in which they would discover another kind of transformation. Chapter 6 describes the children's encounters with narratives featuring dynamic characters whose transformation is associated with growth and inner change. Moss's goal was to introduce the children to characters who mature; gain insights; and develop new traits, attitudes, or values. A question that guided her as she planned this unit was, To what extent would the study of the literary motif of transformation enhance the quality of the children's responses to more complex stories with dynamic characters? She planned to look for answers to this question in Fenster's written records of group dialogue in these sessions and of the children's involvement in the collaborative writing project that would conclude this unit.

CHAPTER 6

The Transformation Tale Unit: Encountering Dynamic Characters

haracter development is a literary term that means "showing the character—whether a person or animal or object—with the complexity of a human being" (Lukens, 1999, p. 80). *Dynamic character* is another literary term defined by Lukens as "one who changes in the course of the action" (p. 89). According to Lukens, this dynamic character may "change from being shy to being poised or even domineering; or from cowardly to brave, from selfless to selfish. The character may demonstrate a new realization about himself or herself, or about his or her personal values" (p. 89). During the first read-aloud sessions in the Transformation Tale Unit, Moss introduced the children to six fairy tales in which the human characters were transformed through magical intervention. In these tales, one of the characters was transformed into a dog, whereas the others were transformed into various kinds of birds. In tales from the oral tradition, characters are usually shown in flat dimension and are referred to as "stock characters" or "character types." Huck and colleagues (1997) write, "Qualities of character or special strengths or weaknesses of the characters are revealed quickly [in folk tales], because this factor will be the cause of conflict or lead to resolution of the plot" (p. 274). This means that these characters usually symbolize good or evil or specific qualities such as power, trickery, wisdom, courage, selfishness, or selflessness, and their actions are predictable. Lukens (1999) reasons that "perhaps because of the necessity to keep the spoken story moving along with suspense, the folktale relies upon stock characters" (p. 95). In most traditional tales, therefore, transformation involves mainly external changes. Conversely, central characters in modern fiction for the most part are well developed and multidimensional. Many of these characters are remembered for *the way they have changed* in the course of the events in the story. During the second part of this unit, Moss focused on stories that featured dynamic characters. Although Moss did not use this specific literary term with the children, she did provide literary experiences that enabled them to discover the difference between external transformation in traditional tales and inner transformation or change in modern fiction. In the course of these sessions, the children themselves invented their own terms to distinguish between these two types of transformation—*outside transformation* and *inside transformation.*

Experience with the transformation motif in traditional tales during the first part of this unit set the stage for literary experiences with modern fiction. Moss continued to encourage the children to make use of their growing knowledge of literature and key reading strategies to respond to the literary texts. She also invited the children to continue to identify the transformations in the stories and to think about the three questions about transformation that she had introduced during the first session of this unit (see chapter 5).

This chapter ends with an assessment of the Transformation Tale Unit as a whole, as well as an assessment of the children's overall literary/literacy development in the library and in the classroom. A section titled "Literature in the Transformation Tale Thematic Unit Collection" also is included at the end of the chapter to provide an easy reference for the texts used in this unit.

Session Seven: Introducing a New Kind of Transformation Tale

When Moss held up *Prince Sparrow*, by Mordicai Gerstein (1984), the children predicted that the story would be about a prince who is transformed into a sparrow. As they examined the front cover, Jonathan noted the absence of the word *retold*. Moss explained that unlike the "retold tales" introduced in the previous sessions of this unit, this one was an original story written by a known author, not a retelling of an old folk tale that had been passed along from one storyteller to the next across time and space. Jonathan responded, "So it's a *new* story instead of an old, old story." The pictures on the front cover and on the title page prompted the following comments from other students:

Clarissa: That princess looks mad! Her hands are like this [makes a fist].

Tamara:	And the doll and the vase on the floor are broken. Maybe *she* broke them.
Nik:	She's looking up at that little sparrow in a really mean way. Maybe *she* turned the prince into a sparrow.
Jonathan:	It's too bad there's nothing on the back cover for more clues.
Tom:	[pointing to the picture on the title page] There's the sparrow again, sitting on a crown. Maybe it's *his* crown.

The children also were interested in the dedication: "For my mother, FAYE, who was called Faygeleh, which means Little Bird." They wondered if this was the reason the author had decided to write a story about a bird.

As Moss began reading this story of a spoiled and selfish princess whose tantrums intimidate her servants and tutor and cause the people in the kingdom to pray that "she'd never become Queen" (n.p.), the children mimed the Princess's extraordinary facial expressions and body language. At her eighth birthday party, "the Princess had her worst tantrum. She smashed all her presents and threw them at her guests" (n.p.). She then orders her tutor to read her a fairy tale. As he reads the Princess a story about a witch who changes a Prince into a bird, a little sparrow flies through the window. Here, the children predicted that "this must be the prince! It's just like the [other] stories *we've* been reading." The next line in the story, "'It's the enchanted Prince!' yelled the Princess" (n.p.), confirmed the children's prediction. When the Princess puts the sparrow in a cage, the bird beats against the bars, and the Princess yells, "You stop that immediately!" (n.p.). The children's response to the Princess's attempt to keep the sparrow in the cage suggested their comprehension of the difference between wild birds and pet birds. The children also recognized the parallel between the Princess's tantrum and the sparrow's outburst. Later, several children wondered if the Princess realized how much her own behavior resembled the outburst of the sparrow.

Jonathan:	The bird does the same thing almost...like *her* tantrum!
Tom:	He lives in the wild.
Sean:	He wants his freedom.
Usha:	But she thinks it's a prince, too!

Later in the story, the Princess releases the sparrow from the cage, and when the sparrow eats a strawberry from her spoon, "the Princess laughed. She had a sweet laugh" (n.p.). At this point, the children discussed the change within the Princess's demeanor:

Tamara: She's usually so bratty. That's the first time she laughed!

Jonathan: Her face usually looks like this [frowns], and now it looks like this [smiles].

The Princess gradually begins to treat the bird like a prince and then like a friend until "Prince Sparrow became her first and best and only friend" (n.p.). From then on, they are always together and the Princess tells the bird all her secrets at night. The day before her ninth birthday, however, the sparrow wants to leave; the Princess reluctantly opens the window for him. That night, she has a dream that the sparrow changes into a real prince, and she tells him that she loved him as a sparrow. As the children carefully examined the illustration of this transformation, Moss reminded them that this was only a dream. When the Princess wakes up the following morning, the sparrow returns and never leaves again. The last lines of the story reveal that "for the rest of his life he remained what he was, a sparrow. The Princess grew up to be a Queen" (n.p.). This ending prompted a number of comments about transformation:

Nik: So, he really is a sparrow, not a prince.

Tamara: At the beginning of the story, she told everybody she was going to be a witch and turn them all into toads. But at the end of the story, she became a queen.

Jonathan: A *good* queen!

Samantha: First she was mean and then nice.

Moss: What was the transformation in this story?

Usha: The sparrow turns into a prince.

Nik: That was in the dream, Usha. He changed to a prince in the dream, but she wanted him to be her friend the sparrow.

Usha: So it was only in the dream?

Nik: Yes. [He points to the illustration of the dream scene, and Moss reads the text again.] It's like a dream bubble. It didn't actually happen.

Jonathan: So the transformation is she turned from a princess to a queen, and she turned from mean to nice.... She changed nice *inside*...like an inside transformation, sort of.

Clarissa: She changed inside because the sparrow came to her, and she didn't want him to leave...because he was a friend. She *smiled*. That was a big clue that she was changing. She got nice to the maids and the tutor. [This last point was not actually in the text.]

Tom: She changed in two ways: one, from mean to nice, and two, she changed to a good princess from a bad one. I think the story was good.... She'd be really, really mean if she had turned into a witch with magic powers. As a queen, she'll become a fair queen.

Moss: How do you know?

Tom: She was fair to the sparrow by letting him go out of the cage, eat with her, play in her bathtub, and use her hair as a towel. And then she opened the window for him!

Sean: So he could be free.

Moss then changed the focus of the discussion by asking the children, "Is this fantasy or realism?" The goal of this question was to invite them to use their prior experiences with different kinds of literary texts to identify the genre and to support their interpretations. The children's responses follow:

Samantha: Fantasy...a bird couldn't get close enough to eat your food in real life.

Jonathan: But he became like other birds that people have for pets. And he became her friend. Like telling secrets at night. A pet can be like a friend.

Charlene: My dog lives with us, and he is part of our family.

Tamara: It must be realism because there's no magic.

Moss:	What about the transformation?
Mason:	It couldn't happen in real life. People don't change.
Jonathan:	It *could* happen! One of my friends used to be mean, and now he's nice. This story can be realism, Mason, because people *can* change...and birds *can* be friends.
Tamara:	There's no magic in the story, and everything that happened in the story *could* happen in real life!
Charlene:	So, it's realism. It's *not* like the other stories.
Usha:	But it seemed like it at first!

This dialogue continued until the end of the session. Most of the children seemed to have grasped the notion of *inside transformation* (the term introduced by Jonathan) and that in real life, people can change. The children drew from their own experiences, thus using literature-life connections, to provide Mason with further examples to support this idea. At the end of the session, however, Mason remained unconvinced. In the ongoing dialogue that was the core of the literary experience in the library, the children learned to support their interpretations with evidence from texts or personal experience. Disagreements during the discussions enabled the children to discover multiple perspectives of individuals within the group, as well as the multiple interpretations a single text can generate. In this supportive environment, Mason apparently felt comfortable enough to hold onto an opinion, even if it seemed to run counter to the opinions expressed by his peers.

Session Eight: Exploring the Nature of Inside Transformation

The Sparrow's Song by Ian Wallace (1986), which Moss selected for this session, is a brief but poetic tale set in Niagara Falls, near Rochester, New York, USA. The story opens when Katie, one of the main characters, finds an orphan bird and learns that her brother, Charles, had killed the bird's mother with his slingshot. When Katie confronts her brother, he tells her, "It's only a sparrow" (n.p.). Charles's comment initiated a rash of comments from the children, which illustrates their emotional involvement in the story world, as well as their use of inferential thinking:

Nik: He hit it with his slingshot; he's not even sorry!

Sean: For him it's just like a target.... He was *practicing* [expresses this word with heavy sarcasm].

Clarissa: Katie was so mad at him because he killed the mother bird, and then he didn't even care!

As the story unfolded, the children learned that Katie eventually is able to forgive her brother, who joins her in taking care of the sparrow. Together, they watch it grow and teach it to fly. Toward the end of the story Charles and Katie's mother convince them to let their bird fly free. The following scene, which describes the bird as it flies free, also reveals Charles's transformation:

> Beating its wings against the fateful wind, the bird soared triumphantly, long and high. From his pocket, Charles pulled his slingshot. Katie gasped in fear, but instead of aiming the slingshot, Charles hurled it away. End over end it tumbled through the air until the river swallowed it. (n.p.)

The illustration that accompanies this scene shows Charles reaching for his slingshot. As the children experienced this moment of tension, their faces revealed their initial fear that Charles would hurt the bird, and a few whispered, "Oh no! Don't!" They heaved a collective sigh of relief when Charles hurls the slingshot away. This was another example of the children "talking back to the story or characters" (Sipe, 2002, p. 477). The ensuing conversation demonstrated not only their active involvement in the story world, but also their growing ability to think critically, as they tried to understand the nature of the transformation:

Nik: I thought he was going to kill it! But I thought he would miss.

Tom: It seemed like he didn't change at all when he pulled out the slingshot.

Usha: When he threw it [the slingshot] away, it showed he didn't want to kill anymore. He really did change.

Nik:	He feels bad for what he did before. He's changing his mind about killing birds.
Tamara:	He doesn't like killing anymore. *That's* why he threw it away.
Jonathan:	He's *showing* her [Katie] that he's changed and doesn't want to do that again.

After the bird flies away, Katie and Charles worry about it. Although the sparrow returns to them one day, it is the only and last time they see it. The last page of the story features an illustration of a bird with its mate and a nest with eggs. The children eagerly responded to the clues in this illustration to make predictions about what had happened to the bird, especially because the author does not reveal this in the text. Note how Clarissa especially drew attention to the craft of the author:

Nik:	He found a mate. He's OK!
Usha:	The bird had eggs. *We* know, but they [Katie and Charles] don't know.
Clarissa:	The author should have let *them* know that their bird was happy. But it was still a good ending.

Next, Moss specifically asked the children to identify the transformation that had occurred in the story.

Mason:	The sparrow transformed from a not-flying baby into flying. Charles transformed from bad to good; he was bad when he killed the bird's mother.
Nik:	It's an inside transformation.
Moss:	Is this realism or fantasy?
Tamara:	Realism—the boy changed the way people really do change.
Samantha:	People *can* teach birds to fly. And birds *can* die.
Jonathan:	People *can* hit a bird with a slingshot.
Tom:	And Niagara Falls is real. Katie called it a magical place.
Tamara:	But there was no magic. Katie called it a magical place, but there was no magic like in those old stories.

Clarissa: The other one [*Prince Sparrow*] was more like a fairy tale with the princess in the castle. But this one is at a place we know.

Sean: It's definitely realism.

The preceding dialogue showed how the children worked together to support their decision to identify the story as realism, and in the process, to clarify their understanding of the differences between fantasy and realism. Although Mason did not enter into the fantasy-realism discussion, he was very attentive to the interchange, according to Fenster's observation notes. We wondered if he was pondering this issue and simply had not yet come to a conclusion. As a whole, the children's responses to this story suggested their growing understanding of the nature of inside transformation, as well as the symbolic nature of Charles's act of throwing away his slingshot.

Session Nine: Exploring Turning Points in Inside Transformation

In this session, Moss introduced Sonia Levitin's *The Fisherman and the Bird* (1982). The children examined the front and back covers and talked about the setting for this story. Tom noted that the fisherman, his fishing boat, and the bird portrayed on the covers look realistic and predicted that this would be a "realism story." Jonathan, Clarissa, and Riley predicted that the fisherman and the bird would become friends like the Princess and the sparrow.

The Fisherman and the Bird tells the story of Rico the fisherman, who rejects the friendship of the other fishermen and villagers and therefore, leads a lonely life. One day, a large, beautiful bird builds its nest on the mast of Rico's fishing boat, and he shouts at it, "You cannot stay here! No fish will come near my nets when they see you above the water! Everyone knows that birds like you eat fish!" (n.p.). When Rico sails home, the villagers laugh at the sight of the bird's nest. Rico picks up a long pole to destroy the nest, but the village teacher stops him and explains that this is a rare bird that is in danger of extinction. When Rico finds two eggs in the nest, the villagers plead with him not to move his boat. The transformation begins when he reluctantly becomes the guardian of the nest. Rico no longer leads a lonely life, as the other fishermen share their catch with him, their wives bake bread for him, and the children in the village keep him company. And Rico now uses the long pole to frighten away birds that might try to harm the eggs in the nest. When the eggs hatch, Rico runs to the church tower to ring the bell. Looking down at the villagers

> with his arms outspread he shouted joyously, "Arrived!" Overcome with happiness, Rico began to sing in a voice so strong it echoed from the distant hills.... The people joined hands, laughing, dancing and singing with Rico, "All is well! All is well! All is well!" (n.p.)

Because Fenster came into the room after the first few pages of the story had been read aloud, many of the children tried to tell her about important events within the story, as well as their significance. For example, Clarissa explained to her that Rico was so unhappy and unfriendly because "he fell in love with a girl who left him. She married a different person. So now, he doesn't trust anyone, even the people who invite him for a meal or to church." Tom and Samantha further explained that the bird on the mast of Rico's boat was in danger of becoming extinct. (The children understood the concept of extinction because they had studied endangered species in the unit on bears earlier that year. Thus, they used their prior knowledge to make meaning.) Sean specifically noted Rico's transformation, by observing that the same pole Rico was going to use to *destroy* the nest was the one he was using now to *protect* the eggs. The children's eager explanations of the parts of the story Fenster had missed seemed to imply their concern that she had missed important information in the story. As the children retold these parts of the story, they revealed (a) their own understanding that Rico had been hurt by rejection when he was a younger man, (b) their use of knowledge gained in a classroom unit of study, and (c) their discovery of another example of symbolism used to highlight the inside transformation of the central character. Retelling a story not only reveals the nature of children's understandings, but also helps them organize their thoughts (Calkins, 2001). According to Calkins, retelling or reconstructing a story helps children "read with understanding" (p. 351). Whenever the situation was appropriate, we encouraged retellings. For example, whenever a visitor joined the group, we invited the children to briefly retell one or more of the stories that preceded the read-aloud selection for the day.

When the read-aloud concluded, Moss invited the children to talk about the transformation in this story. Throughout their discussion on transformation, they continually used intertextual links to the other stories containing dynamic characters to generate meaning about the nature of this story's transformation.

Mason: Rico changed inside—from wanting to hit the birds off—to defending the birds so they wouldn't get attacked by other birds.

Sean: He used that same pole to protect the eggs instead of destroying the nest.... It shows he changed...like when Charles threw away the slingshot.

Jonathan: He transformed from being mean.... He wouldn't do things with other people. He feels they'll just go off like the other people did...the girl he wanted to marry. But now he does things with other people.

Tom: There was another transformation...from the people teasing him because of the birds to people helping him with his birds. *They* changed, too.

Riley: In the beginning he was so lonely, and in the end he had friends.

Tamara: He sang because he was happy inside. That *shows* he changed...like when Charles threw the slingshot away.

Clarissa: And when the Princess [from *Prince Sparrow*] smiled.... It showed she was starting to change.

Sean: All these stories are about characters that change inside because of a bird—the Princess, Charles, and Rico.

Clarissa: It's a pattern!

As evidenced from their discussion, the children seemed to enjoy each new discovery of a recurring pattern among the diverse tales they encountered during the sessions in the library. In an explanation of the value of folk literature for children, Huck and colleagues (1997) write,

Traditional literature is a rightful part of a child's literary heritage and lays the groundwork for understanding all literature.... As you meet recurring patterns or symbols in mythlike floods, savior heroes, cruel stepmothers, the seasonal cycle of the year, the cycle of a human life, you begin to build a framework for literature. Poetry, prose, and drama become emotionally significant to you as you respond to these recurring archetypes. (p. 268)

As the discussion continued, Moss asked a question to call attention to the genre of this story:

Moss: It is an interesting pattern! Is this realism or fantasy?

Tom: It's realism. You can tell by the pictures of the fishing village, and the people, and the birds. It's all in real life.

Mason: It's realism because a bird *can* put their nest on a boat, and a person *can* live alone like Rico did.

Samantha: And a bird does hatch eggs, and a man can be alone because a woman marries someone else.

Mason: And a person can change from living alone and not friendly to living with people and being friendly.

From this discussion about genre, it appeared that Mason has stretched his thinking to include another perspective about the human experience. According to Fenster's notes, Mason revealed an emotional connection to the central character's dilemma, and Rico's transformation seemed to be compelling for him. The literary experience in this session apparently had served as a turning point for Mason. At the same time, throughout the session, the other children explored inside transformations and were able to identify and explore the turning points that foreshadowed or confirmed these transformations.

Session 10: Studying Subtle Meanings and Human Qualities in a Complex Traditional Tale

Moss used Brett's retelling of *Beauty and the Beast* (1989a), an old French fairy tale, in the final read-aloud session of this unit. Because most of the children had seen a play or the Disney movie based on the original story, Moss asked them to think about the differences between these dramatizations and

Brett's illustrated retelling as they listened to this tale. The children then examined the front and back covers, the endpapers, and the title page. Tamara commented, "The girl on the front is holding a fan that has a picture of a warthog and roses, and she's got a peacock feather in her hair!" Several children noted that "roses and peacocks must be important in the story because they're on all the pages!" This cover-to-cover examination allowed the children to make important predictions about what would happen in the story. By this time, the children understood that the details an artist includes often provide significant clues about the story as a whole and that repetition is a literary technique used by storytellers, authors, and artists. The children's comments about the details included in the peritext of *Beauty and the Beast* revealed their focus on the craft of this artist, Brett, who offers a new interpretation of an old tale. The children were familiar with this old tale, and their observations, recorded in subsequent dialogue excerpts, reflected their careful examination of the way Brett created this imaginative new retelling.

Moss began reading the text, which describes Beauty as "lovely and kind" (p. 5). Mason's response to this description, "The storyteller says she's pretty and *kind*. That means she's nice on the inside," reflected his understanding of inner qualities. As the story continued to unfold, the children noticed that in the illustrations the engravings on the stone wall in the Beast's garden and the scenes on the tapestries in his palace reveal humans engaged in the same actions as the animals that serve and play music for Beauty. They noted the central role of the peacock in each illustration, and after examining the tapestry on page 15, Tamara said, "I think that fairy in the tapestry is the peacock that's taking Beauty to her room." Using these visual clues to infer meaning, the children soon discovered the parallels between the characters and the people on the engravings and tapestries. Nik, for example, wondered if the animals were under a spell. The children also focused on the written messages on the tapestries, which were revealed as the story unfolded. For instance, the written message on one of the tapestries included in the scene in which Beauty first encounters the Beast is, "Do not trust to appearances" (p. 16). The children then used the words *inside* and *outside* to discuss this message: They talked about qualities of individuals and noted that outside qualities, or appearances, could hide inside qualities. Mason returned to his earlier comment about Beauty and concluded that she was nice "inside and outside." After a discussion of the meaning of the phrase *appearance*, several children wondered aloud what this message had to do with the story. Jonathan anticipated Moss's response by noting, "We'll just have to read the rest of the story to find out!" His comment demonstrated that he was attending to the craft of the storyteller, as he predicted that this would be revealed while the children listened to the story and examined the illustrations.

As Moss continued reading the story, the children identified a picture of a prince on the tapestry behind the Beast and noted excitedly that this was the first tapestry that had included a prince. Tamara interjected, "Look! The Beast is the warthog on her fan on the front cover." Their excitement and involvement with the story world grew as Moss read the words printed on top of the tapestries on this two-page spread: "Your happiness is not far away" and "Courage, Beauty" (p. 19). At the end of the story, Beauty tells Beast that she loves him, thus breaking the spell that had transformed him from a young prince into a beast. At this point, the prince explains to Beauty that a fairy,

> displeased with people for trusting too much in appearances, has cast a spell over the palace and everyone in it.... The spell would only be broken when a beautiful woman forsook all others and promised to marry the Beast in spite of his appearance. (p. 31)

When the children heard these words, their eyes widened in recognition. This textual clue unlocked the significance of "Do not trust to appearances."

Returning to the questions Moss had asked at the first session of this unit, the children then discussed *why* the spell had been cast and *how* the spell had been broken. The children again used *inside* and *outside* to describe the changes that took place in this story, as well as in other stories from this unit and the Dog Tale Unit:

Nik: She [the fairy] put a spell on everyone in the palace. All the transformations happened *before* the story starts.

Tamara: The fairy probably put those messages on the tapestries. Maybe it's the fairy in the picture.

Sean: The fairy was saying don't just worry about your outsides. Think about your insides more. The fairy caused the transformations

	because she thought the people cared too much about how they *looked*...or how other people looked.
Riley:	And Beauty learned to love the Beast because he was nice on the *inside* and good...even though he's ugly on the *outside*.
Nik:	She could see that he acted like a human on the inside.
Clarissa:	This is fantasy. It's one of the old, old stories. It had magic in it and a fairy that cast magic spells.
Usha:	It's outside transformation. They were all changed from humans to animals. But did they stay the same inside?
Clarissa:	The fairy probably *wanted* them to change inside, but it doesn't say. But, if the fairy *is* the peacock, she's *helping* them to change.
Jonathan:	When that Princess in the other story [*Prince Sparrow*] changed from bratty to nice, she changed on the inside, but you could see the change on the outside. She smiled instead of frowned. [He demonstrates this change by mimicking the Princess's facial expression.]
Nik:	It's sort of like in that story about Gelert. Remember when the prince told his son that even a dog can be a great hero on the inside even though he doesn't *look* like a hero on the outside?

Although the children had not explored Prince Llywelyn's statement, "And mind you this—the mightiest heart can come in the humblest vessel" (n.p.), when *The Mightiest Heart* (Cullen, 1998) originally was read aloud during the Dog Tale Unit, it seemed that Nik's understanding of this prior text was deepened as a result of his encounter with this current text. According to Hartman (1995), "Understandings of one passage can influence or color understanding of subsequent or previous passages—implicitly or explicitly—throughout the reading encounter.... A reading is always open to further interpretations" (p. 558). Nik's intertextual comment also prompted the other children to draw from their discussions of inside and outside qualities to expand their own understandings of a story they had heard months earlier.

At the end of this session, the children returned to Moss's original request and compared this retelling with the films and plays they had seen of this story, as well as with other illustrated retellings that Moss had brought to the story circle. Although the theme of the story was similar in all versions, the children found significant differences among the dramatizations. This discussion helped set the stage for a later session in which Moss introduced the children to the cultural differences found in variants of the Beauty and the Beast tale from different countries, such as *The Scarlet Flower: A Russian Folk Tale* (Aksakov, 1989), *Snowbear Whittington: An Appalachian Beauty and the Beast* (Hooks, 1994), and *The Dragon Prince: A Chinese Beauty and the Beast Tale* (Yep, 1997). She encouraged the children to borrow these books for family reading. When the children shared in this group session the stories they had enjoyed with their parents (one child proudly referred to this experience as his "homework"), it was apparent that their prior knowledge helped them identify the recurring theme throughout these stories, even through the many cultural differences. For example, the children who had read *The Donkey Prince* (Craig, 1977) on their own noted that in this tale, "love broke the spell just like in *Beauty and the Beast*."

Assessment of the Transformation Tale Unit: Revisiting Our Objectives

As discussed, assessment was an ongoing process for us and helped inform our teaching. For example, after the seventh session in this unit, we specifically discussed Usha's difficulty with the dream sequence in *Prince Sparrow*. We realized that she had not been with us in the first semester when the children were introduced to stories with speech, thought, and dream bubbles. Once we recognized this gap in her literary history, we were able to provide her with relevant literary experiences that enabled her to bring an understanding of this literary concept to subsequent transactions with literary texts. The children who already had been exposed during the Dog Tale Unit to the ways authors distinguish between what characters say out loud and what they think, feel, or dream seemed to have no difficulty understanding the role of the dream sequence in *Prince Sparrow*. The cumulative literary experiences in our literary/ literacy program provided the children with a shared literary history to prepare them to respond to subsequent transactions with literary texts.

Following the last read-aloud session in the Transformation Tale Unit, we met to reflect on this cumulative experience as a whole. Did the children grow? What did they learn? Which objectives had been met? As we examined the observation notes Fenster had recorded throughout this unit, as well as her notes from the Dog Tale Unit, we found interesting patterns.

Personal Enjoyment and Growth

Fenster observed that as the quality of the children's involvement in the group sessions improved, their delight and enjoyment increased. As they moved from passive listening to active, expressive engagement in the stories introduced in the sessions, the children began to enter into each story world and became emotionally involved in the lives of the characters, often talking back to the story or characters or miming characters' facial expressions and body language. Their excitement grew as they gained the literary skills and necessary background knowledge to explore beneath the surface of each story, to search for deeper meanings, and to gain new insights as they explored connections between the experiences of these characters and their own experiences. As previously noted, Fenster recorded the children's body language—as well as their words—during these sessions, which provided further evidence of their emotional involvement in the stories. As the children became more involved in these literary experiences, they began to make predictions throughout the development of each story's plot. At times, the children were predicting their way through the text almost as if they were creating the story along with the storyteller. Fenster noted the children's excitement as they began to "read like writers" (Smith, 1984, p. 51). According to Smith, "To read like a writer, we engage with the author in what the author is writing. We anticipate what the author will say, so that the author is in effect writing on our behalf" (pp. 52–53).

Although the children revealed their enjoyment through smiles and laughter, they also revealed the pleasure they derived from undertaking the intellectual challenges inherent in their study of increasingly complex tales. The children's pleasure was obvious when they figured out a puzzling element in the story, filled in gaps left by a storyteller, or discovered the significance of a detail in the peritext that seemed to have little or no meaning to them when they first examined this material prior to hearing the story.

Student-Initiated Book Exploration, Inquiry, and Discovery

The children developed the habit of cover-to-cover reading to explore books and generate meaning. They searched for clues as they examined front and back covers, dust jackets, endpages, title pages, and dedication pages. The children also looked for clues as they studied all the illustrations within books, searching for implied meanings and characters' feelings and thoughts not revealed within the text. They used these clues to predict their way through the text and to revise these predictions as new information was revealed in the text or illustrations. When details in the text or illustrations that the children had noticed but did not realize the significance of were illuminated as the story unfolded, they made sure to return to them and discuss the newfound significance of these details. For example, during the session featuring *The Brave Little Parrot* (Martin, 1998), the children noticed that the parrot on the cover had gray-white feathers and that a single red-and-green feather was at the bottom of the front flap. They used these clues to predict a transformation in which the parrot would gain colorful feathers. As the text unfolded, they returned to these clues and confirmed and expanded on this initial prediction. This cover-to-cover strategy allowed the children to be more thoughtful readers when they explored books on their own. Indeed, when the children began to initiate their own search for clues in this cover-to-cover reading of the stories introduced in the library, they also began to use this strategy in their spontaneous response to stories introduced in the classroom or read independently.

Critical Thinking

Fenster's notes also revealed that the children had grown both as individual learners and as a group throughout the school year. For example, children who rarely volunteered to share their personal responses or to respond to Moss's questions or comments of their peers in the beginning of the year gradually became regular contributors to the discussions. Children who started out as marginal members of the group became increasingly tuned in over time, and the quality of their responses improved. Several children whose responses during the first semester were limited to literal thinking gradually began to engage in more abstract or inferential thinking as they explored multiple perspectives and new possibilities in the meaning-making process. Although this growth was particularly striking in some children, Fenster's notes demonstrated that *all* the children had become active listeners and had grown in terms of the quality of their thinking, the nature of their response to literature, and their ability and willingness to express their understandings and interpretations in this group setting.

Community of Readers

Over the course of the year, these children learned to work together as a community of readers. As previously discussed, in the beginning of the school year, few children volunteered to share their ideas during the group sessions. Generally, they waited for Moss to ask a question, directed most of their responses to Moss, and rarely listened when other children shared their responses. As the children developed a shared literary history and became more comfortable as students of literature, however, they began to respond spontaneously to each new story as it unfolded or at its conclusion. Many of these spontaneous responses reflected the children's growing understanding of the literary concepts introduced in the teacher-initiated questions introduced earlier by Moss in these sessions.

More important, however, the children began to talk to one another. They really listened to one another and responded to the ideas and insights of others, often using the name of the child to whom they were directing their response. The children were building on the comments of their peers to generate meaning in a collaborative dialogue. For example, they worked together to search for clues as they examined books from cover to cover, to discover subtle meanings in the text and illustrations, and to figure out the puzzles inherent in these complex tales. The three new children who entered the class in the middle of the year seemed to be accepted as integral members of the group from the first day they arrived. The other children reached out to the newcomers in an attempt to help them catch up with the class on this literary journey. As a result, these new children seemed to feel quite comfortable entering into the ongoing dialogue and thus, became active participants in this study of literature. In her book *The Kindness of Children*, Vivian Paley (1999) explores the way children make connections with other children and reach out to them with kind deeds. According to Paley, "I've been watching young children most of my life and they are more often kind to each other than unkind. The early instinct to help someone is powerful" (p. 129). According to Fenster, the ongoing literary dialogue that was initiated within the group session in the library extended into informal interactions in the classroom, in the cafeteria, on the playground, and during independent book selection in the classroom or in the library. The children drew the newcomers into these interactions, and because of the "kindness of children," they became active participants in the community of readers that had been evolving since the beginning of the school year.

Exposure to and Awareness of Diverse Literary Genres

In the context of the literary program, Moss introduced the children to diverse literary genres and provided opportunities for them to discover distinguishing characteristics of traditional and modern literature; fiction and nonfiction; folk tales, fables, legends; and fantasy and realism. Therefore, the children gradually initiated their own discussions of genre in the sessions. Their growing awareness of genre also was reflected in their conversations as they selected books for independent reading in the classroom or at home, and Fenster noted that this awareness was carried over in their discussions of the books read aloud in the classroom.

Exposure to Literary Heritage

As previously noted, "Traditional literature is a rightful part of a child's literary heritage and lays the groundwork for understanding all literature" (Huck et al., 1997, p. 268). With this in mind, throughout the literary units developed in the library, Moss introduced the children to a variety of traditional tales from diverse cultures. Some tales she read aloud in the library, although others she brought to Fenster's classroom to include in the collections set up for the Dog Tale and Transformation Tale Units, respectively, and to be used for the children's independent reading selections. Many of the children identified stories that reflected their own diverse cultural backgrounds such as Indian, Russian, Irish, Japanese, Chinese, Italian, Ukrainian, French, Welsh, Native American, and Greek. In addition to the thematic-unit displays set up in the classroom, Moss set up another display in the library that included samples of traditional tales representing the cultural histories of all the children in the program. In response to requests of individual children, Moss demonstrated how to use the library computer to search for books in the 398 section that represented the particular countries from which they, their parents, or their grandparents had come. The children enjoyed sharing these stories with their families and their classmates. This cultural interchange allowed the students to take the first step in developing a global perspective through an exposure to their literary legacy from around the world.

Independent Reading and Personal Reading Interests

The literary units provided a context in which children discovered new possibilities for independent reading. That is, they discovered the rich resources available in the 398 section of the library, because of their new understanding of the book classification system, and the variety of topics available for exploration in nonfiction. The children became familiar with the names of particular authors and artists and the titles of favorite books in the picture book section.

The literary dialogue initiated in the context of the thematic units became an integral part of independent book selection in the library and in the classroom. In the beginning of the year, the children generally selected books in isolation from one another and in a random fashion. However, the nature of this process gradually changed to a social experience dominated by literary dialogue. The children exchanged reading recommendations and helped one another locate books by specific authors, such as Susan Meddaugh, Maggie Smith, or William Steig; or about princesses in the 398 section, or dogs or cats in the 636 section; or favorite "I Can Read" books. They shared discoveries about a book with speech bubbles, a story with a transformation, a book about a working dog, or book by one of the authors or illustrators of a book listed on the chart next to the story circle. They then referred to the chart to identify connections between the shared texts read in the sessions and their self-selected stories. (Many of the children also enjoyed choosing books listed on the chart to reread in the classroom or at home.) For example, when Sean found a book with a picture of a peacock the day after Brett's *Beauty and the Beast* was introduced, he was very excited and shared his find with his classmates. Brett's illustrations of peacocks in her retelling had sparked in Sean a special interest in peacocks. These independent reading choices also provided the opportunity for the children to engage in independent writing. For instance, after Sean discovered another book with pictures of peacocks, he decided to do research on the computer for more information so he could write his own book about peacocks.

As they engaged in this process of selecting books for personal enjoyment, the children carried on a running dialogue as they examined the covers, title pages, and illustrations of possible book choices. After choosing a book, a child would sit with one or two classmates to share his or her selection before putting the book on the "saving shelf" until it was time for solitary reading in the classroom or at home. Each child kept his or her books, papers, notebooks, and folders in the classroom in a saving shelf labeled with his or her name. (Teachers interested in creating saving shelves for their own students can purchase large, stackable, plastic shelves similar to the ones that Fenster used at hardware or discount stores.) Because our first objective was to provide opportunities for children to experience personal enjoyment and growth through literature, we were pleased to see that the children's enjoyment within the group sessions had been carried over into book selection and independent reading.

The Human Experience and Literature-Life Connections

As the children explored the stories selected for this unit, they encountered story characters who offered a range of diverse human qualities and experiences. For example, they met Beauty who was able to see beneath Beast's ugly and fearsome exterior to discover his gentle inner qualities and ultimately learns to love him. They also met the spoiled and selfish princesses in *Prince Sparrow* and in *The Boy Who Knew the Language of the Birds*. One princess changed when she gained a friend and learned to care about him, whereas the other continued to be self-centered and insensitive to the end of the story. Through these characters, the children were able to see how all types of people have the ability to change for the better, although some choose not to. They compared the thoughtless wishes of the queen in *The Glass Mountain* and the father in *The Seven Ravens* and then linked these emotional responses to experiences in their own lives. This literature-life link allowed the children to see the inherent difference between the characters' similar actions: They noted that the queen's wish was more selfish because "she just wanted peace and quiet for herself," but the father made the wish "because he wanted his little daughter to have peace and quiet so she could get well." The children discovered that storytellers and authors incorporate themes about the human experience into their stories. For example, after listening to *The Six Swans* (San Souci, 1988), *The Glass Mountain*, and *The Seven Ravens*, in which three of the characters in these stories bring about the transformation of children into birds, the children recognized that the only one with an evil motive was the new queen from *The Six Swans*. They concluded that when similar deeds are performed by characters with different motives, these motives must be evaluated accordingly. As they were confronted with Colum's dilemma in *The Boy Who Knew the Language of the Birds*, they once again put themselves in a character's shoes by pondering whether *they* would use the last wish to change back into a human or to rescue the king's three sons. Indeed, the children continued to find these literature-life links throughout the program, as they encountered examples of jealousy, cunning, cruelty, greed, courage, loyalty, determination, generosity, and kindness.

Literature, Literary Analysis, and the Craft of Authors and Artists

The observation notes also revealed that the children had learned to incorporate the language of literary analysis in their responses to stories. For example, they identified characters as "villains," "helpers," "heroes," or "heroines." They talked about a story's *setting* and the importance of the setting within the story. They talked about the *problem* in the story and how it was solved. Further growth in the children's literary learning was demonstrated in their ability to differentiate between what story characters say and what they think, feel, or dream. This understanding evolved out of their focus on speech and thought bubbles in the early sessions of the Dog Tale Unit. When they began their in-depth study of transformations in the Transformation Tale Unit, the children began to distinguish between characters' inside and outside qualities and the inside and outside transformations of these characters, as well as real-life people.

The children learned about the craft of authors and artists, or what they do to create meaning and to elicit reader response. For example, the children discovered that illustrations often provide information that is not included in the text. In *The Sparrow's Song*, the artist provides a picture of the sparrow with a mate and a nest with eggs at the very end of the story; however, this information is not provided within the text and is withheld from the characters. Also, in *Beauty and the Beast*, Brett weaves into the illustrations clues that are not within the text about the characters' transformations. Looking for clues within both the text and the illustrations allowed the children to discover significant gaps in many of the stories. For example, in *The Glass Mountain* (Hogrogian, 1985), readers are left with a number of questions, such as "Did the princess ever find her mother and father after the spell was broken?" "How did her mother feel after she made that awful wish?" "Who caused the transformation when the queen made that thoughtless wish?" "Why didn't the storyteller tell you what happened after they got married?" In response to these questions and similar questions they had when they heard other stories, the children learned to look for clues in the illustrations or text to help them fill in the gaps. *The Seven Ravens* (Geringer, 1994) triggered a similar question about who caused the transformation in the story, but no clues were discovered in the immediate text or illustrations to help them find the answer. Eventually, however, they found answers to other questions as the narrative unfolded. For example, *The Seven Ravens* concludes with a reunion of the children and their parents, unlike the ending in *The Glass Mountain*. The children used various gap-filling strategies to help them figure out answers to questions raised by the narrative. Sometimes they drew from their own experiences, literary backgrounds, or imaginations to fill in the gaps. They discovered that storytellers, authors, and artists often provide clues to help readers deduce the inner thoughts and feelings of characters, predict what will happen later in the story, and make inferences about implied meanings.

The children also learned that storytellers of traditional tales use recurring patterns such as transformation, warnings, magic objects, wishes, and quests and character types such as heroes or heroines, helpers, and villains. Because Moss emphasized that storytellers and authors make choices about the kinds of stories they create, the children identified the genre of each story introduced in the read-aloud sessions or selected for independent reading. They discovered that repetition was an important tool of storytellers, authors, and artists, who used it to call attention to significant elements in the story. For example, in *The Seven Ravens*, the artist includes pictures of a jug, a loaf of bread, a wooden stool, a baby's rattle, and a raven on the cover, the front flap, and the pages prior to the story text and used them to decorate the first letter of the story. The children picked up on the fact that the artist used this repetitive device to highlight the central role of these items in the story. Another of the children's discoveries, which evolved out of their cover-to-cover study, was that the pictures on the front and back covers often provided clues that could be used to make predictions about the story. For example, the children found that a number of artists use the back cover to portray the problem in the story; thus, they developed the habit of returning to this picture after a story's completion to figure out the picture's significance.

The children also identified techniques used by storytellers, authors, and artists to elicit an emotional response from their audience. For example, as the children listened to the scene in which Katie and Charles let their bird fly free in *The Sparrow's Song*, they gasped in fear and disbelief when they saw in the illustration and heard in the text about Charles reaching into his pocket for his slingshot. Several children addressed Charles with "Oh no! Don't!" Later, they had the same response during the scene from *The Fisherman and the Bird* when Rico picks up his pole to destroy the nest. Toward the end of this cumulative unit, the children began to notice connections among scenes like these that were scary or suspenseful. Samantha, for example, noticed that after a scary moment, the author "told something else so you could breathe again!" In each story, the author provides new information that enables his or her audience to experience feelings of relief. The children identified this technique when they revisited some of the realistic dog stories introduced in the Dog Tale Unit, such as *Jojofu* (Waite, 1996) and *The Mightiest Heart* (Cullen, 1998). As the children engaged in the collaborative process of creating their own transformation tale at the conclusion of this unit, they talked about ways to use this technique to make their story "scary, but not too scary." The craft of authors and artists was not only providing the children with a context for learning about literature, but also preparing the children for creating original narratives.

Comparative Analysis and Intertextual Links

Throughout this unit, Moss observed the children responding to each new story in light of previous stories and using their expanding literary histories to enrich their understanding of literature as a whole. For example, they compared the witch in *The Six Swans* to the evil fairy queen in *The Boy Who Knew the Language of the Birds* (Wetterer, 1991), noting that both villains were involved in the theft of the three children of the king and queen in each story. Then, using comparative analysis across thematic units, they compared Colum, the hero in *The Boy Who Knew the Language of the Birds*, to Jojofu, the dog that saved his master, and Gelert, the dog in *The Mightiest Heart* who saved the baby as well as his master. The children noted that both Gelert and Colum (in the shape of a dog) had been falsely accused of murder in the course of each story.

Because of the students' growing knowledge of literary analysis, their comparative analyses grew more sophisticated. For example, the children's knowledge of helper characters allowed them to identify the two giants in *The Glass Mountain* and the witch in *The Canary Prince* (Nones, 1991) as helper characters. They identified the courage and unselfish nature of heroes and heroines such as Colum in *The Boy Who Knew the Language of the Birds* and the sister in *The Six Swans*. Engaging in comparative analysis further allowed the children to discover that the warning is a recurring pattern, or motif, in traditional tales. For example, they recognized that Colum was warned not to reveal his secret gift in *The Boy Who Knew the Language of the Birds*; the man in *The Glass Mountain* was warned not to take anything from the old woman to eat or drink for three days; the sister in *The Six Swans* was warned not to speak or laugh for six years; and in *Beauty and the Beast*, Beast warns Beauty to "return before the moon is full, faithful Beauty, or you will break your poor Beast's heart" (p. 22). The children noticed that the sister in *The Six Swans* was the only one who heeded the warning. As they listened to the other stories, the children responded with "Oh no!" when the characters ignored their warnings. Because of their attentiveness to the recurring pattern of the warning in these traditional tales, the children also discovered another pattern: Many of these characters were given a second chance when they did not heed the warning. Other recurring motifs the children discovered include magic objects, quest-journeys, wishing, and transformation. It was clear to us that without these comparative analyses, the children would not have been able to grasp the complexity within each of these tales.

Opportunities to Study
Literature With a Writer's Eye

In keeping with the final objective, Moss invited the children to study the transformation tales with a writer's eye in preparation for creating their own transformation tale. Throughout this unit, the children focused on the craft of the storytellers, authors, and artists who created or retold the stories Moss introduced. Portalupi (1999) calls attention to the important role of "knowledge of literary craft" (p. 5) in the writing process and of the role of literary discussion in building this knowledge. With this in mind, the purpose of the final writing project was to provide the children with an opportunity to draw from their growing knowledge of literary craft, as well as traditional motifs and patterns, to engage in creative writing.

Assessing Growth in the Classroom

Literacy Development

Fenster noted the relationship between the children's growth as literary learners and their development as literacy learners. This group of children was very diverse in terms of reading ability, experience, and learning style. For example, when Tamara entered the first grade, she was just beginning to use sound-symbol correspondence to decode words. Her experiences in the readers' and writers' workshops in the classroom as well as regular practice of sound-symbol correspondence helped her develop decoding skills and build a store of sight words. By the end of the first semester, however, there was a significant turning point in her growth as a reader when she realized that the goal of reading was to generate meaning. By the end of the second semester, she was reading at grade level and enjoying story content. Tamara actively applied many of the reading strategies that Moss had introduced in the sessions in the library—using context clues to decode new words and using prior knowledge and experience to generate meaning in her transactions with literary texts meant for beginning readers. She also identified with many of the characters she encountered in the stories she read, making literature-life connections. Even though her skills as an independent reader were limited during the first semester, Tamara was always an active participant in the literary discussions in the library. She entered into the stories introduced in these sessions and contributed thoughtful and perceptive comments to these group discussions. When she began to read independently, Tamara was able to apply the meaning-making strategies she practiced in the library sessions to her transactions with literary texts.

At the other end of the spectrum was Mason, who entered first grade as a talented reader. His literal recall of factual information was excellent, and he enjoyed reading nonfiction. Unlike Tamara, however, Mason was not initially an active participant in the sessions in the library. Although he contributed to some of the discussions during the early sessions, he did not enter into these stories and did not seem to enjoy "these make-believe stories." Exploring multiple layers of meaning and the craft of authors and artists was difficult for him, and he articulated his preference for nonfiction. Therefore, his challenge during the first semester was to learn to appreciate the multiple meanings and subtleties of literary texts and to focus on plot and character development.

Gradually, Mason moved beyond the boundaries that seemed to define his sense of himself as a reader. By the second semester, he had become an enthusiastic and motivated reader willing to explore both new genres and authors. Moss helped Fenster select challenging and appealing titles for Mason to read during readers' workshop in the classroom. He read, for example, a variety of chapter books at advanced reading levels and developed new personal reading interests in mysteries and humorous stories. The diverse titles that he selected for independent reading reflected his growth as a reader and his willingness to explore the world of literature. He still continued to read nonfiction, integrating it with his fiction choices, and wrote lengthy reports in connection with the thematic units in the classroom. The growth Fenster observed in Mason's independent reading also was reflected in his responses to the literary experiences in the library. That is, he was ready to become emotionally involved in the lives of the story characters and to enter into the story world. We saw Mason become an active and enthusiastic participant in these sessions, as he contributed thoughtful and insightful comments to the discussions. He also grew more flexible in his thinking, ready to explore deeper levels of meaning and to consider new possibilities and perspectives suggested by literary texts.

Similar to the children described in the previous paragraphs, *all* the children had special needs and learning styles and strengths and weaknesses. Also, they all seemed to benefit from the literary/literacy program that bridged learning between the library and the classroom and provided appropriate challenges and support for each child. The children's entries in their Literary Notebooks, described below, illustrated one of the ways Fenster integrated the literary experiences in the library with the literacy experiences in the classroom. Each notebook also served as a record of individual growth.

The Literary Notebook as Further Evidence of Growth

Fenster used the Literary Notebook as a vehicle for reader response during readers' workshop. Within this notebook, the children were invited to respond to the books read aloud in the library and in the classroom, as well as those selected for independent reading. At the beginning of the school year, the children included more drawings than text in their notebook entries, and many of them dictated their responses to Fenster. Also, most of the entries were prompted by teacher-initiated questions, such as

- "Who was the helper in this story? Draw a picture of this character."
- "What was your favorite part of the story? Draw a picture and tell something about it."

- "Who was the heroine in this story? Draw a picture of this character and explain why you think she is the heroine."

Or, sometimes Fenster invited the children to experiment with techniques used by the authors whose books they had experienced in the read-aloud sessions. For example, because the children expressed their interest in the speech, thought, and dream bubbles found in the stories about Martha (from the Dog Tale Unit), Fenster suggested that they experiment with this technique in their notebooks. Following this suggestion, the children created their own cartoon characters with speech, thought, and dream bubbles. During sharing time, the children were able to explain their use of this technique to the other children. However, Fenster noticed a significant change after this notebook activity: The children continued to experiment with these bubble pictures and texts without her direction.

Over the course of the school year, Fenster observed significant changes in the nature of the children's notebook entries, which also involved a gradual shift from teacher-directed responses to student-initiated responses. For example, rather than wait for Fenster's questions, the children opened and wrote in their notebooks on their own. They looked forward to responding to the stories they had enjoyed hearing or reading. Some even reached for their notebooks as soon as they had finished a story they had selected for independent reading. The children also began to move away from dictation and to use invented spelling to write their own comments, and they often started with the written text before working on a drawing to illustrate it. As they gained competence and confidence as readers and writers, their entries became more complex. They often drew from their literary experiences in the library to generate their own questions or to engage in comparative analysis of two stories. Although Fenster continued to introduce questions to prompt the children's written responses in the notebooks over the course of the school year, she made it clear to them that these questions were intended for those who felt they needed help getting started. By the second semester, most of the children were, in fact, ready to start writing on their own. Therefore, these questions often served as reminders of the different ways stories were studied in the sessions in the library. For example, a question about the problem in one story prompted a child to respond directly to the character about his problem and to offer an alternative solution.

The children also used their notebooks in a variety of ways. They used the back of their notebooks to record the titles and authors of the books they selected for independent reading. Fenster asked the children to respond to their favorite selections by drawing and writing about them in the notebook. And during the thematic unit on bears, the children used their notebooks to write notes, as well as a draft of the report about the specific bear they selected to study. Indeed, she found that the Literary Notebooks were useful for recording more than just reader responses, and the children often brought their notebooks to writers' workshops to work on an entry.

We observed a connection between the children's growing involvement in the cumulative literature sessions in the library and their growing involvement in the reading and writing experiences in the classroom. The active, expressive engagement we observed in the sessions in the library by the second semester was observed concurrently in the classroom workshops and read-alouds.

Looking Ahead

The Transformation Tale Unit concluded with a collaborative writing project in which the children worked together to create an original transformation tale. The goal of this writing project was to fulfill our final objective, which was for the children to create an original narrative using the experiences they had to study literature with a writer's eye. This writing project is the focus of chapter 7.

Literature in the Transformation Tale Thematic Unit Collection

Fairy Tales

Aksakov, S. (Retell.). (1989). *The scarlet flower: A Russian folk tale*. Ill. B. Diodorov. New York: Harcourt Brace Jovanovich.

Ash, J. (Adapt.). (1983). *The frog prince*. London: Andersen Press.

Bodkin, O. (Retell.). (1998). *The crane wife*. Ill. G. Spirin. San Diego: Harcourt Brace.

Brett, J. (Retell. & Ill.). (1989). *Beauty and the Beast*. New York: Clarion.

Cooney, B. (Retell.). (1982). *Little brother and little sister*. Garden City, NY: Doubleday.

Craig, M.J. (Retell.). (1977). *The donkey prince*. Ill. B. Cooney. Garden City, NY: Doubleday.

Galdone, P. (Adapt.). (1974). *The frog prince*. Ill. L. Crane. New York: McGraw-Hill.

Geringer, L. (Adapt.). (1994). *The seven ravens*. Ill. E. Gazsi. New York: HarperCollins.

Goble, P. (1978). *The girl who loved wild horses*. New York: Bradbury Press.

Grimm, J., & Grimm, W. (1974). *The frog prince* (E. Tarcov, Retell.). Ill. J. Marshall. New York: Scholastic.

Grimm, J., & Grimm, W. (1989). *The frog prince, or Iron Henry* (N. Lewis, Trans.). Ill. B. Schroeder. New York: North-South Books.

Hogrogian, N. (Retell. & Ill.). (1985). *The glass mountain*. New York: Knopf.

Hooks, W. (Retell.). (1994). *Snowbear Whittington: An Appalachian Beauty and the Beast*. Ill. V. Lisi. New York: Macmillan.

Isele, E. (Retell.). (1984). *The frog princess*. Ill. M. Hague. New York: Crowell.

Langton, J. (Retell.). (1985). *The hedgehog boy: A Latvian folktale*. Ill. I. Plume. New York: Harper & Row.

MacGill-Callahan, S. (Retell.). (1998). *The children of Lir*. Ill. G. Spirin. New York: Dial.

Martin, R. (Retell.). (1998). *The brave little parrot*. Ill. S. Gaber. New York: Putnam.

Mayer, M. (Retell.). (1978). *Beauty and the Beast*. Ill. M. Mayer. New York: Four Winds Press.

Nones, E.J. (Retell. & Trans.). (1991). *The canary prince*. New York: Farrar, Straus & Giroux.

Pearce, P. (Retell.). (1972). *Beauty and the Beast*. Ill. A. Barrett. New York: Crowell.

Rayevsky, I. (Retell.). (1990). *The talking tree: An old Italian tale*. Ill. R. Rayevsky. New York: Putnam.

Richard, F. (Retell). (1994). *On Cat Mountain* (A. Levine, Trans.). Ill. A. Buquet. New York: Putnam.

San Souci, R.D. (Retell.). (1988). *The six swans*. Ill. D. San Souci. New York: Simon & Schuster.

San Souci, R. (Retell.). (1990). *The white cat: An old French fairy tale*. Ill. G. Spirin. New York: Orchard.

Wetterer, M.K. (1991). *The boy who knew the language of the birds*. Ill. B. Wright. Minneapolis: Carolrhoda.

Yagawa, S. (Retell.). (1981). *The crane wife* (K. Paterson, Trans.). Ill. S. Akaba. New York: Morrow.

Yep, L. (Adapt.). (1997). *The dragon prince: A Chinese Beauty and the Beast tale*. Ill. K. Mak. New York: HarperCollins.

Tales With Dynamic Characters

Craft, C. (Retell.). (1999). *King Midas and the golden touch*. Ill. K.Y. Craft. New York: Morrow Junior Books.

Cristaldi, K. (1994). *Samantha the snob*. Ill. D. Brunkus. New York: Random House.

Erickson, R. (1998). *A toad for Tuesday*. Ill. L. Di Fiori. New York: Lothrop, Lee & Shepard.

Gerstein, M. (1984). *Prince Sparrow*. New York: Four Winds Press.

Godden, R. (Retell.). (1970). *The old woman who lived in the vinegar bottle*. Ill. M. Hedderwick. New York: Viking.

Hewitt, K. (Retell.). (1987). *King Midas and the golden touch*. San Diego: Harcourt Brace.

Hort, L. (1987). *The boy who held back the sea*. Ill. T. Locker. New York: Dial.

Keats, E.J. (1967). *Peter's chair*. New York: HarperCollins.

Levitin, S. (1982). *The fisherman and the bird*. Ill. F. Livingston. Boston: Houghton Mifflin.

Lionni, L. (1968). *The biggest house in the world*. New York: Pantheon.

Paterson, K. (1992). *The king's equal*. Ill. V. Vagin. New York: HarperCollins.

Stewig, J. (1999). *King Midas*. Ill. O. Rayyan. New York: Holiday House.

Wallace, I. (1986). *The sparrow's song*. New York: Viking.

CHAPTER 7

From Reader Response
to Collaborative Writing

The planning process for the literary/literacy program, described in the Introduction, began with the formulation of the list of objectives. At the beginning of the program, this list provided guidelines for developing the program; during the program, it provided a set of criteria for the ongoing process of assessment; and at the end of the program, it provided the basis for evaluating the effectiveness of the program as a whole. The final item on this list of objectives—to provide opportunities for children to study literature with a "writer's eye" (Portalupi, 1999, p. 6) in preparation for creating original narratives—set the stage for the collaborative writing project, which was designed as a natural extension of the literary study in the Transformation Tale Unit, as well as a natural ending for the cumulative literary experience. This writing project, which is described throughout this chapter, also offered the children an opportunity to reflect on their literary journey and to move from analysis to synthesis as they engaged in the process of constructing their own literary text. The full text of the children's story, "The Magic Library," concludes this chapter.

Developing Knowledge of Literary Craft

As previously noted, Portalupi (1999) focuses on the role of "knowledge of literary craft" in learning to write and the role of literary discussion in building knowledge of literary craft. According to Portalupi, "We build our knowledge of craft each time we engage in discussion of literature" (p. 5). She also highlights the value of rereading texts:

When we read and reread in order to dwell in a text we develop a new and deeper relationship with that text. Read once to experience, understand, enjoy. If you decide the book is something to aspire to, return to it and study it with a writer's eye. (p. 6)

At the conclusion of her article, Portalupi argues that both teachers and students need to become "students of craft who continually ask the question, What is good writing?" (p. 6). Portalupi is also the coauthor of two excellent resources for teachers of writing: *Craft Lessons: Teaching Writing K–8* (Fletcher & Portalupi, 1998) and *Writing Workshop: The Essential Guide* (Fletcher & Portalupi, 2001). Calkins (1994) uses the term *touchstone text* to refer to texts that can "teach students about dialogue, language, drama, detail, and everything else there is to learn from literature" (p. 278). She further suggests that children can use favorite authors as mentors for their writing. As previously discussed, one learns to write by reading like a writer and discovering the knowledge that writers require (Smith, 1984).

Throughout the literary/literacy program described in this book, the children enjoyed listening to, and reading and talking about literature. In the context of the sessions in the library, they discussed literary texts in terms of the craft of storytellers, authors, and artists. They were learning about what authors do to create literary texts and how to "read like writers" in preparation for becoming writers. The children's year-end writing project to construct their own transformation tale was, therefore, intended as an invitation and opportunity to make use of their growing knowledge of literature and literary craft. To enable the children to participate in a composition process unlimited by differences in writing proficiency, Fenster recorded their words as they collaboratively constructed this original narrative.

Preparing for Collaborative Writing

Sessions One and Two: Questions for Getting Started

When the children met in the library to begin writing their story, Moss invited them to review the shared stories from the Transformation Tale Unit listed on the chart next to the story circle. She then asked them to rethink each story in terms of a series of questions written on another chart:

- "What kind of story is it?"
- "Who are the important characters?"
- "What is the problem? How is the problem solved?"
- "What is the transformation? Who or what causes it? Why?"
- "What *kind* of transformation is it?"

As the children reviewed each story, they responded to these teacher-initiated questions and added other details and discoveries on their own. For example, they talked about magical objects in different stories, clues they had used to fill in gaps in each story, the villains who caused the problem in different stories, the helper characters, conditions for breaking the spells, warnings that were ignored or obeyed, and the consequences of characters' thoughtless wishes. In their discussions of these stories, the children included interesting phrases and direct quotes that they remembered from listening to the stories, as well as relevant literary concepts that had been discussed during the group sessions. It was clear that the children had developed a "deep relationship" (Portalupi, 1999) to these stories. The children also discovered how *much* they knew and how well they could express themselves as they worked together to pull out the most important elements of each story. Every child contributed to this lively session of reviewing and retelling the transformation tales.

At the conclusion of this review, Moss asked the children the first question that had been listed on the chart for review of the transformation tales. Her goal was to use this question to spark ideas for their story. In fact, Moss would use these review questions throughout the writing sessions to guide the children before and during the writing process and to foster discussions.

Moss: Now we need to begin thinking about our *own* story that we are going to write together. We have learned that authors make choices about the kind of story they will write. So, first, we need to decide what kind of story we will write. Is our story going to be realism or fantasy?

Mason: I think a fantasy because more things can happen when it's a fantasy. Not as much can happen when it's realism.

Nik: I think realism because you can do the same things. Mason was saying you can't do as many things but I think you can.

Riley: We could do a little bit of both.

Usha: We could do realism and fantasy because maybe someone could have a dream...like in *Prince Sparrow* [Gerstein, 1984].

Jonathan: Even if you do realism, you can do transformation. A human can change on the inside, and it can show on the outside.

Sean: Let's do realism because I think it is more interesting with realism. I like to read nonfiction books because they are more interesting.

At this point, Moss suggested they vote for one of the three possibilities they had discussed: (1) fantasy, (2) realism, or (3) realism with fantasy. Because the majority of the children voted for fantasy, this was the kind of story they began to write when they met in the library for the next collaborative story-writing session.

In the second writing session, Moss reminded the children that they had voted to write a fantasy story and suggested that they begin by focusing on the questions about the transformation that would be featured in this story.

Riley: We could do both inside and outside transformations in our story.

Clarissa: All of us could be in the story.

Riley: How about a mystical bird could cause the transformation?

Clarissa: All the children could be brothers and sisters like in *The Six Swans* [San Souci, 1988].... Maybe three of them could be changed into animals.

Tamara: Maybe we could have a wicked witch.

Mason: We don't know *what* the mystical bird is transforming!

Jonathan: So we have a wicked witch and three children, and the three children change into things...maybe one into a toad and one into something else and one into something else, and the wicked witch could turn herself into anything...like in *The Six Swans*.

Samantha: And the mystical bird...it could be an evil villain or a helper character.

At this point, Moss asked the children to raise their hands if they would like to include these ideas in their story. Most of the children raised their hands, and the composing process continued. Throughout the composing process, the children came up with many ideas for characters, setting, and plot development. However, along the way they had to decide which of these ideas they would use to construct their story. Because this was a collaborative writing project, Moss provided opportunities for the children to make these choices through a democratic procedure. Each time the children engaged in the voting process, they accepted the majority opinion without comment and quickly returned to the composing process. Notice in the following excerpts, when the children returned to this process, how they built on one another's ideas for this writing project just as they had as a community of readers during the literary sessions:

Jonathan: The children could change into things that start with "T," like toad.

Tom: *Toad, tiger, turtle.*

Tamara: We could all be in the story like Clarissa said, and one of our teachers could be the mom.

Clarissa: Would we have a dad?

Tom: Or our parents could be divorced or our dad died?

Mason: So if three kids get transformed, eight kids don't get transformed.

Nik: Could we act this out when it's finished?

Jonathan: Maybe we could add Tamara's ideas to Clarissa's ideas to my ideas because they're all pretty big ideas and then...

Nik: We just have to act this out!

Jonathan: I was thinking we could go with Tamara's idea, and maybe our school could be the setting.

Riley:	We could combine all our ideas together, and it'd make a great story!
Sean:	Let's get back to *what* and *who* is going to transform [pointing to the chart].
Moss:	Raise your hand if you like the idea of the three children being changed into a toad, tiger, and turtle by a wicked witch. [Only one child raises his hand.] Now raise your hand if the witch is going to cause the transformation. [Seven children raise their hands.] OK, so now we have to figure out what the transformation is going to be. How many want human to animals? [Ten children raise their hands this time.] Now we have to decide who is going to be changed into animals.

After a lively discussion about this issue, the children finally voted to have all the children change into animals. They also decided that each child would choose the animal he or she wanted to be. The children chose a wide range of animals: a tiger, a shark, a cheetah, a cat, a dolphin, and two wolves and two turtles. The exceptions to this were Riley, who wanted to be "a mystical bird who breaks the spell—the helper character," and Nik, who decided that he did not want to be transformed (the children accepted his choice without comment). After the children made their choices, Nik pointed out that "this won't work because all these animals wouldn't live in the same place." But Moss reminded Nik that because this story was a fantasy, "we could work it out. For example, because the setting is at school and we have a pool, maybe the dolphin and the shark could live there." Also, the children's decision to use real children as the central characters in their fantasy suggested that their story would be a blend of fantasy and realism. However, at this point in the composing process, it was not clear if they wanted to be in the story as the central characters or if they preferred to use generic children as the characters. That is, some of the children used first person to refer to the characters, whereas others used third person. Moss noticed this shift in viewpoint throughout the composing process and realized that the children would need to make a decision about the identity of the children and the viewpoint they would use when they were ready to move from creating their outline of the story to creating the actual narrative.

Even though the second session had ended, the children continued to talk about their story as they walked back to the classroom. Some were already calling the story a play and considering how it could be performed. The dialogue from these first two sessions showed how the children seemed to have internalized the language of literary analysis, as they used terms such as *villain, helper character, setting, transformation, realism,* and *fantasy* as integral parts of their discussion. They also were borrowing ideas from their favorite stories.

Session Three: Building on One Another's Ideas and Using Writing to Capture Original Ideas

The third writing session opened with a review of the story elements on which the children had voted during the previous writing session: the setting, the central characters, the villain, the helper character, and the transformations. Moss pointed to the question chart and suggested that the next step was to decide *why* the witch would change the children into animals, *where* that would happen, and *how* the spell would be broken.

Mason: The children were doing something the witch didn't like, like playing basketball, and she didn't like it because it was right on top of her little secret house that was underground— under the playground?

Samantha: The witch could have a secret castle that nobody knows about except the children, and the children sometimes go there in the daytime.

Sean: Maybe our witch could have a secret castle in the library, and so if you pull books apart a little, you see a secret tunnel to get to this castle. Maybe the children take out some books and see the tunnel.

Nik: [shivering] That sounds like it could be real scary.

During the read-aloud sessions in the library, the children identified the scenes in which the babies are stolen in *The Boy Who Knew the Language of the Birds* (Wetterer, 1991) and *The Six Swans* as scary. Nik also uses the word *scary* to identify this tense scene that Sean had described. Sean's idea showed us that as the children composed their own narrative, they too considered ways to create suspense and to "make it scary but not too scary."

The children and Moss continued to discuss ideas:

Sean: Maybe they go through the tunnel, into the castle, and stay there a few days.

Moss: Wouldn't the parents worry?

Sean: Maybe there are time changes so a few days in witch time is only an hour in our time...like in *Rip Van Winkle* [Locker, 1988].

Usha: Maybe there would be a whistle that the witch owns and doesn't want the kids to touch, and the witch gets really mad and turns the kids into animals because someone touched the whistle.

Riley: How about if one of us steals the magic whistle, and there is a barrier at the tunnel entrance, and we need to blow the whistle a special way to open the barrier, and the whistle is locked in a special drawer that the kids open—only the blow of the whistle opens the barrier. The whistle is passed from witch to witch.

As Riley's ideas poured out, he was pointing to the card catalog behind the story circle. Although a computer had been introduced to replace the card-catalog system in our library, the old card catalog was not discarded. The children still enjoyed using it to search for titles and authors in the small drawers. Moss was pleased to see that one of the children thought the card catalog important enough to include as an integral element of the story.

Moss: So the whistle would be found in the card catalog when someone looks up a book? And then someone blows the whistle, and the tunnel opens?

Tamara: Yes! They blow the whistle, and the card jumps out, and the book comes right off the shelf.

Charlene: And then you could see the tunnel.

Tamara: And maybe the witch lives in the little library office [points to the window in the wall that separates the small library workroom from the rest of the library], and she watches the children through those curtains.... And she hears the basketball on the court, and it bothers her because she doesn't like the sound...like Mason said.

Mason: Maybe we could use Tamara's idea, and the witch traps them in a net so she can turn them into animals.

Moss: So she has a secret castle at the end of the tunnel and a secret stairway that goes into the library office so she can watch the kids. And her castle is under the basketball court so the sound is too loud for her?

Usha: Yes! So the book opens, and they go down the tunnel and get trapped in the witch's castle, and they get changed into animals!

Sean: Behind the shelf is another world and only the witch knows about it and then *we* know about the land and we get changed into animals and we don't know how to get back to the library.

Tom: They get trapped and can't get back to the books because she wants them to just be animals so they can't play basketball if they can't get back.

Throughout this session the children demonstrated growing excitement as they saw their story take shape. They were building a clear mental image of the setting and the action in the story that was emerging through their dialogue. Also, the children clearly were engaged in a collaborative effort. Their comments—"like Mason said" and "maybe we could use Tamara's idea"—acknowledged each child's ownership of a new idea as they built the story. Indeed, at the end of this session, most of the children had ideas to add to the ones that had been shared already. Moss invited the children to record these ideas so they could be shared in the next writing session. The children responded to this invitation by writing these ideas on notepaper as soon as they returned to the classroom so they would not lose their ideas. Fenster encouraged the children to use invented spelling for these notes so their limited knowledge of conventional orthography would not interfere with the flow of ideas. When all the children finished, two children volunteered to collect the notes and take them to Moss. The following excerpts provide a sampling of the children's ideas:

- "Mabey the kids blow the wisel and the books move and the kids go in the tunel and the wich turns the kids into animals. Charlene"
- "Dear Mis Moss. I do not no how to put my words on papr from Clarissa."
- "I say that there is an opsticel cours and they get shrunk and the books open and a net comes down so the witch can turn them into animales. And let them go. Mason"
- "I wod like to be cang [changed] into a monkey, not a wolf. Love Sean."
- "Dear Mrs. Moss. Nik and Tamara play a toon on the wisl. Then the books open. The papre in the books has cloos [clues]. Nik and Tamara."
- "Dear Mrs. moss. I forgot what I sed. Alos this is going to be a cool store [story]. Love Tom."

Session Four: Building on Literary Histories and the Craft of Authors

The fourth writing session began with a review of the ideas that the children had discussed during the previous session. Following this, Moss read aloud the written notes that the children had recorded at the end of the last session. To reduce the number of different ideas being considered for the narrative, Moss asked the children to vote for one of the ideas suggested for (a) the *location* of the witch's house or castle, (b) the *reason* the witch transforms the children into animals, and (c) the way the children *reach* the witch's house or castle. After discussing the various suggestions, the children decided that the witch would live part of the time in the library office, which would have a secret staircase leading to her underground castle and a tunnel between the castle and the library bookshelves. Then, they decided that the witch's motivation for transforming the children was because they discovered her secret castle.

Jonathan added another idea just prior to the children's discussion about how the children reach the witch's castle: "The children could find the tunnel while playing basketball." His comment indicated that he seemed to want to include Mason's original idea. However, drawing from Charlene's idea in her note, the children ultimately decided that they would prefer to have the discovery of the tunnel in the library; that is, when the children selected a specific book, the tunnel would be revealed. Clarissa then elaborated on this idea:

> Somebody goes to the card catalog to find *There's a Witch Under the Stairs* (Smith, 1991) [this was a favorite title among these children]. When they find the card, they see a whistle in front of it. When they blow the whistle, the books on the shelf move, and they see the tunnel.

All but Jonathan voted for Clarissa's elaboration. Throughout the writing process, the children's comments revealed their appreciation of the ideas contributed by their classmates. By abstaining from the vote for Clarissa's elaboration, Jonathan showed support for Mason's idea. According to Fenster's observation notes, Mason seemed pleased that his idea had not been ignored. In the process of building a community of readers, the children learned to encounter their classmates as unique individuals, and as evidenced by Jonathan's response in the preceding excerpt, they made an effort to understand and respect the viewpoint and feelings of others.

After the children made their decisions about this part of the story, they continued to work on the story's details:

Tamara: When the tunnel opens, there's a roller coaster that takes them down the tunnel to her castle.

Samantha: When the kids come in, the witch is horrified. She zaps them with her finger.

Jonathan: The witch pretends to be nice, but she's not and gives them food that changes them.

Usha: She gives them food to make them go to sleep.

Tamara: Like in *The Glass Mountain* [Hogrogian, 1985]. And then she pours powder over us while we're sleeping.

Riley: I don't think she'll want to turn me into a mystical bird. This is a problem we have to solve.

Clarissa: He could be a mystical bird to start with.

[Riley's and Clarissa's comments led to a discussion of *The Brave Little Parrot* (Martin, 1998), specifically the god who changed into a bird and became a helper.]

Riley: I know. I would be invisible so the witch couldn't see me, but the kids could. Only the *good* people could see me, not the evil people.

This dialogue revealed that the children continued to draw from their literary histories as they generated ideas for their story. Riley's solution, for example, reflected his knowledge of a basic literary motif (good versus evil) found in traditional literature. The children liked Riley's idea and then identified stories they had read in which this motif also was embedded. They voted for Riley's idea, as well as for Samantha's "magic finger" idea.

The next step in the children's story-writing process was to figure out how the witch's spell would be broken. The children discussed different approaches to how they could solve the *problem* that they had created within the story:

Usha: The mystical bird has a special feather that he pulls from himself and touches each animal, and they're transformed back into humans.

Sean: Maybe we knock down the witch's castle and her magic stuff so she couldn't do any harm, and she'd have only one magic thing left that would be used to change us back.

Tom: Maybe *she* changes back to a regular person who thinks kids are really nice. So she's the one who changes the animals back to kids.

Moss: Are you suggesting that the witch had been under a spell that made her evil and now she likes kids again?

Moss intended for this question to call attention to Tom's idea to use inside transformation in the children's story, which illustrated his knowledge of literary craft.

After discussing Tom's idea about the witch's transformation, the children voted for the idea derived from this discussion: The mystical bird would break the spell on the witch, and the witch would change the kids from animals to humans. They then continued to discuss the details of the bird's transformation. Notice how Usha used details from another story to create ideas for this story. This demonstrated that similar to Riley, Usha was using her literary history to generate writing ideas:

Riley: The mystical bird stays a bird and lives in a special egg in the library by the tunnel hole.

Usha: He uses the feather once, and it regrows into a regular feather. Remember when Tico [from *Tico and the Golden Wings* (Lionni, 1964)] gave away his gold feathers and they grew back to regular black feathers?

Riley: Maybe the magical feather always comes back to me so I can always help.

The children expressed their approval of Riley's and Usha's ideas and moved on to figure out how the children would get back to the library. In the following dialogue, it was clear that Mason recognized many literary elements that the children had used in their story:

Mason: This story has outside *and* inside transformation: The witch changes on the inside, and she's nice now. And she has a special wand that she uses for good instead of evil like when the fisherman used the pole to protect the eggs instead of to destroy it [*The Fisherman and the Bird* (Levitin, 1982)]. And she makes stairs for the children to go up because the tunnel used to be slippery.

Samantha: The roller coaster could take them up.

Sean: Maybe the mystical bird can fly us back?

[The children responded with great excitement to this idea and connected it to the scene in *The Seven Ravens* (Geringer, 1994) in which the raven takes his brothers and sister on his back, and they fly home.]

Mason: And if it's fantasy, it could happen that he has the power to get himself bigger!

After the children voted for this solution, they then focused on what would happen to the witch. Eventually, they decided that the mystical bird would stay with her like a pet or a friend "like in *Prince Sparrow*," and the children would visit her and decorate her castle.

When the children moved on to discuss a possible ending for the story, several of them remembered the ending of a story introduced in the library program when they were in kindergarten, *The Hungry Otter* (Ezra, 1996). In response, Moss located the book and read aloud the last pages of the story. At the end of this picture book, Little Otter returns to his family with the fish he managed to catch despite the fact that ice covered the surface of the river. His brothers and sisters ask, "How did you catch a fish when the river is frozen over?" (n.p.). The last line of the story is: "Then, as the hungry family sat down to eat, Little Otter told them his story" (n.p.). After listening to the ending of this story again, the children agreed that it would be an interesting way to end their own story. Later, Sean came up with the idea of ending their story on Grandparents' Day so the children could tell the whole story to their grandparents: "On Grandparents' Day, they find the tunnel in the library, and the kids tell the whole story about the witch and the mystical bird!" During this session, Jonathan added another idea to "have the beginning and ending the same like in the story about Gelert." Again, Moss located the book *The Mightiest Heart* (Cullen, 1998) and read aloud the opening and last lines of the text, respectively. The children liked the storyteller's use of repetition to connect the beginning and ending of this legend and decided to use this literary technique for their own story. At the conclusion of this final session during the preparation stage, Moss asked the children to write down ideas for a title for their story and for characters' names.

It was clear throughout these sessions that the children drew from their literary experiences and from their awareness of the craft of storytellers and authors to create their own story. They used the language of literary analysis as they engaged in this creative process. They used ancient storytellers as mentors for their writing: From them, they first learned about the recurring patterns, motifs, and themes found in traditional tales and then used what they learned to compose their own story. From modern authors, the children learned about inside transformation and incorporated this form of transformation, along with outside transformation, into their story. The children learned to study literary texts with their writers' eyes by thinking about the craft of the authors who had created the stories introduced in the read-aloud sessions. For example, during the read-aloud sessions, it was clear that when the children considered their favorite parts of stories such as *The Six Swans* and *The Boy Who Knew the Language of the Birds*, they noticed that authors use literary techniques to make readers laugh or feel scared, relieved, happy, angry, or surprised. Using their knowledge of these techniques, the children created scenes in their story that they hoped would make readers laugh or feel scared or relieved. In their study of authors' craft, they also noticed the interesting ways authors started and ended their stories. Therefore, when they constructed their own story, they wanted their beginning and ending to be interesting, too. Because Moss had carefully *prepared* the children for the creation of this original narrative, she felt that she had been successful in fulfilling our final objective.

Writing and Illustrating the Story

The fifth writing session opened with a review of the basic outline of the story, which had been constructed in the previous sessions. From this outline, the children developed the setting, plot, and characters and added dialogue and descriptive details as they dictated the whole story to Fenster. The children decided to use their own names for the children in the story, thus clarifying the identity of these characters. By this time, the story had become very real to the children. Indeed, they had entered into their own story. In the words of Rosenblatt (1982), their experience was a "lived-through transaction with the text" (p. 272): They entered into the story and lived through it as a personal and emotional experience. After this first draft was typed and read to them in the next session, the children revised it until they felt it was ready to be published in the school's "publishing center." To help the children get started on the revision process, Moss asked several questions about this first draft—"What did the witch look like," "What happened when the children returned to the library? Was Mrs. Moss there," and "Who is telling this story?" The first two questions prompted the children to discuss how they wanted to describe the witch and where and what kind of dialogue was needed in the story. The third question prompted the children to talk about this scene in more detail and then revisit their story to look for other gaps that needed attention. The fourth question, however, puzzled them. Moss, therefore, began to reread their story, emphasizing the points in the narrative in which there was a shift from first person ("We started screaming.") to third person ("Everyone started talking at once."). When the children detected the different viewpoints, although they were unaware of the literary language used to identify viewpoint, Moss asked them to decide if they wanted their story told "as if by a storyteller" or "as if they were talking to the reader." The children decided the story would sound more similar to other stories they had heard if it were told as if by a storyteller. Once they made this decision, they could edit the text to ensure that the viewpoint was consistent throughout the narrative.

The children added other revision questions to the list that Moss started. For example, when one child noticed that the setting was "pretty complicated," another child added the question "Is the setting clear?" to the list. The children also returned to the questions about the nature of transformation on the chart that Moss used to introduce this writing project and considered their story in terms of these questions. Finally, after making various revisions, they asked Moss to reread their story a few more times so they could decide if it would make sense to someone listening to or reading it. That is, they were learning to write with a sense of reader (Holt & Vacca, 1984). When the children agreed that others would not only understand their story, but also enjoy the funny and scary parts within it, they decided it was ready to be published. The next step was to send the story to the publishing center, a parent-run effort at our school in which students in kindergarten through grade 4 have an opportunity to have their own stories published. A parent volunteer who serves as the coordinator of the center solicits, trains, and coordinates the other parent volunteers. After working with their teachers to meet classroom standards for publication, the children bring their stories to the center to be typed, photocopied, and bound and then returned to the classroom for the student authors to illustrate.

Because theirs was a collaborative story, the children in our program worked on illustrations before it was photocopied and bound. Each child drew a scene in which he or she had a part. They looked at favorite books to get ideas for the illustrations, just as they had reviewed the transformation tales to get ideas for their story. After experimenting with water colors, crayons, colored pencils, and markers, and after much discussion and debate, the children decided that everyone should use colored pencils with newly sharpened tips to create a detailed, precise look for all the illustrations. The children spent several days planning and working on these illustrations, often completing two or three drafts before feeling satisfied that they had a finalized version. They used one another as coaches as they worked on these drawings, by soliciting opinions and suggestions. The children were respectfully critical of one another's work and set high standards for themselves; in fact, they accepted criticism as useful feedback. Fenster did not have to intervene at any point as they engaged in this collaborative process, which had started in the library. Nik and Usha, who created the illustrations of the mystical bird, provided further proof of the children's growth in working with and learning from one another, as they worked side by side, planning the design and colors for the bird with precision and care and drawing and coloring segment by segment to ensure that their illustrations would be comparable.

When the book was published, each child was given a copy of it to take home. Copies also were placed in Fenster's classroom and in the library. To assign the children's creation the same significance as the other books in the Transformation Tale Unit, Moss gave the library copy a bar code and pocket. Of course, the children shared their story with other classes, although they did not have the time to present their story as a play because it was not finished until the last week of school. Nonetheless, they were proud to share the story they had created and to receive encouraging feedback from the children and teachers who heard "The Magic Library."

Assessment: Did the Children Use Their Knowledge of Craft to Inform Their Writing?

During the read-aloud sessions in the Transformation Tale Unit, the children entered into the story worlds created by the storytellers and authors. That is, they became emotionally involved in the lives of the characters in these stories and often felt compelled to talk back to the story or the characters. Moss then invited the children to step back from this aesthetic experience with each literary text to study the story objectively and to shift to a critical/analytic stance. As the children discussed each text, they considered the craft of the storyteller or author in terms of the following types of questions:

- What kind of story is this?
- What recurring patterns or motifs did the author weave into the tale?
- What techniques did the author use?
- How did the author develop the characters, the problem, the solution?
- What deliberate choices did the author make about the beginning and ending of the story?
- Why did the author leave out important information, or leave gaps, in the story?
- What clues did the author or artist provide to help the reader fill in these gaps?
- What was the nature of the transformation in the story?

As the children explored these elements of craft, they not only became increasingly aware of what authors do to create literary texts, but they also discovered the knowledge that writers require. The story they wrote reveals their knowledge of literary craft and what they learned from their mentors. Although "The Magic Library" was the culmination of the literary/literacy program, for these children, it was only the beginning of their literary/literacy learning as both readers and writers.

"THE MAGIC LIBRARY"

It all started the day Clarissa was looking for There's a Witch Under the Stairs in the Lower School Library. Mrs. Moss said, "Why don't you look in the card catalog to find out the author's name, so we'll know what shelf the book is on." Tamara said, "I'll help you, Clarissa. I've done that before." So the girls went over to the card catalog and opened up the "T" drawer. When they found the card with the title they wanted, Clarissa said, "It says the author is Maggie Smith.... But, look, Tamara!! There's a little whistle here...right in front of the card. I wonder what it's doing here!?" Tamara looked in the drawer and reached in to pull out the whistle. She blew the whistle. It sounded like somebody whistling.

The moment Tamara blew the whistle, Sean called out, "Hey! Look at this!" Sean had been searching for a book on the "S" shelf when all of a sudden, the book by Maggie Smith fell off the shelf and Sean saw a hole in the wall behind the bookshelf. Mason glanced up from the book he was looking at and said, "What's the matter, Sean?" Sean replied, "Just when that whistle blew, this book fell on the floor and...." Samantha said, "Tamara blew the whistle. You should do that outside, Tamara. Not in the library." Charlene asked, "Where did you find that whistle?" Nik said, "It looks sort of strange." Clarissa said, "We found it in the card catalog drawer!" Sean continued, "So-o-o...as I was <u>trying</u> to tell you.... When Tamara blew the whistle, this book fell on the floor and there's a hole in the wall where that book was and...." Jonathan came over to look at the book, and he said, "I know this book! It's about a witch under the stairs. I read it. It's really good." Sean said, "I <u>know</u> it's a good book, but look what was <u>behind</u> it!" By this time, all the children had gathered around Sean and were looking at the hole in the wall. Tom said, "Look! The hole is getting bigger. What <u>is</u> this???" Usha peered into the hole and said, "It looks like a tunnel. I wonder where it goes." Jonathan said, "Let's climb in and see where it goes!" Tamara said, "It's pretty dark in there." Clarissa said, "I've got a little flashlight on my chain. Let's go. It'll be a good adventure!" "I'll go," said Nik. "Me too!" said the others.

The children were quite curious about this strange tunnel behind the bookshelf, and they were anxious to see what was at the other end. Clarissa led the way because she had the flashlight, and the other children followed close behind her. Suddenly, the light went out and the children found themselves on a roller coaster ride down through the tunnel! The children started screaming, but then the light went back on and the ride stopped, and everyone started talking at once: "That was scary!" "I don't like this." "Where are we?" "How come the light went out?" Then Nik called out: "Look! There's a castle!" Charlene said, "Let's go knock on the door. Maybe a king and queen live there and they'll help us." Sean said, "I think you're right, Charlene. Anyway, I'm hungry. Maybe they'll give us something to eat." "I don't get it," said Jonathan. "How can a castle be down here? And how did we get on that roller coaster ride?" "I thought I was dreaming!" said Samantha. "Me, too!" said Mason. While they were talking, Tom went up to the door of the castle and knocked. Everybody stopped talking. Tom knocked again. Then he knocked a third time. The door opened. It was not a king. It was not a queen. It was a witch!

The witch was wearing a black hat and a raggedy black dress with spiders crawling on it, and she was carrying an old broomstick. The makeup on her face was bright green, and she had rosy cheeks and warts all over. On one hand, her long fingernails were painted dark pink. On her other hand, her fingernails had black polish. But her pointing finger on her right hand was bright yellow. The witch looked at the children and said, "I know who _you_ are! You're the first graders! I watch you whenever you come into the library for a story!"

Nik said, "But...but...how can you see us from this castle? Are you a _spy_?" The witch replied, "Every Wednesday, I go up a secret staircase from my castle to the library office, and I look through the window in the office, and I listen to the stories. But now it's time for _you_ to answer _my_ question. How did you find my castle?"

The children began to explain about the book and the whistle and the bookshelf and the tunnel and the roller coaster ride, but the witch screamed, "Enough! No one is allowed in _my_ castle. It's mine! I will not have children in my castle!" And with these words, the witch raised her hand and pointed her bony finger with the bright yellow fingernail right at Samantha. ZAP!!! Samantha was transformed into a tiger! Then the witch pointed her finger at Charlene. ZAP!!! Charlene became a shark and plunged into the moat surrounding the castle. And before the startled children knew what was happening, the witch had pointed her finger at each of them. Mason became a cheetah. Tamara became a little

cat. Jonathan became a wolf. Clarissa and Tom became turtles. Sean became a monkey. Usha became a dolphin. Just as the witch turned toward Nik and was about to point her finger at _him_, the wolf started howling. The witch stopped and looked around to see what the wolf was howling at. Nik and all the animals looked, too. They saw a mystical bird flying through a window and into the castle.

The mystical bird circled around the witch. But the witch could not see the bird. To her it was invisible. Only the children could see the beautiful bird. As the bird circled around the witch, she did not move. She stood as still as a statue. Then, the bird pulled a feather from his body with his beak and touched the tip of the witch's nose with the feather. The witch sneezed three times, and then she looked around and stared at the animals. Very slowly the witch said, "O-o-oh no-o-o! What have I done!" Nik said, "You changed my friends into animals! That's what you've done! You said you didn't want us here. But then the bird came

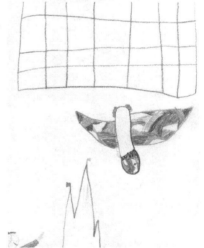

and...." Suddenly the witch cried, "The bird! I can see the bird now!" As the witch stared at the bird in wonder, the bird settled on the back of an oak chair and said to the witch: "I am the mystical bird. I am a friend of the firebird. I live in the Lower School Library. My home is an egg on the 'S' shelf. With a touch of my magic feather, I have lifted the enchantment that changed you into an evil witch. The fact that you can see me is <u>proof</u> that you are no longer evil. Although you have not really changed on the outside, you are very different on the inside." Then the mystical bird began to circle around the tiger, the cheetah, the cat, the wolf, the turtles, the monkey, and the shark and dolphin swimming together in the moat. The bird called to them and said: "I saw you in the library. I saw you climb into the tunnel, and I followed you. I have used the power of my magic feather to break the spell that put evil in the witch's heart. But it is the witch who must undo the spells she used to transform you into animals." The bird and all the animals looked at the witch and waited.

The witch said to the mystical bird, "Thank you very much for helping me. A wizard cast a terrible spell on me years ago. I almost forgot what it is like to be nice! But now I will use the magic I have left to help the children." And she pointed her bony finger at each animal.... ZAP!!! ZAP!!! ZAP!!! They were all children again! The witch said, "Come. Let me show you my castle."

The children had a wonderful afternoon running in and out of all the rooms in the castle, although Charlene and Usha were still a bit wet. When the big clock in the tower struck three, the mystical bird said, "It is time to return. Climb on my back, and I will take you to the library." As the children flew off on the mystical bird, they all waved farewell to the witch who was standing at the great door of the castle. A big tear rolled down her cheek as she called out, "Please come back and visit me. You will always be welcome at my castle. And bring some books next time. I love listening to stories!" The children called out to her, "We'll come back!"

When the mystical bird brought the children back to the library, they all said, "Thank you! Thank you!" Usha said, "Are you going to stay with us, Mystical Bird?" "No," said the bird. "I have decided to return to the castle to stay with the witch. She is very lonely and needs a friend. But I'll come with the witch every Wednesday for the story in the library. And I hope you will come and visit us in the castle!" Tom said, "Yes! We will come." Tamara added, "And we'll decorate the castle so it won't look so dreary." Sean said, "We'll bring some pizza, and we can have a party!" Suddenly, Usha looked very closely at the bird and cried, "Look, Mystical Bird! Your feather grew back!" The mystical bird said, "Yes. I will always

have a magical feather to use if you need help. Goodbye. Goodbye." And then there was a light so bright, the children shut their eyes. When they opened their eyes moments later, the bird was gone. But where the bird had been, there was now a big window! Mrs. Moss came over to the children to take them back to their classroom. She said, "How did this window get here? This is wonderful! I've always wanted a window like this in the library!"

Several months later, the children entertained their grandparents and special friends at school. When they brought their guests into the library, Jonathan said to his grandparents, "I want to show you one of my favorite books. It's called There's a Witch Under the Stairs." When Ben took the book off the shelf, his grandfather said, "There's something strange here. Look! There's a hole in the back of the bookshelf. I wonder where it goes." Ben looked at the other children and they all said in unison, "Well, it's a long story. It all started the day Clarissa was looking for...."

CHAPTER 8

• • •

Reflections From the Library and the Classroom

At the end of the school year, we met to share our personal reflections about the literary/literacy journey we had shared with the children whose voices are at the heart of this book. We both identified our collaborative partnership as a source of pleasure and professional growth, as well as a source of new insights and perspectives about the children. Because Fenster, as the classroom teacher, had extensive contact with the children, she was able to provide Moss with relevant information about individual children. For example, Fenster shared information about the special interests, strengths and weaknesses, and learning needs and styles of individual children, as well as evidence of children's growth she observed in the readers' and writers' workshops over the course of the school year. This knowledge deepened Moss's understanding of the children and helped her to plan her literature program and to individualize her responses to each child in the group sessions in the library. Joining her students in the sessions in the library each week enabled Fenster to gain additional insights about her students as well, as she observed and recorded their responses to new challenges in an environment outside the classroom.

We concluded that our collaboration enriched the ongoing process of planning and implementing our literary/literacy program. Over the course of the school year, we continued to explore ways to deepen children's responses to the shared texts and to help them develop literary awareness and appreciation in the library and in the classroom. Because of her extensive experience as a student of children's literature, Moss was able to introduce Fenster to a wide variety of literary selections that had been unfamiliar to her but would be incorporated into her classroom curriculum in the months to come. As Fenster observed her students becoming increasingly immersed in the literature Moss had suggested, she knew that these children had surely benefited from this collaborative partnership between teacher and librarian.

Moss shared other reflections about what this literary/literacy program had meant to her. For example, she noted that this experience confirmed for her the value of demonstrating to the children personal responses to literary texts, the cover-to-cover study of literary texts, and the search for layers of meaning and subtle clues about characters and themes. In the course of this program, the children learned to reflect on their own experiences with literary texts and internalized meaning-making strategies. They used these strategies to enter into the story world that unfolded between the covers of each new book they encountered and engage in a thoughtful study of each story as a literary work. Moss also discovered the power of the group interactions that emerged in an environment in which literature study is viewed as a journey, an exploration, and an adventure. As the children caught on to the notion that they were being invited to work together as explorers searching for meaning or as detectives discovering clues in the text or illustrations, they began to listen to one another and to engage in genuine dialogue. Through this dialogue, they discovered multiple layers of meaning and multiple perspectives, and they learned from one another by building on the interpretations of others. They truly became a community of readers in their quest to build meanings.

Fenster also shared her reflections about the impact of the collaborative partnership on her teaching. As a result of this experience, she observed that she now provided her students with more diverse literary materials for independent reading in the classroom and used her book talks to stimulate excitement about the content of the selections in the classroom collections. Fenster found that as the children's interest in these selections grew, they began to take more risks as readers. She also realized that the read-aloud sessions in her classroom were enriched by her observations of the group sessions that Moss conducted in the library. For example, she began to use the cover-to-cover study of literary texts; she invited discussion of genre, intertextual links, clues in the text and illustrations of a story, and the craft of authors and artists; and she reinforced the literary language and vocabulary that had been introduced in the library sessions.

We discovered another significant outcome of our collaboration: The children seemed to view the library as an integral part of their classroom experience and seemed to feel as comfortable in one place as in the other. What they learned in the library was carried over into the classroom; what they learned in the classroom was used to respond to the shared texts in the library sessions. They used their classroom and library experiences to engage in thoughtful selection of books for independent reading in school or at home. The children's excitement about books they discovered in the library sessions carried over into the classroom and vice versa. It became clear to us that the link between the library and the classroom was a natural and valuable dimension of the total educational experience for these children. Thus, we decided to continue our collaboration in the years to come.

Follow-Up With the Children Involved in the Literary/Literacy Program

Since the conclusion of our original program, we have continued to meet regularly to discuss our students, our own teaching, and the literary/literacy experiences that have evolved as a result of our ongoing partnership. We also have had the opportunity to observe the children featured in this book as they moved into second grade and beyond.

In the elementary school where we work, the first-grade children in the three combined K–1 classrooms are regrouped in order to move into the two second-grade classrooms. As the school librarian, Moss worked regularly with all the children in kindergarten through grade four; therefore, she was able to observe the involvement of the new second graders in the read-aloud sessions, literary discussions, creative writing, and book selection that took place in the library. Although most of the children in the second-grade classes had grown as students of literature during their first-grade year, the 11 children who participated in our program seemed to stand out in terms of the quality of their participation in the library activities. Moss noticed that these children were often the ones who initiated the literary dialogue with their peers in the literature program in the library. For example, in the first literature session, our 11 students were the first ones to identify and talk about the transformation motif that was embedded in the legend that Moss had selected to introduce the thematic unit featuring sea tales. The children from our original program also seemed to be more fully engaged in the reading and writing activities that were part of their second-grade program; that is, they made good use of the meaning-making strategies and literary language that had been demonstrated by Moss in the first-grade library sessions and reinforced in the classroom with Fenster. Moss's observations led us to conclude that even though *all* the first-grade children had participated in similar literary experiences in the library with Moss, only Fenster's students had experienced follow-up of these experiences in the classroom between the weekly library sessions. Moss's observations provided further proof that these children had benefited from the collaborative partnership between their classroom teacher and their librarian.

As Moss watched the former first graders select books in the library, she noted the thoughtful way they searched for a book to take home, how they helped one another in these searches, and the pleasure they derived from talking about books with their classmates. She also enjoyed ongoing dialogues with these children as they shared with her their current literary experiences. They often found connections between the new books they were reading as part of their second-grade year and the stories they had studied together in the first-grade literary sessions. Discoveries of intertextual links continued to be part of the dialogues that extended into their third-grade year. For example, when Clarissa, as a third-grade student, read the new library acquisition *Lady Lollipop*, a chapter book by Dick King-Smith (2001), she told Moss that this story reminded her of a book they had studied during the Transformation Tale Unit, *Prince Sparrow* (Gerstein, 1984). Clarissa explained that both stories were about spoiled, selfish princesses who learned to think more about others and less about themselves. Another link she found between the books was the character most responsible for the inside transformation in each story: In Gerstein's book, a small sparrow inspired the reform of the princess; in King-Smith's book, a pig named Lollipop brings about the transformation of the princess. After sharing her response to *Lady Lollipop*, Clarissa said she would like to read other books by the author of this book. She clearly was excited when Moss showed her a library shelf filled with other books by King-Smith. When other third-grade students discovered another new library acquisition *The Dog Prince: An Original Fairy Tale* (Mills, 2001), they also identified the intertextual links between the inside transformation of the spoiled prince in this story and of the spoiled princess in *Prince Sparrow*.

Moss made further observations of the students from the original group as participants in the third-grade literature program in the library. They brought to the group discussions the literary histories they had developed in the context of the first- and second-grade literature programs. Using this prior knowledge, they made predictions, inferences, and interpretations and continued to identify intertextual links to generate meaning. The children from the original program seemed to be especially excited to discover familiar literary patterns and motifs as they explored the more challenging stories introduced during these sessions in the library. They drew from their experiences with inside and outside transformation and knowledge of characters' inner thoughts and feelings to engage in critical analyses of narratives with dynamic characters, internal conflicts and dilemmas, and complex plot patterns. For example, when Moss introduced *Mufaro's Beautiful Daughters: An African Tale* (Steptoe, 1987) during one of these sessions, these children initiated a discussion of the nature of the transformation found in this tale, which is an African variant of the Cinderella tale. In an effort to find the most worthy young woman to become queen, the king in this tale transforms himself into a snake, a hungry boy, and an old woman to discover the inner qualities of the candidates who desire to be his wife. After listening to *The Luminous Pearl: A Chinese Folktale* (Torre, 1990)—the story of two brothers who reveal their inner qualities when they respond to tests of honesty and courage as part of a quest to win the hand of a princess—the children demonstrated not only their knowledge of the literary motif of transformation, but also their experience using intertextual links to generate meaning. For example, the children noticed that like the two sisters in *Mufaro's Beautiful Daughters*, these two brothers are "similar on the outside, but just the opposite on the inside." In addition, the children engaged in gap-filling strategies to deduce that "the princess must have set up this conflict [in the story] to test the brothers' inside qualities just like the king's test in the African tale." Also, when several children talked with Moss about the novels they were reading independently, one child commented, "The authors tell *a lot* about what the characters are thinking. Remember the thought bubbles we did in first grade?" In response, Moss shared with them something she had read recently by Katherine Paterson, which she hoped would help in their readings of these more complex texts: "Each character in a novel has a visible self and an invisible self. It is the peculiar nature of novels that they allow the invisible self to be open and available to the reader" (Paterson, 2001, p. 43).

When Moss shared with Fenster her experiences with these third graders who had continued to use and build on the literary/literacy learning documented during their first-grade experiences, she learned that Fenster also had the chance to observe her former students, who continued to visit her and to engage with her in conversations about "good books." During these conversations, they shared favorite passages from books they had read or asked for comments about a piece they were writing. They asked her about the kinds of books she was sharing with her current students and suggested titles that she could read to them. Sometimes, they even stopped her in the hallway or cafeteria to tell her about a new title they had discovered in the library or to recommend a new book for her to read. Fenster also shared an interesting sequel to the story of the collaborative writing project described in this book. When the first graders were working on "The Magic Library," the kindergartners in this combined K–1 classroom were very interested in this project and loved listening to the story when it was finished. The following year, when the kindergartners became first graders, they asked Fenster if *they* could do a "big story" together. Later that year, they worked on a story about an overnight adventure at the art gallery with Moss, Fenster, and the art teacher. Although the children's story was different from "The Magic Library," they used the magic-finger motif found in this story to create a new tale called "The Magic Finger." Similar to the first-grade class before them, these first graders had become part of a long tradition of storytellers who had engaged in the building-borrowing process to produce the oral tradition that is our literary heritage. When the former first graders heard "The Magic Finger," they were delighted that their story had been the inspiration behind this new tale. Samantha, in particular, was pleased that her magic-finger idea had become a central motif in this story. The following year, when the authors of "The Magic Finger" became second graders, their story was selected as one of the major literary sources used in the creation of the script for the annual second-grade play. The authors of "The Magic Library" experienced a great sense of pride when they learned of the legacy of their writing project.

Our encounters with the former first graders involved in our program convinced us that they loved to read and talk about books. It also was clear that they continued to respond to the challenges of literary study with the same enthusiasm revealed during the implementation of the literary/literacy program. In the article "Understanding Reading," Barbara Kiefer (2001) states, "To become lifelong readers, [children] really need to be invested in the power of books within a community of others that love reading" (p. 49). In the same article, Kiefer also highlights the "important role that librarians can play in helping children learn to read and learn to love reading" (p. 50). She concludes her article with the following:

> Librarians have the power to give children a rich experience with literature, to share their enthusiasm for fine books, and to develop readers who will find a lifetime of pleasure in the reading of good books. In the end, that is the most precious reading lesson that librarians can teach. (p. 52)

We based our literary/literacy program on a theoretical foundation constructed from decades of research about linguistic, literary, and literacy learning. The studies of young readers, cited in chapter 1, demonstrated the significant influence of literary experiences on children's linguistic and literacy development. Many of these studies reveal the important role of parents and teachers as providers of these rich literary experiences. Kiefer's article, however, calls attention to the school librarian as another important provider of these literary experiences.

Our program was a product of our collaboration as librarian and classroom teacher. We discovered the value of this collaboration for our students, as well as for our own professional development. As a result, we have continued this partnership and have planned and implemented a literary/literacy program for and with each new group of first graders. This book is an invitation to other school librarians and classroom teachers to build partnerships and to initiate their own collaborative endeavors to provide rich and fulfilling literary/literacy experiences for the children whose lives they touch.

REFERENCES

• • •

Adams, M.J., & Collins, A. (1977). *A schema-theoretic view of reading.* Urbana, IL: University of Illinois at Urbana-Champaign.

Anderson, R.C., & Freebody, P. (1981). Vocabulary knowledge. In J.T. Guthrie (Ed.), *Comprehension and teaching: Research reviews* (pp. 77–117). Newark, DE: International Reading Association.

Ausubel, D.P. (1960). The use of advance organizers in the learning and retention of meaningful verbal material. *Journal of Educational Psychology, 51,* 267–272.

Beach, R. (1990). New directions in research on response to literature. In E.J. Farrell & J.R. Squire (Eds.), *Transactions with literature: A fifty-year perspective* (pp. 65–77). Urbana, IL: National Council of Teachers of English.

Beck, I.L., McKeown, M.G., McCaslin, E., & Burkes, A. (1979). *Instructional dimensions that may affect reading comprehension: Examples from two commercial reading programs.* Pittsburgh, PA: University of Pittsburgh, Learning Research and Development Center.

Calkins, L.M. (1994). *The art of teaching writing.* Portsmouth, NH: Heinemann.

Calkins, L.M. (2001). *The art of teaching reading.* New York: Longman.

Carroll, J., & Freedle, R. (1972). *Language comprehension and the acquisition of knowledge.* Washington, DC: V.H. Winston.

Cazden, C. (1981). *Peer dialogues across the curriculum.* Unpublished manuscript, Harvard University, Cambridge, MA.

Cazden, C. (1988). *Classroom discourse: The language of teaching and learning.* Portsmouth, NH: Heinemann.

Chambers, A. (1985). *Booktalk: Occasional writing on literature and children.* New York: Harper & Row.

Charney, R. (1992). *Teaching children to care: Management in the responsive classroom.* Greenfield, MA: Northeast Foundation for Children.

Chinn, C.A., Anderson, R.C., & Waggoner, M.A. (2001). Patterns of discourse in two kinds of literature discussion. *Reading Research Quarterly, 36,* 378–411.

Chomsky, C. (1972). Stages in language development and reading exposure. *Harvard Educational Review, 42*(1), 1–33.

Clark, M. (1976). *Young fluent readers: What can they teach us?* London: Heinemann.

Cohen, D.H. (1968). The effect of literature on vocabulary and reading achievement. *Elementary English, 45,* 209–217.

Cullinan, B.E. (1995). Foreword. In N.L. Roser & M.G. Martinez (Eds.), *Book talk and beyond: Children and teachers respond to literature* (pp. ix–xi). Newark, DE: International Reading Association.

Denton, P., & Kriete, R. (2000). *The first six weeks of school*. Greenfield, MA: Northeast Foundation for Children.

Dickinson, D.K., & Tabors, P.O. (1991). Early literacy: Linkages between home, school, and literacy achievement at age five. *Journal of Research in Childhood Education, 6*, 30–46.

Durkin, D. (1961). Children who read before grade one. *The Reading Teacher, 14*, 163–166.

Durkin, D. (1978/1979). What classroom observations reveal about reading comprehension instruction. *Reading Research Quarterly, 14*, 481–533.

Durkin, D. (1981). Reading comprehension instruction in five basal reading series. *Reading Research Quarterly, 16*, 515–544.

Farrell, E.J., & Squire, J.R. (1990). *Transactions with literature: A fifty-year perspective*. Urbana, IL: National Council of Teachers of English.

Fish, S. (1980). *Is there a text in this class? The authority of interpretive communities*. Cambridge, MA: Harvard University Press.

Fletcher, R., & Portalupi, J. (1998). *Craft lessons: Teaching writing K–8*. York, ME: Stenhouse.

Fletcher, R., & Portalupi, J. (2001). *Writing workshop: The essential guide*. Portsmouth, NH: Heinemann.

Frase, L. (1967). Learning from prose material: Length of passage, knowledge of results, and position of questions. *Journal of Educational Psychology, 58*, 266–272.

Freppon, P.A. (1991). Children's concepts of the nature and purpose of reading in different instructional settings. *Journal of Reading Behavior: A Journal of Literacy, 23*, 139–163.

Golden, J.M., & Guthrie, J.T. (1986). Convergence and divergence in reader response to literature. *Reading Research Quarterly, 21*, 408–421.

Goodman, K.S. (1967). Reading: A psycholinguistic guessing game. *Journal of the Reading Specialist, 6*, 126–135.

Goodman, K.S. (Ed.). (1973). *Miscue analysis: Applications to reading instruction*. Urbana, IL: National Council of Teachers of English.

Goodman, K.S. (1985). Unity in reading. In H. Singer & R.B. Ruddell (Eds.), *Theoretical models and processes of reading* (3rd ed., pp. 813–840). Newark, DE: International Reading Association.

Graves, D.H. (1983). *Writing: Teachers and children at work*. Portsmouth, NH: Heinemann.

Graves, D.H., & Hansen, J. (1984). The author's chair. In J. Jensen (Ed.), *Composing and comprehending* (pp. 69–76). Urbana, IL: National Council of Teachers of English; ERIC Clearinghouse on Reading and Communication Skills.

Hansen, J. (1987). *When writers read*. Portsmouth, NH: Heinemann.

Harste, J., Short, K.G., & Burke, C.L. (1988). *Creating classrooms for authors: The reading-writing connection*. Portsmouth, NH: Heinemann.

Harste, J., Woodward, V.A., & Burke, C.L. (1984). *Language stories and literacy lessons*. Portsmouth, NH: Heinemann.

Hartman, D. (1995). Eight readers reading: The intertextual links of proficient readers reading multiple passages. *Reading Research Quarterly, 30*, 520–561.

Harwayne, S. (1992). *Lasting impressions: Weaving literature into the writing workshop*. Toronto: Irwin.

Heller, M.F. (1991). *Reading-writing connections: From theory to practice*. White Plains, NY: Longman.

Hepler, S.I., & Hickman, J. (1982). "The book was okay. I love you"—Social aspects of response to literature. *Theory Into Practice, 21*, 278–283.

Higonnet, M.R. (1990). The playground of the peritext. *Children's Literature Association Quarterly, 15*(2), 47–49.

Holdaway, D. (1979). *The foundations of literacy*. Sydney: Ashton Scholastic.

Holt, S., & Vacca, J.L. (1984). Reading with a sense of writer: Writing with a sense of reader. In J. Jensen (Ed.), *Composing and comprehending* (pp. 177–181). Urbana, IL: National Council of Teachers of English; ERIC Clearinghouse on Reading and Communication Skills.

Huck, C., Hepler, S.I., Hickman, J., & Kiefer, B. (1997). *Children's literature in the elementary school*. Madison, WI: Brown & Benchmark.

Iser, W. (1978). *The act of reading*. Baltimore: Johns Hopkins University Press.

Kiefer, B. (2001). Understanding reading. *School Library Journal, 47*, 48–52.

Langer, J.A. (1995). *Envisioning literature: Literary understanding and literature instruction*. New York: Teachers College Press.

Leal, D.J. (1993). The power of literary peer-group discussions: How children collaboratively negotiate meaning. *The Reading Teacher, 47*, 114–120.

Lee, D.M.P., & Van Allen, R. (1963). *Learning to read through experience*. New York: Appleton-Century-Crofts.

Lukens, R. (1999). *A critical handbook of children's literature* (6th ed.). New York: Longman.

McGee, L.M. (1995). Talking about books with young children. In N.L. Roser & M.G. Martinez (Eds.), *Book talk and beyond: Children and teachers respond to literature* (pp. 105–115). Newark, DE: International Reading Association.

McKeown, M.G., Beck, I.L., Sinatra, G.M., & Loxterman, J.A. (1992). The contribution of prior knowledge and coherent text to comprehension. *Reading Research Quarterly, 27*, 79–93.

Morrow, L.M. (1992). The impact of a literature-based program on literacy achievement, use of literature, and attitudes of children from minority backgrounds. *Reading Research Quarterly, 27*, 250–275.

Moss, J.F. (1972). Growth in reading in an integrated day classroom. *The Elementary School Journal, 72*(6), 304–320.

Moss, J.F. (1975). A general language arts program in an informal classroom. *The Elementary School Journal, 75*(4), 238–250.

Moss, J.F. (1996). *Teaching literature in the elementary school: A thematic approach.* Norwood, MA: Christopher-Gordon.

Moss, J.F. (2000). *Teaching literature in the middle grades: A thematic approach.* Norwood, MA: Christopher-Gordon.

Moss, J.F., & Oden, S. (1983). Children's story comprehension and social learning. *The Reading Teacher, 36,* 784–788.

Noden, H., & Vacca, R.T. (1994). *Whole language in middle and secondary classrooms.* New York: HarperCollins.

Paley, V.G. (1999). *The kindness of children.* Cambridge, MA: Harvard University Press.

Paterson, K. (2001). *The invisible child: On reading and writing books for children.* New York: Dutton.

Pearson, P.D., & Johnson, D.D. (1978). *Teaching reading comprehension.* New York: Holt, Rinehart and Winston.

Peterson, R., & Eeds, M. (1990). *Grand conversations: Literature groups in action.* New York: Scholastic.

Plecha, J. (1992). Shared inquiry: The great books method of interpretive reading and discussion. In C. Temple & P. Collins (Eds.), *Stories and readers: New perspectives on literature in the elementary classroom* (pp. 103–114). Norwood, MA: Christopher-Gordon.

Pollack, H.L. (1988). Questioning strategies to encourage critical thinking. *Insights into Open Education, 21,* 1–11.

Portalupi, J. (1999). Learning to write: Honoring both process and product. *Primary Voices K–6: Teaching Young Writers the Elements of Craft, 7,* 2–6.

Probst, R.E. (1990). Dialogue with a text. In T. Newkirk (Ed.), *To compose: Teaching writing in high school and college* (pp. 163–176). Portsmouth, NH: Heinemann.

Rosenblatt, L. (1978). *The reader, the text, the poem: The transactional theory of the literary work.* Carbondale, IL: Southern Illinois University Press.

Rosenblatt, L. (1982). The literary transaction: Evocation and response. *Theory Into Practice, 21,* 268–277.

Roser, N.L., & Martinez, M.G. (Eds.). (1995). *Book talk and beyond: Children and teachers respond to literature.* Newark, DE: International Reading Association.

Rothkopf, E.Z. (1970). The concept of mathemagenic activities. *Review of Educational Research, 40,* 325–336.

Rumelhart, D.E. (1976). *Toward an interactive model of reading* (Tech. Rep. No. 56). San Diego: Center for Human Information Processing, University of California.

Sanders, N. (1966). *Classroom questions: What kinds?* New York: Harper & Row.

Saul, E.W. (1995). "Why did Leo feed the turtle?" and other nonliterary questions. In N.L. Roser & M.G. Martinez (Eds.), *Book talk and beyond: Children and teachers respond to literature* (pp. 24–31). Newark, DE: International Reading Association.

Sipe, L.R. (2000a). The construction of literary understanding by first and second graders in oral response to picture storybook read-alouds. *Reading Research Quarterly, 35*, 252–275.

Sipe, L.R. (2000b). "Those two gingerbread boys could be brothers": How children use intertextual connections during storybook readalouds. *Children's Literature in Education, 31*, 73–90.

Sipe, L.R. (2002). Talking back and taking over: Young children's expressive engagement during storybook read-alouds. *The Reading Teacher, 55*, 476–483.

Smith, F. (1978). *Understanding reading: A psycholinguistic analysis of reading and learning to read.* New York: Holt, Rinehart and Winston.

Smith, F. (1982a). *Understanding reading: A psycholinguistic analysis of reading and learning to read* (3rd ed.). New York: Holt, Rinehart and Winston.

Smith, F. (1982b). *Writing and the writer.* New York: Holt, Rinehart and Winston.

Smith, F. (1984). Reading like a writer. In J. Jensen (Ed.), *Composing and comprehending* (pp. 47–56). Urbana, IL: National Council of Teachers of English; ERIC Clearinghouse on Reading and Communication Skills.

Smith, F. (1985). *Reading without nonsense* (2nd ed.). New York: Teachers College Press.

Smith, F. (1988). *Understanding reading: A psycholinguistic analysis of reading and learning to read* (4th ed.). Hillsdale, NJ: Erlbaum.

Snow, C.E., Tabors, P.O., Nicholson, P.A., & Kurland. B.F. (1995). SHELL: Oral language and early literacy skills in kindergarten and first-grade children. *Journal of Research in Childhood Education, 10*, 37–48.

Sternberg, R.J. (1987). Most vocabulary is learned from context. In M.G. McKeown & M.E. Curtis (Eds.), *The nature of vocabulary acquisition* (pp. 89–105). Hillsdale, NJ: Erlbaum.

Taba, H. (1965). The teaching of thinking. *Elementary English, 42*, 534–542.

Teale, W. (1978). Positive environments for learning to read: What studies of early readers tell us. *Language Arts, 55*, 922–932.

Tierney, R., & Pearson, P.D. (1984). Toward a composing model of reading. In J. Jensen (Ed.), *Composing and comprehending* (pp. 33–45). Urbana, IL: National Council of Teachers of English; ERIC Clearinghouse on Reading and Communication Skills.

Wells, G. (1986). *The meaning makers: Children learning language and using language to learn.* Portsmouth, NH: Heinemann.

Wolf, D. (1988). *Reading reconsidered: Students, teachers, and literature.* Princeton, NJ: Report to the College Board.

Zarillo, J. (1991). Theory becomes practice: Aesthetic teaching with literature. *The New Advocate, 4,* 221–233.

Children's Literature Cited

Aksakov, S. (Retell.). (1989). *The scarlet flower: A Russian folk tale.* Ill. B. Diodorov. New York: Harcourt Brace Jovanovich.

Alexander, S.H. (1992). *Mom's best friend.* Ill. G. Ancona. New York: Macmillan.

Aller, S.B. (1997). *Emma and the night dogs.* Ill. M. Backer. Morton Grove, IL: Albert Whitman.

Arnold, C. (1991). *A guide dog puppy grows up.* New York: Harcourt Brace Jovanovich.

Bare, C.S. (1998). *Sammy, dog detective.* New York: Cobblehill Books.

Bjork, C., & Anderson, L. (1987). *Linnea in Monet's garden.* Stockholm, Sweden: R&S Books.

Brett, J. (1985). *Annie and the wild animals.* Boston: Houghton Mifflin.

Brett, J. (Retell. & Ill.). (1987). *Goldilocks and the three bears.* New York: Dodd, Mead.

Brett, J. (Retell. & Ill.). (1989a). *Beauty and the Beast.* New York: Clarion.

Brett, J. (Adapt.). (1989b). *The mitten: A Ukrainian folktale.* New York: Putnam.

Brett, J. (1992). *Trouble with trolls.* New York: Putnam.

Brett, J. (1997). *The hat.* New York: Putnam.

Bushey, J. (1994). *A sled dog for Moshi.* Ill. G. Arnaktauyok. New York: Hyperion.

Calmenson, S. (1994). *Rosie: A visiting dog's story.* Ill. J. Sutcliffe. New York: Clarion.

Chekhov, A. (1995). *Kashtanka—A Russian tale* (R. Meyer, Trans.). Ill. G. Spirin. Harcourt Brace: San Diego.

Cisneros, S. (1994). *Hairs = Pelitos: A story in English and Spanish.* New York: Knopf.

Clutton-Brock, J. (1991). *Dog.* New York: Knopf.

Craig, M.J. (Retell.). (1977). *The donkey prince.* Ill. B. Cooney. Garden City, NY: Doubleday.

Crews, D. (1991). *Bigmama's.* New York: Greenwillow.

Cullen, L. (Retell.). (1998). *The mightiest heart.* Ill. L. Long. New York: Dial.

dePaola, T. (1975). *Strega Nona.* Englewood Cliffs, NJ: Prentice Hall.

dePaola, T. (1999). *26 Fairmount Avenue.* New York: Putnam.

Egan, T. (1997). *Burnt toast on Davenport Street.* Boston: Houghton Mifflin.

Ezra, M. (1996). *The hungry otter.* Ill. G. Rowe. New York: Crocodile Books.

Foster, J. (1972). *Dogs working for people.* Ill. J. Stanfield. Washington, DC: National Geographic Society.

Franklin, K.L. (1996). *The wolfhound.* Ill. K. Waldherr. New York: Lothrop, Lee & Shepard.

Gardiner, J. (1980). *Stone fox*. Ill. M. Sewall. New York: Crowell.

George, J.C. (1994). *Animals who have won our hearts*. Ill. C.H. Merrill. New York: HarperCollins.

George, K. (1999). *Little dog poems*. Ill. J. Otani. New York: Clarion.

Geringer, L. (Adapt.). (1994). *The seven ravens*. Ill. E. Gazsi. New York: Harper-Collins.

Gerstein, M. (1984). *Prince Sparrow*. New York: Four Winds Press.

Goble, P. (Retell.). (1990). *Dream wolf*. New York: Bradbury Press.

Grimm, J., & Grimm, W. (1989). *The frog prince, or Iron Henry* (N. Lewis, Trans.). Ill. B. Schroeder. New York: North-South Books.

Hausman, G., & Hausman, L. (Retell.). (1999). *Dogs of myth: Tales from around the world*. Ill. B. Moser. New York: Simon & Schuster.

Hogrogian, N. (Retell. & Ill.). (1985). *The glass mountain*. New York: Knopf.

Hooks, W. (Retell.) (1994). *Snowbear Whittington: An Appalachian Beauty and the Beast*. Ill. V. Lisi. New York: Macmillan.

Jones, C. (Adapt.). (1997). *The lion and the mouse*. Boston: Houghton Mifflin.

Jones, R. (1992). *Jake: A Labrador puppy at work and play*. Ill. B. Eppridge. New York: Farrar, Straus & Giroux.

Kellogg, S. (1979). *Pinkerton, behave!* New York: Dial.

Kellogg, S. (1981). *A rose for Pinkerton*. New York: Dial.

Kellogg, S. (1982). *Tallyho, Pinkerton!* New York: Dial.

Kellogg, S. (1987). *Prehistoric Pinkerton*. New York: Dial.

Kimmel, E.A. (Retell.). (1992). *The tale of Aladdin and the wonderful lamp: A story from the* Arabian Nights. Ill. J. Chen. New York: Holiday House.

Kimmel, E.A. (Adapt.). (1997). *Sirko and the wolf: A Ukrainian tale*. Ill. R. Sauber. New York: Holiday House.

Kimmel, E.C. (1999). *Balto and the great race*. Ill. N. Koerber. New York: Random House.

King-Smith, D. (2001). *Lady Lollipop*. Ill. J. Barton. Cambridge, MA: Candlewick.

Kramer, S.A. (1993). *Adventure in Alaska: An amazing true story of the world's longest, toughest dog sled race*. Ill. K. Meyer. New York: Random House.

Levitin, S. (1982). *The fisherman and the bird*. Ill. F. Livingston. Boston: Houghton Mifflin.

Ling, M. (1991). *Amazing wolves, dogs, and foxes*. Photo. J. Young. New York: Knopf.

Lionni, L. (1964). *Tico and the golden wings*. New York: Pantheon.

Locker, T. (Adapt. & Ill.). *Washington Irving's* Rip Van Winkle. New York: Dial.

Ludwig, W. (Retell.). (1990). *Good morning, Grannie Rose: An Arkansas folktale*. New York: Putnam.

Manson, A. (1993). *A dog came, too: A true story*. New York: Macmillan.

Martin, R. (Retell.). (1998). *The brave little parrot*. Ill. S. Gaber. New York: Putnam.

Meadway, W. (1990). *Let's look at birds*. New York: Bookwright Press.

Meddaugh, S. (1992). *Martha speaks*. Boston: Houghton Mifflin.

Meddaugh, S. (1996). *Martha blah blah*. Boston: Houghton Mifflin.

Meddaugh, S. (1998). *Martha walks the dog*. Boston: Houghton Mifflin.

Meddaugh, S. (2000). *Martha and skits*. Boston: Houghton Mifflin.

Mills, L. (2001). *The dog prince: An original fairy tale*. Ill. D. Nolan. Boston: Little, Brown.

Nones, E.J. (Retell. & Trans.). (1991). *The canary prince*. New York: Farrar, Straus & Giroux.

O'Neill, A. (1999). *Dogs: Evolution, history, breeds, behavior, care*. New York: Kingfisher.

Osofsky, A. (1992). *My buddy*. Ill. T. Rand. New York: Henry Holt.

Patent, D.H. (1986). *Maggie: A sheep dog*. Ill. W. Muñoz. New York: Dodd, Mead.

Patent, D.H. (1993). *Dogs: The wolf within*. Photo. W. Muñoz. Minneapolis: Carolrhoda.

Patent, D.H. (1994). *Hugger to the rescue*. Photo. W. Muñoz. New York: Cobblehill Books/Dutton.

Patten, B. (1996a). *Dogs with a job*. Vero Beach, FL: Rourke.

Patten, B. (1996b). *The terrier breeds*. Vero Beach, FL: Rourke.

Patten, B. (1996c). *The world's smallest dogs*. Vero Beach, FL: Rourke.

Paulsen, G. (1993). *Dogteam*. Ill. R.W. Paulsen. New York: Delacorte.

Polacco, P. (1998). *Thank you, Mr. Falker*. New York: Philomel.

Rathmann, P. (1995). *Officer Buckle and Gloria*. New York: Putnam.

Rylant, C. (1982). *When I was young in the mountains*. Ill. D. Goode. New York: Dutton.

Rylant, C. (1985). *The relatives came*. Ill. S. Gammell. New York: Bradbury Press.

San Souci, R.D. (Retell.). (1988). *The six swans*. Ill. D. San Souci. New York: Simon & Schuster.

Seymour, T. (1993). *Pole dog*. Ill. D. Soman. New York: Orchard.

Smith, M. (1991). *There's a witch under the stairs*. New York: Lothrop, Lee & Shepard.

Smith, M. (1994). *Argo, you lucky dog*. New York: Lothrop, Lee & Shepard.

Standiford, N. (1989). *The bravest dog ever: The true story of Balto*. Ill. D. Cook. New York: Random House.

Steptoe, J. (Retell.). (1987). *Mufaro's beautiful daughters: An African tale*. New York: Lothrop, Lee & Shepard.

Stone, L. (1993). *Canines: Predators*. Vero Beach, FL: Rourke.

Torre, B. (Retell.). (1990). *The luminous pearl: A Chinese folktale*. Ill. C. Inouye. New York: Orchard.

Waite, M.P. (Retell.). (1996). *Jojofu*. Ill. Y. Ito. New York: Lothrop, Lee & Shepard.

Wallace, I. (1986). *The sparrow's song*. New York: Viking.

Wetterer, M.K. (1991). *The boy who knew the language of the birds*. Ill. B. Wright. Minneapolis: Carolrhoda.

Whelan, G. (1988). *Silver*. Ill. S. Marchesi. New York: Random House.

Wilcox, C. (1999a). *The Newfoundland*. Mankato, MN: Capstone High/Low Books.

Wilcox, C. (1999b). *The Samoyed*. Mankato, MN: Capstone High/Low Books.

Wood, T. (1996). *Iditarod dream: Dusty and his sled dogs compete in Alaska's Jr. Iditarod*. New York: Walker.

Yep, L. (Adapt.). (1997). *The dragon prince: A Chinese Beauty and the Beast tale*. Ill. K. Mak. New York: HarperCollins.

INDEX

• • •

Page references followed by *f* indicate figures.

D

E

F

G

H